FROM OASIS INTO ITALY

War Poems and Diaries
from Africa and Italy
1940–1946

These Poems

by John Jarmain

You who in evenings by the fire
May read these words of mine,
How let you see the desert bare
In the print-smooth line?

Listen! These poems were not made in rooms,
But out in the empty sand,
Where only the homeless Arab roams
In a sterile land;

They were not at tables written
With placid curtains drawn,
But by candlelight begotten
Of the dusk and dawn.

They had no peace at their creation,
No twilight hush of wings;
Only the tremble of bombs, the guns' commotion,
And destructive things.

Mareth, Tunisia. March, 1943.

WHAT — GO HOME?

'What—go home on leave in an English winter!'

ITALY 1944

"Don't think we'll have much of a leave here, old man"

'Two Types' cartoons by JON

FROM OASIS INTO ITALY

War Poems and Diaries
from Africa and Italy
1940-1946

Editors
Victor Selwyn, Dan Davin, Erik de Mauny,
Ian Fletcher

Advisers
Field Marshal Lord Carver
General Sir John Hackett

Shepheard-Walwyn (Publishers) Ltd

This edition first published 1983 by
Shepheard-Walwyn (Publishers) Ltd
26 Charing Cross Road (Suite 34)
London WC2H 0DH

British Library Cataloguing in Publication Data
From Oasis into Italy.
 1. World War, 1939-1945—Campaigns—Africa, North—
    Poetry
 2. World War, 1939-1945—Campaigns—Italy—Poetry
 3. English poetry—20th century
 I. Selwyn, Victor
 821'.912'080358   PR1195.H5

ISBN 0-85683-063-1
ISBN 0-85683-064-X Pbk

Of this edition the first one hundred and
ten copies have been numbered

This is number

4

Typeset by Grainger Photosetting, Southend-on-Sea, Essex.
Printed and bound in the United Kingdom by Robert Hartnoll Ltd, Bodmin, Cornwall.

An Appreciation

The verses and other literary pieces in this book were written by men serving in the armed forces in the Second World War in the later stages of the campaign in North Africa and in those that followed in Sicily and Italy, including those who served at sea in the Mediterranean in that period. It was a time which tested them, and in which they felt the need to express their personal feelings: to commune with themselves. There could be no doubt that the Anglo-American-Russian alliance would eventually prevail; but how long it would take and whether one would oneself survive to see victory were open questions.

The conditions under which men lived and fought in those campaigns were different from those which the Eighth Army and the Desert Air Force had experienced in the Libyan desert before and after Montgomery's famous Battle of El Alamein. In Tunisia, Sicily and Italy one was fighting where people were living. One was reminded of the rhythm of normal human life, with all its hopes and fears, and at the same time of the misery which war brings to those who happen to live on the battlefield. One was not living a life apart, as if in some military monastery, as one had been in the desert. The climate was severe: cold, wet, muddy and miserable in winter: stiflingly hot at times in summer. The terrain was rugged and provided obstacles to movement of every kind, which favoured the defence. The Italians having surrendered, one was up against only the Germans, experts in defence, and fighting with their backs to the wall. The conditions in which the men who wrote these pieces lived and fought came nearer to those experienced by their fathers in the First World War than in any other campaign of the Second. Their achievements should not be forgotten. This book will help us to remember them and to see through their eyes what war meant to those who fought for freedom.

FIELD MARSHAL LORD CARVER

Acknowledgements

We say thank you to the Dulverton Trust (Maj. Gen. Douglas Brown), the Esmée Fairbairn Charitable Trust, Derek Bryant, Hunt & Ford of Ipswich and the many members of the 7th Armoured Division Officer's Club without whose generosity the task of collecting the material for this book would not have been completed. It has taken nearly three years. We have been helped by so many whom we have not met, who responded to appeals in the media for manuscripts or sent books of the time and service magazines.

Without the media these poems, diaries and other material would not have reached us. The first appeal for manuscripts by Field Marshal Lord Carver and General Sir John Hackett appeared in *The Times* in April 1981, to be followed by the *Sunday Mirror, Daily Mail, The Listener, Daily Telegraph* and *Yours*, the magazine of Age Concern. We acknowledge the support of BBC Radio 4 and Radio Brighton (Keith Slade).

We are grateful to Professor Geoffrey Best of Sussex University for telling us of Professor Norman Hampson at York (thanks to British Rail's delay at East Croydon which prompted Geoffrey's memory); to Michael Croft for Lawrie Little; to Jim Barker for his artist cousin George Meddemmen; to Mrs Bramley for her late father William Godrey's poem; and to Rosemary Meynell for advice on John Strick. John Moyniham kindly sent us Alan White's *Garlands and Ash* and at least ten *Sunday Mirror* readers sent versions of 'The D-Day Dodgers'. And a special mention of Hamish Henderson for the Scots poets and the Italian Partisan songs. Finally, David Morgan, staff poet and assistant editor of *The Oak*, magazine of the 46th Division who presented us with a complete set of *The Oak* just two weeks before he died. Finally, we thank Richard Hoggart for prompt delivery of his Introduction to the Arts in Italy and Captain Simmons for the loan of this copy of *The Four Winds*. A special word of thanks is due to four actor volunteers, all former members of the National Youth Theatre, who have reached a wider audience through their reading of the poems on radio and through their recording on casette of *Return to Oasis*: Martin Jarvis, Mick Ford, Edward Wilson and Irene Richard. We gratefully acknowledge the help of Michael Croft and staff, Keith Slade and Simon Vance in this respect.

For secretarial aid we have to thank Judith Greenhalgh, Denise Stratton and Bev Wood; for designing the jacket and colour insert, as well as proof-reading, Trixie Selwyn; for sorting and listing all the contributions, Norman Morris; for office space, Jack Pearce of Rottingdean Lions. We owe a debt of gratitude to the staff at the Imperial War Museum—Messrs Suddaby, Reed, Wood, Moody, Lucas, Dowling *inter alia*—where the material sent to the Trust has been deposited, 'a literary windfall' as *The Times* has called it. And thanks to publisher, Anthony Werner, for patient assistance.

We acknowledge prior publication of the following and have applied for permission to reproduce where possible. *Poems from the C.M.F.* (T. I. F. Armstrong, Norman Morris), 8th Army; *The Four Winds* (W. Nelson Cheesman, H. Darby, Trefor Davies) Arts Centre, Naples; *Salamander* (John Waller), Cairo; *Pulp in Bosnia* (R. K. Brady), Fortune Press; *Poems of Drummond Allison*, White Knights Press; *A Map of Verona* (Henry Reed), Jonathan Cape; *Flowering Cactus* (Michael Hamburger), The Hand & Flower Press; *The Years of Anger* (L. Randall Swingler), Meridian Books; *Garlands and Ash* (Alan White), *And the Morrow is Their's* (Sue Ryder); Fortune Press; *The Devil's Own Song* (Quintin Hogg), Hodder & Stoughton; *Mediterranean Songs* (John Papasian), Cairo; *Dancer's End* (Enoch Powell), Falcon Press; *Two Men and a Blanket* (Robert Garioch), South Side, Edinburgh; *Songs of Soldiers* (C. P. S. Denholm-Young), published privately; *Poems* (John Jarmain), Collins; *Poems from Italy* (Robin Benn, A. W. Crowther), Harrap; *Poems* (John Strick), Percival Marshall; *Autumn Leaves* (Erik de Mauny), Lindsay Drummond; *Goon for Lunch* (Harry Secombe), Michael Joseph. We acknowledge, too, published poems of H. Compton and Richard Shuckburgh. We apologise for any omissions or if we have failed to trace the publisher.

Finally we acknowledge the permission of the Imperial War Museum to reproduce the portraits by Sam Morse-Brown, the paintings by George Meddemmen and the cartoons by JON. We also appreciate the personal assistance of JON and the family of Sam Morse-Brown, to whom we were referred by Nicholas Bagnall, Literary Editor of the *Sunday Telegraph*; and thanks to Gough Malcolm Associates, Brighton, for use of art facilities.

The Salamander Oasis Trust and Friends

The Salamander Oasis Trust (a registered charity of volunteers) produced first *Return to Oasis* and now *From Oasis into Italy*. In doing so it has begun the rescue of the little known writings of a generation and endeavoured to put the literary record straight, challenging the myth that only World War One produced the poets.

The Trust was launched in 1976 from among those who took part in the original *Oasis*, as editors or writers, in the Middle East forty years ago. The first chairman was John Cromer Braun O.B.E., leading light of the Salamander Society in Cairo. Of the Trust's founders, G. S. Fraser, John Rimington and George Norman have now passed on.

Dan Davin, M.B.E., took over as Chairman in 1980. Erik de Mauny, Sir John Waller Bt, Professor Ian Fletcher, Louis Challoner and Dr Darrell Wilkinson have remained as Trustees as has Victor Selwyn, who manages the Trust.

The 'Friends of Oasis' have aided the Trust. Peter Rost, M.P. sponsored the launch in the House of Commons, chaired by Lord Carver. Andrew Bowden, M.P. helped the Trust in Sussex. Most of the Friends are from the 7th Armoured Division Officers' Club. The Club's Hon. Sec., Major Christopher Milner, has been especially helpful as have Major General Patrick Hobart, Colonel Joe Lever and Major Nigel Neilson. Sir Kenneth Cork, former Lord Mayor of London, introduced the Trust's books and tapes into the City Library.

Contents

Foreword

Every war is a private war. Every man, woman or child in any way involved in it lives in a unique and private world among experiences inaccessible to others. Wartime pressures, physical, moral, spiritual, can be very high, often so high that the vessel upon which they are brought to bear collapses under them. Even when they can be borne they leave no-one unmarked. As they move in growing degree towards the limit of human tolerance they generate an intensity of feeling that cries out for relief of self-expression. None of this experience can be shared. It is private, personal, unique and in its essence uncommunicable. But if the experience itself cannot be shared it is still possible to lighten the load by saying something about it, to seek out the places where truth, pain, beauty, anguish, wonder lay and try to indicate them to others. It brings a measure of relief not only to those who do it but also to those before whom it is done, for it shows them that others too were under the hammer and have cried out in language they can understand.

In World War Two the volume of such self-expression must have been very great. Much of it—no doubt most—has gone beyond recovery, but the effort to preserve what can still be found has brought to light an amount which suggests that the whole output was enormous. What we have put together from British and Commonwealth sources in the Middle East and Mediterranean theatres, and published in these two collections (*Return to Oasis*, followed by the present volume, *Oasis into Italy*) varies greatly in kind and quality. There is prose and verse, carefully worked on and complete, side by side with rough and uncouth fragments. There is poetry on a respectable—and even a high—lyrical level and plain doggerel. The sad, the seamy, the savage, even the simply funny reflections of individual experience in active theatres of war which we offer here have been assembled for two reasons. It was important to rescue and preserve what still remained of this wartime self-expression, even if not all of it was of the highest literary quality. Just as important, to me at any rate, was the need to fill out the human backdrop against which great events were played, by sketching in something of the characters of those playing in them. Without this these events will soon be no more than dates and battles in history books. But wars are made and fought in by people. It is people who suffer in them, who struggle, endure, behave basely or well and sometimes even find in wars enjoyment as well as tedium and horror, and it is what people have to say about their thoughts and feelings at these times that endows the record with reality. I think of this collection in all its variety, at all its levels of quality, as a glimpse at part of the structure within which the 'history' was made, a sort of environmental archive without which all the factual chronicles of events and all the hardware on display have little meaning.

GENERAL SIR JOHN HACKETT

In Memory

Drummond Allison	(Lieut.)	killed in Italy, 1943
Keith Douglas*	(Capt.)	killed in Normandy, 1944
Tony Goldsmith	(Lieut.)	killed in North Africa, 1943
John Jarmain*	(Capt.)	killed in Normandy, 1944
Sidney Keyes*	(Capt.)	killed in North Africa, 1943
John Strick	(Capt.)	killed in Italy, 1944
Alan White	(Lieut.)	killed in Italy, 1944

These published poets had established themselves before they joined up. They took part in many actions in the Mediterranean and other theatres of war and were writing until the end. In these pages they live on.

* See *Return to Oasis*

Introduction

From Oasis into Italy, the second volume prepared by the Salamander Oasis Trust, is a sequel to the earlier book, *Return to Oasis* (1980). Appearing some forty years after the end of the war in Africa and the Allied landing in Italy in World War Two, it consists of poems, prose, drawings and sketches from the British and Commonwealth forces in the Middle East, North Africa, the Balkans, Sicily and Italy. As with the earlier volume, an essential condition for inclusion has been that the pieces should have been written or drawn by those serving in the relevant war-theatres and written or drawn at the time. The editors have occasionally relaxed the conditions *slightly* so as to be able to include material written later but based on letters, diaries[1] and other re-collections of the wartime period. In contrast to many collections, the selecting and editing of this series has also been carried out by people who themselves served in these campaigns and have written about them and during them, and so they are familiar with the subject material.

The fact that most of the contributions were written at or near the time of the events with which they deal, gives them, or so the editors hope, an added quality of immediacy and authenticity. By definition we would expect a collection from a sector of a war to exhibit a range of literary skills. We are putting on record the facts and feeling of war. There is one feature common to all the pieces: a direct relation to experience. They are sincerely written, true to themselves and to their background. The editors re-jected material that strained to achieve an effect. Often this endeavour killed an otherwise promising ms—and, as with the first volume, the editors rejected poetry and prose which they suspected was written from a distance and no doubt by a professional at home. This had been the experience of others. However, the editors felt that having shared the background of the contributors they were in a position to judge. If they have erred, they apologise. But the volume would otherwise lose its point. We have gathered in the writings and art of a generation and present in this series a range of experience,

---

[1] Officially, all ranks were forbidden to keep a diary on active service, for obvious security reasons. In fact, the rule was often disobeyed (by the enemy also, incidentally) and such diaries have been very useful to the editors. It is perhaps of interest that diaries of infantrymen are the scarcest. This is not surprising. Not only can the foot soldier carry little with him but many of them did not live to tell their tales. Proximity to the enemy also made the security rules more important.

feeling and accomplishment. But the accomplishment has had to reach a standard and make its point.

When *Return to Oasis* was published there was some complaint in the more knowledgeable (or knowing) quarters that many of the more outspoken popular ballads—comparable in some ways to the gamy rugger songs which in our less reticent age are by now better known than the game itself—had not been included, although they were as characteristic a product of war in the Middle East as its slang, its sweat and its swagger. The editors in the present volume have tried to meet this criticism by publishing some of the more or less printable specimens. They felt, however, perhaps squeamishly, that even today's tolerance—if it is not stunned indifference— might take exception to the rude ditty which dealt rather too explicitly with King Farouk's more private proclivities and parts and which was sung, rather too faithfully, to the tune of the Egyptian national anthem.

Another ballad, however, although not without its contentious aspects, has been included: 'The D-Day Dodgers'. The fact that we received ten different versions, mainly from readers of the *Sunday Mirror*, will afford some idea of its popularity among the troops. That popularity is at once a confirmation of and the obverse of Lady Astor's unpopularity at the time: for it was firmly believed by the British forces in Italy that she had referred to them as the 'D-Day Dodgers', with the offensive implication that they preferred to avoid taking part in the forthcoming invasion from Normandy of *Festungs-Europa*. They were also convinced that she had suggested that all men returning from India, the Middle East or Italy should be made to wear yellow arm-bands, to give fair warning that they might be carriers of V.D.[2] Needless to say, Lady Astor herself was much pained by these rumours and allegations—her wartime corres-pondence (at Reading University) indicates that she appealed to the Ministry of Information to refute them—but she was indeed somewhat impetuous and over-righteous of speech; and these maybe exaggerated but widespread legends reflect the vulnerable sensibilities of men at war, how quick the men are to resent unjustified criticism by those not themselves at risk and how often this is forgotten except by those who are in immediate contact with them. The editors felt that, for these reasons and because such phenomena are an essential part of wartime folklore, the ballad demanded inclusion; as does another, somewhat acid, piece about the good lady.

Return to Oasis was an attempt to reveal to most and to remind the few how much poetry and prose had been produced—though by no means always published, given the circumstances in which it was written, the paucity of

---

[2] This allegedly stemmed from a belief, obviously untrue, that a female relative of the good lady contracted V.D. from an officer in India.

outlets, the more clamorous insistences of military action, by the forces in the Middle East; and how vital—whatever its shortcomings—Cairo had been as a cultural base in the critical years of the Western Desert struggle and the Greek and Cretan campaigns which drained the desert of essential resources and, whatever the other consequences, prolonged the desert war.

The poetry published in that volume, in all its variety, struck a strong chord of surprise and appreciation in many quarters and was praised by discerning readers like Dr. John Rae,[3] who has pointed to our prevailing tendency to think of war poetry as the product principally, almost exclusively indeed, of the First World War and, so far as the Second War is concerned, associated only with two or three poets like Alun Lewis and Keith Douglas or Sydney Keyes. He pointed out also how the poetry of *Oasis* reflects the response of an essentially unwarlike people forced to fight in defence of their freedom but doing so in *full awareness* and without the initial naiveté of poets like Rupert Brooke or Julian Grenfell. *Oasis* presented in many ways a more mature and truthful reaction to war. As the late George Fraser, himself a poet and critic of distinction who knew the Middle East well, remarked, the writing of his war came from a more aware and literate generation, people who read and with fewer illusions—though with no less resolution, it might be added.

It was therefore the hope of the editors that *Return to Oasis* would challenge such received notions and dispel the idea that such good writing as did emerge in the Second World War was a kind of second-best which in any case appeared only in London. Such myths are not easily dislodged, however, even if we allow for the inevitable prejudices of the World War One generation that Robert Graves represents, writing in 1949 to the effect that poets seem to have been absent from the Eighth Army's Libyan campaigns. No doubt this comment reveals the deep feeling we are granted as a consolation for growing older that nothing is as good as it used to be and that it would be impudent to look at any evidence that might displace this reconciling delusion. We could add that one characteristic of the expert is not to dig for facts, especially those which contradict his thesis, in the belief—too often justified— that as an expert he is less likely to be challenged. A similar complacency of ignorance is less pardonable in a younger generation of critics and writers.

---

[3] Headmaster of Westminster School and a specialist in wartime literature. He made this observation at the launching of the cassette *Return to Oasis*, a selection of the poems from the Middle East introduced by Field Marshal Lord Carver, read by Martin Jarvis, Irene Richard, Edward Wilson, Mick Ford and Erik de Mauny, arranged by Michael Croft, Director of National Youth Theatre of Great Britain. The tape includes Field Marshal Montgomery's own recording of his speech assuming Command as General, 8th Army, 13th August 1942. Pipe music from Tom Smith, Gordon Highlanders. Produced by Keith Slade and Simon Vance, BBC Radio Brighton: Talking Tape Co/Hayward.

The second volume is an attempt to continue the process of recovery, redemption, revelation, and adjustment to long-established prejudice. The accident of material available, and changes of military scene, have produced some differences: the proportion of prose to verse is greater and it is noticeable that, for whatever reason, the poems tend to be written by those who had written before serving in North Africa and Italy. The spontaneous act of creation in the Western Desert and in Cairo would not be repeated. It had become a different war. Other factors may be at work. For there was no one steady cultural centre in Italy that could fulfil the role of Cairo in the earlier period. Naples had it's Services' Arts Centre, as Richard Hoggart describes in this book; and later there were centres elsewhere, in Perugia and Florence for example. The Army by now wanted to patronise the arts, especially the opera, which revived in lively fashion with the enthusiastic patronage of men from the forces: indeed, as our poet Norman Morris recalls, soldiers at Cassino would often get a day-pass, hitch-hike to Naples, have a bath, read the newspapers, go to the opera, and return to the field of battle, to be killed soon after.

In the Desert campaign, until the fall of Tunis and the end in North Africa, Cairo had always remained the intellectual capital. The ebb and flow of the desert fighting had somehow always returned there, whether the tide was low or at the full, giving a certain security of physical base, a permanence behind the veiling *khamseens* of sand and dying. And the fact also that Cairo was there meant that it could contain editors to advise, printers and publishers to produce and a readership with some understanding of what was trying to be said.

Italy was different; for, although Naples was central for a time—say till the fall of Cassino and the general break-through of May, 1944—the front kept moving forward, and never as too often in the desert backward; so a firm centre was impossible to establish as Rome fell and in their turn the northern cities of Italy. In such a situation, or series of situations, journals like those that had existed in Cairo could no longer be established.

There was a further difference: the old simple relationship of Cairo and the Eighth Army was gone. Apart from its own truncation in Italy (caused by the transfer of some of its most important components such as 7 Armoured Division), it had been conflated with formations from the First Army which, though battle-hardened in Tunisia, naturally enough retained a different tradition and the emphatic pride in their identity, that divisions which have long served together eventually achieve and are right to set store by. The conditions of their service in North Africa had not, however, been favourable—if only because of their relative brevity—to the establishment of a literary tradition such as had existed for the Eighth Army, though of course there were individual writers snatching the exiguous moments to try and save something of their experience and feeling from ephemerality—as some of the pieces in this volume will make clear.

Now embattled in Italy, many had still only recently (within a year) come from Britain and therefore altogether strange to the legend, myth and traditional eccentricities that had developed on the other side of the Mediterranean, untouched by the accumulated memories and what had by now become a jealously treasured nostalgia (the legend of the Eighth Army and the Desert). This nostagia is clearly reflected in the cartoons by JON, where the Two Types, to the men of Eighth Army recognisably representative, must have meant less to the other and fresher formations. The cartoons expressed the tendency to look backwards to the earlier phase and what many of the then survivors had come to think of as a kind of home, Cairo, Egypt, Libya and the sand.

There was another basic difference in experience between those who came through North Africa to Italy and those who had served in the Desert. The soldiers and the writers among them who had fought in the Western Desert had soldiered in a world almost without any population but for the enemy and, except in battle itself, there was between the two opposing forces a decent and prudent interval. Such inhabitants as constituted the sparse population of those sandy wastes had on the whole developed a skilful art of invisibility—except for the occasionally trading of midget eggs against tea and the pungent, free-issue V-Cigarettes. And so there had been a special climate or ambience of space and freedom, often illusory and sometimes depressing as well as dangerous, but nonetheless in its better moments peculiarly favourable to a feeling of inspiration, a desire to create—something perhaps savoured long before by the prophets and saints whom the deserts have always notoriously nurtured.

In the comparative absence of a settled population, too, and the fact that Arabic was a language inaccessible to most of the troops they were able to create their own world with its own special vocabulary, terms of reference, techniques of survival and social communication, a life independent of any mode of living except their own. In Italy, the case was very different: they had entered a world already rich in tradition, and a tradition with a certain familiarity even to those unconscious of it: the classical and the Christian, cultures stratified upon each other, had also done much to form the civility on which the British themselves had been bred, even unaware. The language of the country, compared with Arabic, was almost easily accessible, and it was not too difficult for the newcomers to enter almost directly into the local way of life, as is clear from some of the writings in this book, which look outward beyond the army world. The people so recently classified as an enemy could now be accepted as allied: the activities of the partisans, of which we have been able to give some glimpses here, became more effective and better known to our own forces as the fighting struggled agonisingly northward. And, perhaps most important of all, where in the desert destruction had been mainly something for the contending armies themselves, in Italy almost no military action was possible without some tragedy to the civilian population and destruction to the magnificent monuments of the ages as well as to the sometimes more shocking annihilation of humble but treasured homes. Hardly a day could pass for many a soldier in Italy without his sensibilities being assaulted by some evidence of the terror of war, some compelling demand upon his compassion.

There is a further observation that might not be at once apparent to the reader of today who happens not to be old enough to recall the years of that war. The writings in this volume, as in *Return from Oasis*, come from men who belonged to the last generation before television, transistor radios, and cassettes, and all that visual world whose distanced reality has gone so far to re-place the world of the book, the world of the written word. The soldiers had enjoyed more independence and silence than is possible for their civilian counterparts today; and many of them had used that silence to read and to re-flect, and perhaps to be more self reliant in both activities, less overwhelmed by the pressure of converging and conventional opinions from without, than is easily possible today. Their present had a deeper dimension, included more past, was less vulnerable to instant obsolescence, to the pose of changing fashion, and therefore had a more extended perspective, even though the immediate future was subject to constant threat.

With a strange combination of the starry-eyed and the realistic—they had shed the illusions of their fathers— they really did believe they were fighting for a better world, a more compassionate society, the possibility of an international organisation to defend the peace. It was more than a war against Hitler. There was a positive belief in freedom and caring for others and the pamphlets that came from the War Office itself fostered such beliefs, especially the work of Beveridge and Butler.[4]

So, however on the surface they might scoff, affect cynicism, they were in fact the last generation to be able to think in terms of hope without looking over their shoulders, without that despairing apathy which endless disappointment has afflicted not only the survivors but even more the young who were not there. And the certainties of that period, the innocence of their aspirations, and especially so in the services the relative absence of a commercial element, are reflected either directly or by implication in much of what this volume contains.

On other pages the editors acknowledge more formally the help they have

---

[4] Beveridge's war-time report envisaged the Welfare State. The Butler Education Act of 1944 laid the basis of a post-war education for all citizens. The reports of both formed the subject matter of pamphlets from the Army Bureau of Current Affairs.

received from institutions and individuals. The media have aided in presenting our appeals for material, in particular *The Times* and the *Sunday Mirror*, the *Listener* and *Your's* and the BBC itself. The Imperial War Museum gave us access to its own relevant collections and was most helpful with its bibliographical, recording and storage resources.

It is invidious to single out names for special mention in this introduction but this book owes so much to the unstinting aid and encouragement of Field Marshal Lord Carver and General Sir John Hackett, who have throughout displayed that enviable capacity of busy and important men to find time and to do things that lesser men would be too busy to contemplate. We appreciate, too, Richard Hoggart's aid not only in his contribution on the Arts in Italy but also his advice on poetry from his Naples Centre. Let us add the financial aid from the Dulverton Trust—thanks to Major General Douglas Brown—and the Esmée Fairbairn Charitable Trust among those listed elsewhere. Collecting material is time-consuming and costly and the Trust must pay for the preparation of manuscripts for publication and meet a share of book production. But all the efforts would have failed were it not for the co-operation of the members of the war-time forces—and of their families, where they have died, in the search for the often dusty mss, collections of drawings, fading books and all that precious debris which can now carry its message far beyond the immediate kinsfolk who have treasured it so long.

It is largely because of the piety of such people that we are able to present this record, however incomplete, of how men thought and felt in the brief intervals afforded them by a war in distant lands where they risked their lives, and often lost them, for a freedom which, if not yet won, they at least saved us from losing.

Of those who did not come back let us mention the poets, who had developed and written in their brief years before enlisting in the services. Their names are recorded on an earlier page, headed 'IN MEMORY'. They comprise most of what we must term the professional poets who served in the Middle East, North Africa and Italy. Is their death, their inability to return and promote their cause, one reason why their work has been so sadly neglected, one reason we needed to found a Trust to rescue from oblivion what would otherwise be lost in the competing clamour of the endless output of the printed word?

D.D. and V.S.

Reflection

They went to war quietly. The war had to be fought. Not a flag in sight! It was a job to be done and the poets and writers in this book and their colleagues, who survived, would return just as quietly—some four or five years later—and a man would shake their hand as they queued in a closed, dusty building, and say 'thank you'—and that was it—before they went on to collect a suit, a ration book, clothing coupons and maybe a Post Office book with £100. Then down the road to heaven—a pint of bitter at 4 pence (less than 2p) and then the train and home to family and children who were strangers.

Glory? They would have laughed. Heroes? A ribald response! When the bombs drop or shells come over there is only one thing—dig in and duck!

V.S.

I
Middle East Forces

Frank Allridge

Tank

Metallic cold, and mud-caked silhouette.
Rust, where rain and dew absorb into
An unresponsive juggernaut!

Deep-pressed into indented ground,
Bereft of life, and frictional sound,
Iron tracks rust red!

Power, to rend, and crush and kill!
Ponderous birth of mechanic skill.
Armed walls of steel!

Fumed air, with smoke, and racking roar,
She lurches from her mud-gripped floor.
Automaton, born for war!
An oil-stained driver's paramour.

J. H. Bailey

From My Middle East Diary

Mena is on the very edge of Cairo. At the end of the tram line. At least it was and I suppose still is. A luxury hotel called Mena House was forbidden territory. It was outside our price range, anyway. Full we were told with high up base wallahs and our own straight from the Western Desert Correspondents. The Sphinx and Pyramids Guide business was flourishing and the donkeys and camels worked overtime.

About thirty of us had been allocated to the 8th Hussars. The adjutant spoke to us briefly. Something about having won two belts instead of one at the Charge of the Light Brigade.

We were the first conscripts the 8th had experienced. The previous year, a number of territorials had joined them. Mostly mechanics, fitters and the like.

They had recently come back from their first trip into the Western Desert—the 'Blue', as it was called. Wavell was the General in charge, and apparently we had won. At least we had taken thousands of Italian prisoners, smashed up their Army at Beda Fomm, and chased them out of Cyrenaica. The names the boys dropped sounded quite romantic. 'Fort Maddalena', 'Sidi Omar', 'Fort Cappuzzo', 'Hellfire Pass' and 'The Wire', always 'The Wire'. This was a boundary erected between Libya and Cyrenaica by the Italians.

We new boys were placed two to a tent with ten or so relatively old sweats. They were for the most part well equipped with spoils from the Italian Campaign. Most had folding beds. Mine also had a lurcher-looking bitch and her six pups. But now, for the very first time, we were on the ground. In England there had been beds of a sort. On the boat there had been bunks. Or had there? We in the good ship 'Samaria' had zig-zagged our way from Liverpool across the Atlantic and back, paused for a day or two at Freetown, and moved on to Durban. And in the five or six weeks this took I doubt if I slept in the same place twice. Our official hold was 'E' deck. When the hammocks were slung there was no room to move. One had to crawl around between the mess tables and forms. Every night, some of us crept out with our blanket and found some place on deck. The 'Samaria' was a 20,000 ton Cunard boat and carried some 4500 officers, men and crew. The 4000 or so men occupied one half. The rest the other. We did not relish being torpedoed.

The 8th Hussars were encamped at Mena without a tank to call their own. I cannot recollect that anyone was frantic with worry; or particularly anxious to go up the Blue again. In any case the tanks did eventually turn up. They were American 'Stuarts', or 'Honeys' for some reason or other. Someone said their 37 mm gun wasn't a match for the German Mk. III's 50 mm. Someone else said the Stuart was 10 miles an hour faster than the Mk. III . . . So you could take your pick.

We gave each tank the name of a racehorse. A Squadron began with 'A', B with 'B', C with 'C' and HQ with 'H'! These were stencilled on either flank of the tank, and in front the Jerboa, the Desert Rat, the Divisional sign of the 7th Armoured Division. Pennants were flown from the wireless masts and we were more or less ready for off.

The 1940 Wavell Offensive had pushed up beyond Benghazi to El Agheila. But now, in the summer of 1941, things were not so good. Someone called Rommel had appeared and pushed us right back again; right back, in fact, to the Wire. So we went up again. We new boys were for the most part not even driver's mates. I was, at first, particularly unfortunate and spent the first few weeks perched on the spare tyre of an ammunition truck situated between the body and the cab, with a machine gun in my lap and instructions to use it against the Stukas—German Dive-Bombers. I did intitially make the occasional effort. But there really wasn't much point. So I gave it up. After a while the job of cook to the LAD became available. So I volunteered. The LAD—Light Aid Detachment—were for the most part Ordnance Corps men whose job it was to keep up with the tanks and effect such running repairs as were necessary. Needless to say we had a saddler and carpenter on the strength.

During the day life was one of constant movement. We seldom made contact with men from any but our own squadron. A. B. and C. might have been other villages dotted out on the plain. Our main concern was to keep an eye open for ready-made slit trenches, so that we did not have to dig yet another. This and Stukas. When they appeared we ran for such shelter as there was, waited for the bang, and then looked up to see who had been unlucky.

So it went on, all through that late summer and on into autumn. Would we be back in Cairo by Christmas? This was our main concern.

Cairo had everything from the brothels upwards. The OR's[1] official port of call was called The Berka. This was a building very much after the style of a Glasgow tenement, being several storeys high with a wide stone stairway leading up. On the ground floor, sitting in his stall, was the RAMC man doling out one french letter, one tin of ointment, and a pamphlet to each suppliant. There was no excuse if one contracted VD, the pamphlet said. This was a punishable offence. The price the girls charged varied. It ranged from 5 to 30 piastres, 1/- to 6/-, the more expensive young ladies being on the first floor. The higher one climbed, the less one paid.

There was, I am afraid, no Romance of the East, or any other place. One joined the queue for the ones who were said to be the better value. Or walked in at a vacant door if one was pressed for time.

By February Rommel had refitted and pushed us back to Gazala. So in March, having stencilled the names from the 1941 casualty list on our brand new Grants and Stuarts, we returned to the Desert. It was evident that this desert warfare was very much a matter of supplying one's lines of communication. Ours from Egypt. Theirs from North Africa and beyond. Once either side was on the run, the temptation to outstrip one's supplies was very great. And there were no petrol pumps on the one and only road from Agheila to Alex.

The Regiment moved on to the black ribbon which was the Cairo–Alexandria road, turned to the left somewhere around Almeriya, fanned out into the set 40 or so yards between each vehicle and followed our leader, Colonel Kilkelly, up into the Blue once again.

After the ususal here, there and everywhere we ended up near Bir Hacheim, and, to our surprise, made a semi-permanent camp there. The Free French were between us and the 15th and 21st German Armoured Divisions; but apparently there was no panic and we went in batches to bathe in the Mediterranean, some

---

[1] Other Ranks.

40 miles away. The day after our turn orders came to get ready to move; but without any sense of urgency. I had just removed the radiator cap from my truck, to check the water level, when Ginger's strident voice yelled out something about every man for himself. This was perhaps a little premature; but those tanks on the sky-line were not ours. And when the guns opened up we knew they did not belong to the Free French either. We had been caught with the rising sun in our eyes. But our tanks were moving towards them and we of the Thin Skins in the opposite direction up the sides of the escarpment, with Corporal Martin, sitting beside me giving me a running commentary on the battle in the wadi below. And then we saw more tanks in front of us. We appeared to be completely surrounded. Half an hour or so later we ran into a long line of our own trucks only to find that they were in charge of the enemy. So we had no option but to join them.

We stayed for five days with our captors. Somewhere in the Tobruk, Gazala, Bir Hacheim triangle. Montrose, a wireless operator from A squadron, could speak some German, and our two guards were quite affable. Once again, but this time for us, 'for you, the war is over'. We would go, they said, to a POW camp in Italy, and later into Germany. All was well organised. It almost sounded attractive. At least within spitting distance of home. I felt a bit concerned for Montrose, who was a Jew from Glasgow. But if he was worried, he never showed it.

On the third day we had to get out of our trucks and walk. The German guards were replaced by Italians. Walking meant we had to limit our possessions to what we could carry in the heat of the day. Two blankets, a small pack and water bottle was about the limit. The Germans had been very methodical. Officers one way. NCO's another, and then the rest. One of our fitters produced a couple of stripes from his haversack. He had lost them for something or other; but an entry had not yet been made in his Pay Book. NCO's he maintained were the foremen and shop stewards in the prison camps. Nothing was changed. See you in Stalag B.

On the sixth day my Monty and I found ourselves the last in a line of an enormous crocodile of prisoners. We had been back over the same ground twice, and argued this would happen again. So we sat down on the edge of a slit trench. The solitary Italian guard, bringing up the rear, motioned to us with his tommy gun, to get up and join the queue and moved on. We followed. But this time the queue did not turn round, and we found ourselves further and further behind . . . There was a battle going on somewhere on our right and stray shells were dropping around us. So we lay down in a hole made by one of them. Monty, who was the best possible companion to have with one in circumstances such as these, assured me that shells never dropped in the same place twice . . . We stayed in the hole until the shelling stopped. It wasn't very pleasant. For one thing we were out of water and it was the middle of the day. Our queue had vanished in the distance and we were very lonely. Some time later we saw German armoured troop-carriers coming towards us. We stood there, fully expecting a lift. But they were apparently in a hurry. Monty held out his water bottle and called out 'wasser' to the last of the carriers, and someone, who shall be for ever blessed, dropped a Jerrican at our feet. It contained enough water to give us the drink we needed, and to fill our bottles.

And so, once again, we felt very much alone. The odd puff of smoke on the far horizon must, we thought, be coming from our guns and we decided to walk in that direction. Some time later we saw a gun-limber in the distance; it might have been the one we had to hand back. They spotted us but did not come towards us. Instead someone standing on the roof of the limber, waved to us to come in. We thought this uncharitable . . . but our first words of greeting were 'You buggers have just walked across a bloody minefield'.

We had lost about half the regiment and it was being reformed with men from the Gloucester Hussars and reinforcements from home. The missing men meant promotions all round and I found myself having to stitch a stripe on. We learnt that a new General called Montgomery had arrived. He sent round a circular telling us we were going to 'knock the enemy for six'. Rumour had it that he had also closed down the Berka, on the grounds that we couldn't both fuck and fight. Be that as it may I found myself, sometime in July, driving a Honey up to Burg el Arab where Montgomery had his caravan on the sea shore. Rommel had not been able to get any further than El Alamein. The Qattara Depression narrows the gap at this point and it was a thousand miles or so to El Agheila. We went on patrol between the sea and the Depression and when we returned in September it was obvious that there had been a very considerable build up. We had never seen so many planes—'ours'—above our heads as we moved around the Depression and had only made occasional contact with the enemy.

At Burg el Arab the Build Up was going on. Hundreds of the latest American tank—the Sherman—had arrived and we liked it much more than the Grant. Its 75 mm gun was in the turret and more or less a match for the German 88s. Two more troops of the 8th had arrived from Alex equipped with Shermans, but they were almost all strangers. It was impossible to learn who had or had not been killed or taken prisoner; but I could get no news of Monty, my Monty. Months later I knew he had been killed along with most of the troop that went up again from Bardia away back in June.

Harold Ian Bransom

Our Patrols Were Active . . .

An old man raised his eyes and snarled,
 'Orders? Good God, have you no head?
Go out, and fetch me German dead'
 He sent a handful to defeat
The Hun dug-in in his retreat.
 They died, as ordered, without growl.
The 'Brass-hats' said, 'Not a good prowl.'

Smug politicians sit and smoke,
 They listen to the news.
'Roberts! First class! A master-stroke.
 We need old hands to run this show.'
While women kneel in chapel pews
 To mourn for sons whose blood did flow
Because 'old men' refused to 'Go.'

J. E. Brookes

Waltzing Matilda

They said that Sergeant Symington had been
an officer in the Great War. I mean,
well wouldn't it!? From officer in one
of those posh regiments that thought the sun
shone from its arse to Pommie sergeant in
the Aussie Army? Well he'd only win
respect by his example that's for sure.
A prima facie case of kill or cure,
and up you too, mate! All right, granted he
seemed dinkum but appearances can be
deceptive, it's the killing and the noise
of battle sorts the men out from the boys.
And so to Bardia. Poor Morcom had

his head blown off but things were not so bad
once we had got ourselves inside the wire
and right-wheeled down it; the Eyetalian fire
was lessening. But when we came atop
a wadi and fanned out some bloody Wop
had seen us coming. Over open sights
they let us have it—must have seen the whites
of old Ned Kelly's eyes. We'd gone no more
than the length of a cricket pitch before
the Captain realised that this attack
was suicide. He shouted out 'Get back
into the wadi, men, get back and wait
for further orders!' Me, I was prostrate
in some imaginary desert groove
and kept my head down, just too scared to move,
I reckon. Understandable. There fell
around us every single shot and shell
in Mussolini's ammunition dump.
Then looking up I saw a khaki lump
in front of me which asked 'Have you been hit?'
'No, I'm all right' I said but I admit
Melbourne seemed far away. My bloody oath!
I crawled up to the voice so we were both
in it together. Sergeant Symington
it was, poor bastard. He was lying on
his back with both his knees drawn up. Was it
some author bloke who said when you've been hit
the worst thing is the guns keep firing? If
in pain he didn't show it, kept that stiff
uncompromising upper lip a Pom
is noted for and said 'Take a tip from
an old campaigner. Push me on my side
to face the enemy, I won't have died
in vain if you can use me as a shield.'
Famous last words I reckon on the field
of battle. Jesus Christ! But I demurred.
I mean, I couldn't do it, never heard
of such a thing. He said 'No ifs and buts,
I'm done for, soldier!' (it was true, his guts
were hanging out). So that is what I did.
I pushed him round upon his side and hid
behind him while the Eyeties threw the lot.

The bullet or the shrapnel that had got
my name written all over it was stopped
by Sergeant Symington and when he copped
this last lot he just upped and died. Well, thank
the Lord a bloody great Matilda tank
came waltzing up, its armour-plated hull
like some huge battleship, and in the lull
that followed while the Eyeties had a look
and thought that it was time they slung their hook,
I heard old Sgt-Major Byron shout
'Right men, continue to advance! Fan out,
fan out!', so shaking Symo by the hand,
which was a little limp of course with sand
and blood all over it I upped and strode
towards the enemy. No doubt I owed
my life to him. It did not matter much
in military terms to succour such
a tenderfoot as me but bells have rung
for lesser deeds than his and medals hung
on lesser breasts. I mention it because
he WAS a man, my bloody oath he was!
He wasn't decorated. Well I mean,
he wasn't but he bloody should have been!
I tell you, Sport, if it was up to me,
then he'd be Sergeant Symington, V.C.!

Burial Party

The stairs were shot away so someone fetched
a ladder, up we went and found him stretched
out on the balcony. His eyes were closed,
his face serene. You might have diagnosed
it simply as malingering except
that when we turned him over . . . thus we kept
him face up which enabled him to show
his medal ribbons to advantage. So
we took down the Italian flag that flew
forlornly from the flagstaff which we knew
would come in handy as his winding sheet
and tied the rope's end to his booted feet.

He offered no objection so we laid
him uncomplaining on the balustrade,
made a sign of the Cross to please the Pope,
prepared to take the strain upon the rope—
and pushed him off. The trouble was a ledge
projected from the cornice and its edge
lent him a foothold. Hanging by the toes
head down he must have looked like one of those
high-wire trapezists when we hold our breath
below while watching them perform their death
defying feats; indeed a passing troop
of soldiery had gathered in a group
to see the fun. However hard we tried
to work him off the ledge he just defied
the laws of gravity. We hauled him back
a little way and tried creating slack
by jerking hard but this brave officer,
completely 'hors de combat' as it were,
upstaged us and performed on it instead
a 'danse macabre' standing on his head,
and those below, accustomed to a much
more solemn undertaking, seeing such
an unexpected 'tour de force' appeared
to find it entertaining for they cheered
him to the echo. Then the flagstaff broke
and that was that. A funny sort of joke!
Our hero did not take a curtain call,
there was no safety-net to break his fall.
He caught his head a very nasty crack
on his parade ground like we'd dropped a sack
of water melons on it. Someone said
'That's cheating mate, he was already dead!'
War kills of course, but furthermore it warps
men's sense of humour—laughing at a corpse!

B. W. Brown

Wireless

Twiddle-Dumb and Twiddle-Dee,
Twirling knobs with fiendish glee,
Strive, these twain, with efforts tireless,
Extracting noises from the Wireless,
Trying each and every station,
Every language, every Nation,
Weaving patterns kaleidoscopic
Covering every sphere and topic.
The Air is filled with squeals and moans,
Atmospherics, shrieks and groans,
In consequence of faulty Earth,
A hideous row is given birth,
Every time the tap is used
(Just to keep the chaps amused!)
And owing to a wiring short,
The stove itself joins in the sport,
Crackle—every time it's stoked,
Crackle—every time it's poked.
In the road a lorry driving,
Impersonates a Bomber—diving.
Listen to the Caterwauling—
'This is Ghermainey calling',
Interrupting gems of swing
(Gosh, Oh Death where is thy sting?)
Lists of latest Russian slaughter
Drowned in ENSA Concert laughter.
Childish chorus singing 'Yours',
Detracting from some Worthy Cause,
Intermingling with the views
Of Daylight raiding Bombers' crews.
A worthy Politician's speech
Is terminated by a screech.
Concerts given for the Yanks
Overlapping tolls of Tanks.
Plaintive notes upon a Cello
Blasted by a general bellow,
Little bursts of music martial,
Fragmentary opera—faint—impartial.

11

Singers, crooners, stopped mid-voice,
So many Waves—so wide the choice.
When this has gone on Far too long,
'Sorry Chaps—NOTHING ON.'!

"Failing that, I suppose we will have to appeal to their better nature!"

When you embarked they handed you a card with your deck (which could descend to Deck 'E') and within the deck where you slept . . . in a hammock, on the mess table or on the floor. Those prone to sea-sickness were encouraged *by others* to choose the floor.

MTS OTRANTO   Boat Drill

Troopship on the way out to the Middle East round the Cape.

13

Ken Burrows

Stella

I met her first in Cairo,
I fancied her on sight,
But she gave me just a glassy stare,
When my lips met hers that night.
To me she was so beautiful,
Tall, with a golden tan,
And her effervescent sparkle,
Would please 'most any man.
She was so cool and tempting,
Her dress was paper thin,
And as I madly tore it off,
I knew that I would win.
I held her tightly in that bar,
I was hot, my throat was dry,
I took her without a struggle,
There was no protesting cry.
I took her back to share with friends,
She passed from man to man,
She was drained of all she had to give,
As only soldiers can.
Now, as I lay upon my bed,
I wish that she were here,
But I've only the empty bottle,
That was filled with Stella beer.

W. H. Burt

Stane Jock[1]

*For the glory of the Highland Division
on the night of 23 October 1942*

Atween the mune an' the yird[2]
   There is quick steel:
Atween the steel and the yird
There is quick stane!

The man-trap field is fu' o' men
   Walking saftly.
The man-eating mandrakes scream
   As they bite.

The stane Jock o' Beaumont Hamel
   Is fa'en doon.
There's nae mair pipes in France—
   Nae mair sweet croon.

But this nicht stane Jock,
   Walks in the sand!
This nicht I hear the pipes,
   I hear the band!

There's nane deid but his dead e'en
   Glower at the west.
There's nane living but stepping hard
   Towards the west.

For the stane fa'n in France
   Here rises a living stane—
For the mindin' o' men killed
   Here rises a killing stane!

[1]Name of the stone memorial on the Western Front of World War One
[2]Earth

Yon pinke'ed craw, the mune,
    Sees a field o' strange plants—
Fire and sand fused glassily
    Into flowers on a wall.

An' the wa' is o' stane,
    An' the wa' walks
Covered wi' red flowers—
    A stane striding to destiny!

Gallus laddies a'l
    Stanes o' destiny!
Stane Jock in the mantrap field
    Walking saftly.

Send Snow

There's cold here.
But it's the belly cold of night
And it covers nothing.
Send snow
To cover and whiten the graves
The yellow graves.

Louis Challoner and Joe Nugent

The Guns at El Alamein

From early July until mid-October we remained dug in across the desert.

To the East of us there was feverish activity on the part of the civil population of Cairo and Alexandria. They had evidently come to the conclusion that the war was over and that Rommel and his Afrika Korps would be driving up Sharia el Pasha[1] any day now.

---

[1]Main street of Cairo.

To the West the combined might of Germany and Italy waited only for the word of command to advance and smash their way through to the Canal.

Short of ammunition, fuel and water, plagued by the blistering heat, the blinding, suffocating sand and the ubiquitous flies, we spent our days perfecting gun-drill, weaponry and navigation techniques and our nights in interminable guards and pickets.

Mysterious exercises took place in which we drove out to the edge of the minefields, dug gun-pits and arranged camouflage for them and then returned without firing a shot. We saw new airfields laid out in the desert with squadrons of new 'planes' (hastily constructed from packing cases and sacking) designed, perhaps, to trick the enemy into believing that the R.A.F. was being vastly reinforced.

In other places dummy tanks and guns were drawn up in vast numbers as if in preparation for a massive counter-attack and immense quantities of ammunition were stock-piled and concealed.

We heard of fire-plans being drawn up which would call for the expenditure of thousands of shells at an unprecedented rate. By contrast, on the other hand, everyone was adjured to conserve ammunition and even the customary morning and evening ranging shots of the enemy went unanswered.

Despite the back-breaking toil, the itching, smarting sand, the sickening attentions of the flies, which came in clouds from the Qattara Depression, the icy chill of the nights beneath the stars and the murderous heat of the day, morale had never been so good—never had the other ranks been so confident that this was to be the final turning point and that the forthcoming battle was destined to be the beginning of the end.

On the evening of October 23rd the order to 'stand to' was passed in whispers along the whole front. 'Take Post!' and then, after a further three minutes of quivering tension the synchronised command rapped from a thousand throats—'Fire!'

The fury of horrendous sound which assaulted our ears during the following hours was something we had never experienced before. It cuffed, shattered and distorted the senses with throbbing, trembling pain. It loosened one's teeth—and one's bowels—alarmingly.

It was bad enough to withstand without wavering the crack of our own piece, and the concerted roar of the four guns in the troop firing together was worse still, but this, with hundreds of guns almost hub to hub, all bucking and recoiling, spitting fire and snapping like a pack of vicious terriers all at once, it was sheer horror.

More thunder rolled and reverberated across the front as the heavier guns behind us added their base tones to the discord. The very ground trembled and winced, the noise eddied and roared out fan-wise in all directions; massive waves of blast swept sand and smoke into tremendous currents and the moaning undertones of echo from the smoke-cloud and the whine of departing missiles sounded as if even the spirits of the underworld were adding their voices to the tumult.

The thunderous action continued throughout the night, each gun being rested periodically for a few minutes to allow the barrel to cool. Our targets had been enemy guns between four and five miles away, but in the early hours of the morning our range was shortened in order to subdue the Axis machine-gunners and provide our Infantry with cover for their advance. A close watch was kept to ensure that all settings were correct lest any shells should fall short. But we had to shout at the tops of our voices to make ourselves heard for our heads were beginning to feel numb right through and ordinary tones of voice were quite useless.

Those of us who had contemptuously refused to wear ear-plugs were now regretting our bravado. Incredibly a use was found for the unsmokeable 'Victory V' cigarettes, doubled up and pushed into the ears, they afforded some relief.

The Infantry made good progress towards their limited objectives and scout parties who went further forward through the minefields came back with encouraging information. Some enemy units had moved back and there were signs of a more general withdrawal in some areas. Quite a number of very shaken prisoners who had been taken without resistance came back with them, proving that the shelling had been highly effective. This was not surprising, perhaps, considering that on an average every gun had fired six hundred rounds.

Each day, and with infinite caution, we pressed forward a little further. There was no attempt this time to sweep exultantly through the enemy's lines and go fanning out over wide stretches of desert. The line remained solid and just moved forward with the inexorable steadiness of a steam roller.

As we progressed we kept firing, and the Armoured columns and Infantry drove wedges into the enemy formations. The defences were creaking, it seemed, and it would only be a matter of time before they broke completely. But there was no complacency. It was not for nothing that Rommel was known as the 'Desert Fox', and his astuteness had to be taken into account. We suspected that a fox might be most dangerous when it was at bay.

On October 29th the Aussies opened a path for us through the vast minefield. Our passage was strongly opposed and we were heavily shelled and bombed en route. Eighty-eight millimetre shells landed close to us with all the ferocity of old and Stukas made some of the most audacious attacks we had ever known. But nothing was going to stop us now. We noted with satisfaction that we were back in the vicinity of Woodcock and from here on November 1st another tremendous attack was directed upon the disorganised enemy.

A fantastic number of shells poured from our guns—the graft entailed in getting the programme under way at short notice was inhuman and no galley-slaves could ever have surpassed our work-rate. We were close to exhaustion by the time the fire-plan was completed but on this occasion at least we saw something to give us a feeling of satisfaction. Droves of shell-shocked and thoroughly demoralised soldiers from the other side were staggering through our lines. Their weapons they had thrown away, and some of them could hardly raise their hands to put them on their heads. They were surrendering to anyone who would lead them away from the scene of the dreadful shelling and the hell it had created.

Edward Cope

Letter to Fiancée

Sgt. E. Cope, MM,
The Rifle Brigade,
M.E.F.,
12th April 1943[1]

Dear Doreen,

I've got a very difficult job in front of me now, but don't let those words alarm you. You see I've just returned to the Bn[2]. and have received 13 letters from you, practically together (Nos. 1-11 incl.). Now do you see my difficulty—to answer all those in one letter? Still I'll do my best. Your last letter is dated 29th March, so you can see what an excellent service it is.

I was very pleased to hear that practically all my letters have now been received and also the present. I had almost given the latter up for lost and I didn't ask about it so as not to disappoint you if it was. Anyway I knew you would let me know when it arrived and I'm glad it's alright for size.

I find it next to impossible to write when we are moving as you can imagine. I was thankful to have a day's respite which we have today. You've made my mouth water with tales of a Christmas dinner and of other such meals, so I think you justly deserve to be made to feel as I did. I cannot tell of delicious meals other than of tinned meat and veg. or bully fritters but I can describe today and the area we are occupying!

---

[1] Edward Cope corresponded with his girl friend Doreen Roots throughout the War. We also reproduce a letter of his from Italy in a later part of the book.

[2] Battalion.

It's either Saturday or Sunday, I'm not sure which, but it doesn't matter as long as we know it's April and it feels like Sunday, or it will until the bombers come over! It's nearly midday, the sky is clear and blue and the sun is beating down the heat of which however is relieved by a cool wind which keeps a constant freshness. Birds are twittering and insects buzzing around, but not annoying, and from across the valley comes the dull, lazy sound—not of cricket bat against ball—but of steady hammering, and in the distance one can hear trucks moving up.

The valley is covered with stubbly grass and masses of yellow daisies and a white flower and blue and purple flowers as far as one can see. In the centre of the valley is an outfield and olive trees planted in disorder in the field. But a few miles away, quite clear to view are olive groves in orderly ranks, like lines ruled on brown paper stretching for miles. And away on the other side are high rugged hills disappearing into a blue haze.

And then someone tests out their bren gun or fires a rifle and the picture is reconstituted on a war basis!!

Your last letter records the fall of Mareth and by now it seems that the last phase of this campaign is on. What then, is impossible to say and the hope, that many soldiers out here have, is hardly likely to be realised. You can guess what they are looking forward to after this campaign, but they don't quite realise that the war is not over when this African affair is over. But I sincerely hope that the Battle of Europe doesn't take too long.

And now let's scan the letters to see if or rather how many questions I must answer. Oh, here's one in letter 9 (18.3.43), you ask where I spent my last leave, whether in Cairo or not? Yes, it was. I like your remark that Cairo must seem like an old friend now. You're right it certainly does. What I know of Cairo would fill a book, and what I don't would fill another one!! But I have an acquaintance with a new friend now, one that we have fought for from the commencement of the war and that is now in our hands, Tripoli! But it's nowhere near as good as Cairo; still it would have to be good to be that for several old soldiers who have been to India and Malta all say that none of the cities will touch Cairo—for spending leave anyway.

I've received the snap of you and Sunch and Dick and his friend. It's quite good and Sunch certainly seems to be enjoying herself. By the way, if she is ten stone now she'll be as heavy as I am by the time the war's over. Are you sure she hadn't filled her boot with stones, or is it the milk from the dairy that's losing cream?

Mentioning photographs, I didn't know that tinting them was a hobby of yours. I thought tinting was a very specialised job, although you do mention that the glossy ones are difficult. What colouring matter do you use—water colour or a special mixture?

I was rather amused when you said that Pop found Edgar Wallace tame after the Herries Chronicle. I can just imagine the contrast. As a matter of fact I've been lucky enough to get hold of *Nicholas Nickleby* by Dickens and, although I've read it once or twice before, it still comes new, interesting, amusing and refreshing. Do you know, after the end of term examinations at school, we always had a few days of inactivity, while the masters were marking papers, and I always used to get one of Dickens's books out of the library and read it nearly all day. Actually quite a good parallel could be drawn between an exam and our present situation, with today as one of the days of inactivity.

You seem to have seen quite a few good pictures and plays this year, *Dancing Years* and *Desert Victory*, *Cinderella* and *Random Harvest*. Now I wonder if you enjoyed the latter best of all, for you say the tears rolled down your cheeks! Actually, on the three weeks course, we had a small cinema near us, I believe I described the type before! where the film show change nightly. I think we went there every night! what a record. Still there was little else to do. *Desert Victory* has been shown out here, but I haven't seen it yet; by your description it sounds pretty interesting and I would like to see it.

I've just started again on this letter, as we've just had an interlude for lunch. No, you're wrong—it wasn't bully and biscuits! It was cheese and pickles and bread with rice and jam to follow. And as a speical treat we had milk with the rice—not tinned milk or cow's milk, but goat's milk that the people at the local village had given one of our crew. Have you ever tasted goat's milk? I doubt actually if you'd tell the difference, unless, of course, quite a possibility, and that is that we've forgotten what cow's milk tastes like! Anyway it made a lovely rice pudding— and now I feel as much as you probably did after your Christmas dinner!!

You end up your last letter by saying 'I wish you were here so that I could say "thank you" nicely for the dressing-gown'. Well, you know how much I wish I were, but one day, no doubt, it will all come true and like the end of a fairy tale story we'll be able to live happily ever after.

Till then, darling, all my love

Ted

XXXXX

P.S. Would you thank Aunt Tom for her letter, I'll reply as soon as I can.

H. Darby

You Lucky Guys

Now stop your moans, both big and small,
For I don't think, you've a grouse at all,
You work just twenty four hours a day,
And get your food, your clothes, and pay.

You're up each morn, by six o' clock
And right away you have your chuck,
Then all day long, you mooch about,
And growl because you can't go out.

No sirens howl, to break these spells
And all you do, is dodge the shells
You have no stairs at night to pound
Your bed is ready, on the ground.

Now take those workers, back at home,
Who work their fingers to the bone,
To send you all the things that please
Like Bully Beef and Victory Vs.[1]

Their hours are long, and all that's found
For toiling so, is sixteen pound,
They queue for grub, and bacca's dear,
And only get ten pints of beer,

So arnt you glad, you left the Strand,
And rest in such a sunny land,
I guess you all should sign for more,
And go and join the Chinese war.

[1]Army issue cigarettes

Dan Davin

Libyan Epitaph

The snake is dead. The lethal life
Is broken free. The hypodermic teeth
Still hold uninjected death. The knife
So keen-edged rusts by its sandy sheath.

Under the minute scales how fine the bone.
How delicate the spectrum of his spinal bloom.
How rippled his last shudder. How alone
He lies upon his grave, the ancient womb.

Symbol of subtle sin, he has sin's wage,
Who knew no myths of why old Adam died.
His foe was always knowable. His rage
Reached little past his supple, lovely pride.

More deadly I, though clumsier my art.
I fight for causes, less innocent my heart.

8 December, 1942.

Erik de Mauny

Picking up the Pieces at El Alamein

My El Alamein? A blurred jumble of noise, dust, confusion, and a desperate lack of sleep!

Having done my basic training earlier on with the New Zealand Medical Corps, I was by then with No. 1 NZ Casualty Clearing Station. This was, in effect, a small but well equipped mobile hospital, operating as near as possible to the front line, and moving forward every few days to deal with the latest intake of casualties.

Everything had been pared to the bone for the sake of speed and mobility. Our transport consisted of three-tonners, from the back of which canvas awnings could be slung to form tented wards. There was a special blood bank truck, a well-stocked dispensary, and a large generator to provide power for the operating theatre. It was an extremely efficient outfit, staffed by a small team of surgeons who operated round the clock, and a great many badly wounded men undoubtedly owed their lives to their skill and devotion.

Once the battle had begun, with its mind-numbing barrage, ambulances started arriving in a steady stream from the forward RAPs[1], jolting over the rough desert tracks to the additional agony of their suffering occupants. No distinction was made between friend or foe, but only in the varying degrees of injury inflicted. This was indicated by discs of various colours hung round the necks of the wounded. Those not in urgent need of treatment would be given a hot drink, food, a cigarette, and despatched by ambulance convoy back to a base hospital. But those with stomach wounds or grave damage to other vital parts would be rushed as quickly as possible onto the operating table.

I had several spells as a theatre orderly, and among the mingled odours of blood, diesel fumes and anaesthetic, I saw some prodigies of battle surgery. It was always an eerie experience, especially at night, when the ground shook with the impact of high explosives, the sky behind the tent flaps an arterial crimson with gun flashes, and our overhead light blinking and flickering as the generator groaned in the background. Only the surgeons, their eyes dark with fatigue, seemed unperturbed, cutting away sections of blood-soaked uniform, trimming, probing and sewing up the gaping flesh with calm and studious concentration.

But in that first phase of the battle, the entire unit had to make do with a minimum of rest. My main job was to look after one of the tented wards. While the wounded snored and groaned in the darkness, I sat at a small table on the back of the truck, surrounded by medical paraphernalia, and devised desperate stratagems to fight off the encroaching waves of sleep. The only one that seemed to work was to light a cigarette, then catnap with my head on the table until the smouldering butt burned my fingers; whereupon I would light another one and repeat the process. At four o'clock one morning, the RC padre, making one of his rounds, found me asleep on a pile of sandbags beside the truck. I had no recollection of lying down there. The padre pumped up the primus, and restored me with a scalding mug of black coffee.

What struck me most was the dramatic contrast in the way the wounded reacted to their predicament. I saw a lengthy operation on a young German soldier with multiple stomach wounds, in which yards of intestine were hauled out onto a metal side tray, each perforation neatly sutured, then the whole lot

---

[1] Regimental Aid Posts.

unceremoniously shovelled back into the open cavern of the abdomen. It was like watching a seemingly impossible repair of a badly punctured bicycle tyre: but the seemingly impossible worked. A day or so later, in the intensive care ward, I saw the young German, full of drainage tubes, but sitting up in bed and smiling cheerfully. He would survive.

Others wouldn't. A man might have only a minor injury. But bad news from home—the desertion of a wife or girl friend—could be as lethal as a bullet. One says that the spirit is willing but the flesh is weak. At Alamein, and in its aftermath, I learned that the reverse is also sometimes true. The flesh was willing to heal itself; it was the spirit that weakened and withdrew. One knew it from a peculiar expression on a man's face—and that he was about to turn his face to the wall.

Michael Dugdale

In a Little Wadi

In a little wadi
Where the thistles blow,
There's a donkey's body
Lying down below.

All the month of June, dear,
Maturing in the heat,
Very, very soon dear,
'Twill be fit to eat.

Bruce Etherington

Dinner-Dance, Cairo

I observe with my five senses
Scents and the music oozing
Curling like a poisoned lily
Under the jade-green foliage

And dark hair darkly gleaming
And scarlet nails on fingers
And Colonel de Pfoliot Darcy
Dancing with a luscious Greek badly

And Private William Albert
Hawkins happy with a Gipsy
A starlike, flowerlike maiden
Really they rumba superbly

But I cannot help staring for pity
At the solitary lady guzzling
Immortal spirit doubtless
But the body of a hippopotamus

Oh such a tiny driver
To a vehicle so enormous!
With the mane of a dusky lion
The profile of Rameses or Vernepta . . .

The piano tinkles tosh
And the fiddle yearns its slosh
On a flat-faced waiter fawning
On a fat-faced diner yawning—

All these phenomena at G——i's[1]
I observe with my five senses
From my table in the corner
And dribble them delicately on paper.

[1]Groppi's, famed for its ice cream and cakes.

Ian Fletcher

Friends Gone

Philip's slim half-forgotten hand-writing
And Donald courting death like a girl
And Tony when drunk finding God exciting
And Peter whose courtship was too successful

Falling down in a locket of fire;
And Kenneth with his sinister metaphysic;
Jack Gregory loving his gun and his beer
With one or two others out of the wreck
Fashioning some vivid life of their own.

Now what I remember, what runs quick
Round the heart is this much alone:
Some found that death was too lovely, or
Some were bent on trying to believe it so,
Some merely stayed away, uncalled for:
Their time was shortest, having nowhere to go.

1942.

Naked Africa

Naked Africa I lie on you
—the fruit-like body of woman

think of your women, philtres of midday,
dark cinders of their gaze

pressing an earthiness
of eastern flesh upon us

hiding fear between
pincers of their salamandrine sex

this is the source,
emptiness, a nothing
through which we enter on ourselves

gravid the desert

two eyes on a thin khaki stalk
still surprised
like foetuses the dead are coiled.

1944.

E. D. Forster

Prayer from Ground Level

Wing-tilted, light-hearted,
Terrible and gay,
Up and down the column
The fighter-bombers play
One-O-Nine and One-Nine-O
Dancing down the day;
Spitfire come and Hurricane,
And chase these c---s away.

Screaming Stukas stopping
Through the dusty haze,
With the vain winds plucking
At their dive-brake-stays;
The green crescendo whistle,
And the bomb-flower's blaze;
Oh, come and chase these f-----s off,
And speed them on their ways.

Double motors stealing
Down blue lanes of sky,
While the tracer-gardens blossom
And hot splinters fly;
Golden pencils scrawling
On the night wheeling by;
Come, you bloody Beaufighters
And make these b------s cry.

Libyan Desert, 1942.

A Red Cross Doctor's Diary

Nov. 1941 onwards

This was D Day for the British offensive to relieve Tobruk. 151[1] was with the 7th Armoured Division, and each truck carried the Divisional sign, the little red jerboa, as well as the Red Cross. The Division were already desert veterans, the backbone of Western Desert Force, from which Eighth Army was now being built. There were two armoured brigades, and a Support Group motor infantry and guns, commanded by the formidable Jock Campbell, whose name in the Desert achieved at that time a status hardly inferior to that of the enemy commander! My section was attached to Support Group, and on D1 we were at the so-called aerodrome at Sidi Rezegh, a spot hardly to be distinguished from the surrounding waste. From this place we were unable to move, while the armoured battle flowed all round us, for we were tethered by patients from British, South African, New Zealand, German and Italian Forces. The unrecorded heroes were the ambulance drivers, whose vehicles we loaded as we could, and sent away 'in the general direction of', praying for their luck and protection; and for their freight of wounded men, who comported themselves with great fortitude, and displayed the most astonishing optimism; I remember one load in particular, which included a British officer with a shattered arm, who was convinced that he was going to be nursed by a Q.A.[2] fiancée in some hospital beside the Nile. The expectations of a German tank commander, of his early recapture, seemed more realistic. He had arrived on my doorstep the evening before, having stepped out of his 'brewed-up' vehicle, dancing with pain, from his superficial burns, and who now paid me a grateful farewell!

So we were busy enough, marooned in no-man's-land (indeed it was everyman's-land) with little idea of what was going on. Two other doctors, cut off from their units, attached themselves to my Red Cross—Hugh Stanton, the R.M.O.[3] of a gunner regiment, and Guy Berry from a South African field unit. It may be guessed how glad I was of their moral support, to say nothing of their help with the work itself. Guy had two medical orderlies with him who were of the greatest value, for tracer was now zipping through the shelter, and my own section had suffered casualties. My Sergeant had a bullet through his right shoulder, cutting his axillary artery, and damaging his brachial plexus.

While I was trying to arrest the bleeding, a Jerry major walked in and said, 'No one can see your Red Crosses. How are you getting on?'

One of my lads replied, 'Plenty of wounded, and some dead men in the corner.'

---

[1] 151 Field Medical Unit.
[2] Queen Alexandra Nurse.
[3] Regimental Medical Officer.

‧ 'I'm sorry' he said, saluted and walked out.

We had little sense of time. It must have been about now that Rommel sent an armoured column round the back, and into Egypt, and we must have been indeed in enemy territory. We had no more ambulances, and many wounded were lying out in the desert outside the crowded shelter. Our anxious thoughts were on the problem of rations and medical supplies, but there were so many abandoned and burnt-out trucks around, that we were able to collect some food and blankets, and best of all some tins of water. We did what we could with dressings and treatment, and we had between us, thank God, a good supply of morphine. There were stranded combatants as well as medics, and an efficient burial squad was organised, marking the graves with makeshift crosses, and determining the map reference as accurately as possible. Henry Rogers, the chaplain from Support Group, was with us, and his co-operation and courage sustained us all.

One afternoon we came under fire from a few light tanks which popped up over the horizon. I did not enjoy my walk forward with a white rag, for they were by no means prompt with their cease-fire; and when I found that they were British, I expressed myself in unparliamentary terms.

'Well, we didn't know who you were.'

I asked if anything could look less hostile than a canvas shelter, with a crowd of bods upon the ground, to say nothing of my white flag. But they had been in battle too, and those were jittery days. It was only a small patrol, and they promised to report our position, and to underline our anxieties about supplies. Next day some Italians blew in, and they too said that they would report our predicament.

Perhaps they did, for next morning we were officially captured, and were told that transport would come to take us to a staging-post on the way to Italy. Sure enough, some trucks arrived, but luckily the officer in charge was a sensible man, with whom it was possible to negotiate a reasonable procedure. That left the three M.O.s and the two medical N.C.O.s, one of Guy's and my own Corporal; but they took Henry Rogers with the rest of my Section, as well as a mixed bag of all sorts.

Again we were left to our own devices, and though our numbers were now much reduced, our problems were more sharply defined. It seemed too much to hope that the next visitors might be 'some of ours', and indeed it was Italian ambulance transport that arrived the next day. We were moved to a wadi nearer the sea, there to join a New Zealand field medical unit, that had been taken in situ, in toto. Some attempt at organisation was now made by the enemy. An Iti. (combatant) captain declared himself to be Camp Commandant, but he left the medical command to the N.Z. Colonel. Stanton, Berry and I joined up with his team, and we did what we could to sort and treat the wounded. We segregated the 'enemy' in one large shelter, in which I found myself working with a mixed team of N.Z. and German orderlies—'the English Arzt in the red coat'. (I had a maroon wind-cheater, bought in happier days from Patrick Thompson.)

The enemy wounded were exemplary, and the German orderlies competent, and the fact that I was technically their prisoner had no effect on our relations. Though I had difficulty with one lad who was determined to find out when you said 'some', and when you said 'any'. (You try to explain that to an earnest enquirer whose English is limited!)

One night, a battery of British 25-pounders opened up on us, and one shell landed right in the middle of my 'enemy' shelter, with horrible results. Luckily, the New Zealanders had a mobile surgical section, a unit within a unit, which had never before been used. (The Iti's coveted this set-up, and strove to keep it hidden from the Tedeschi[4]!)

Our critical medical situation was compounded by a serious lack of supplies, by extreme shortage of food, and by tiny dwindling supplies of water. We complained to the Camp Commandant, but at no time did we get any replenishment from the enemy, whose own situation must have been precarious enough. A few non-medical bods, with a hope and a prayer (and perhaps with a compass!), slipped away from time to time, and maybe one or two got through. We took blankets to the top of the wadi, and spelled out 'WATER'. It may have helped.

Anyway, one morning, we found that all the enemy had disappeared and not long after a British column arrived. I wish that I could remember in detail the disposal of that unwieldy mixture of humanity on the floor of that dry riverbed; it must have been a feat of desert improvisation. The wounded, the prisoners, the combatants and the medics were all removed to appropriate places, and *I* found myself at Support Group Battle H.Q.! Jock was pretty gruff, as if it had been all my fault, but he put me up for a decoration. This was undeserved, of course, for at no time could I have found any alternative line of action. But if the story that now gained circulation *had* been true (which it was *NOT*) that on being ordered to 'get out and fall back', I had told the Brigadier to 'eff off, and mind his own business', then indeed a Monkey Charlie[5] would have been well and truly earned; I don't remember Guy or my Corporal Dicky Bird going off. Both had been wounded, and so presumably were on the way to some hospital, but Stanton and I were debriefed by a cheerful young man who admired our beards. He had more to tell us than we him. Pearl Harbor had happened on 7th December, and the Repulse and the Prince of Wales had been sunk on the 10th. The Germans in the wadi had been told that Moscow had fallen, but this it seemed was not true. Tobruk had been relieved, cut off, and

---

[4]Germans.
[5]Military Cross.

then relieved again. Rommel was now said to be on the run, and we were organising fast columns to drive him out of Libya. I had been posted to one of these columns as R.M.O. Wilson Column was composed of an element of K.R.R.C.[6], and a battery of 3rd R.H.A.[7] Here I came to understand the merits of the 25-pounder and to know and admire the men who used it to such effect.

Of course, Rommel was not on the run at all, but had decided to fall back into Tripolitania to re-group, preparing a counter-punch which was to come before the end of the year. At this stage there occurred a disastrous failure in public relations. It was thought that some of the Columns might reach Agedabia before the enemy had cleared Benghazi and the coast; but there was never a realistic chance that any considerable body might be cut off. Some British troops, Wilson Column among them, did get near to the sea very quickly, but the situation was wildly distorted by war correspondents, who proclaimed the capture of Agedabia, with the cutting off of the bulk of Rommel's army. It had all happened before, when Wavell's dramatic advance had been turned round at the same point, and then too the publicity had been mishandled. (It was not until the 'third time round', after Alamein, that the advance went through, and ended up with the bottling-up of the whole lot in the Tunisian peninsula.)

Wilson Column was there to see the whites of their eyes, when the Germans came flooding back again (the Iti's never seemed to be an important factor in the equation) and it was only by some nimble motoring that we got back to the Tobruk area, and everyone paused for breath. The line was stabilised at Gazala, and Support Group, with the rest of the Division, came back to the Delta to re-fit. I rejoined 151, already established at Qassassin, in the middle of February, 1942, just in time to hear of the fall of Singapore.

---

[6]Kings Royal Rifle Corps.
[7]Royal Horse Artillery.

Alan Freedman

*August**

Flood-swift and brown with earth-break,
Rock-spun, bridge-cleft and clamouring,
In one great turbulence—thus the Nile.

Down to the arms of the aching delta
Swirls the green-wrack silently.
Yet, river entire, there is no quiet
For water is reft and the whole length
Surfaced with sail and flutter of birds.
But rarely now the weighted oars
And plash of fishnets dropping.
All things wait, feeling the turn
Of season and the coming up of cloud.
Enough and enough of heat and aridity!
Seep, pour, drench down the coolness,
Stride in the bluster of evening breeze
For this is the sign, the months develop
And soon the quick and the cold and the clean.

Underneath the mosque
The cistern cellar is splash
With flooding and still mounting,
While on the palms the tight date clusters
Redden and ripen.
Root sprung with roaring sediment
All things conceive.
Night after night the banks are mad
With multiple voices
And the maize fields yelling with frogs.
Pulse after pulse, like blood beat
Of desire, moves the strong life,
Beats upwards. This is the river
Whose autumn is a strange new spring.

*Wrongly attributed in *Return to Oasis*

Brian Gallie

C.A.N.T.[1]

We looked at the cloud
And someone on the bridge
Said 'Was that thunder?'
Another peal as loud—
And from its lower edge
(So soft and white that it had made him wonder,
Who spoke, the day being cool and clear,
While Zante, on the beam,
Cloud-dappled lay, as lovely as a dream)
There came a silver sea-plane, like a bird,
So low and near
That we could see the fasces on her wings.
Indeed it was not thunder we had heard
(It was not thunder weather)
But three fleet fighters going hell for leather!
Out of the cloud they came,
And we—who'd often longed to see such things—
Cheered wildly when a little tongue of flame
Leapt from her cockpit, grew, enveloped all—
So that her fall
Was hymned by the wild cheers!
It was no time for tears—
Yet, when the splash
Quenched the bright flame, and left poor wreckage of the crash,
Then suddenly the shouts died on our lips
And silence came among the grim, grey ships;
While Zante, on the beam,
Cloud-dappled lay—as lovely as a dream.

H. M. S. Warspite, Summer, 1940.

[1]An Italian Naval Reconnaissance seaplane.

William Godfrey
The Tale of Tobruk 1942

We got in a ship and sailed out to sea,
And each of us then were in spirits of glee,
For 'twas farewell to Egypt, and old King Farouk,
We were bound for the beautiful town of Tobruk.

A night and a day we sailed o'er the waves,
Then arrived in Tobruk with its harbour of graves,
There were ships all around but sad to relate,
They were all under the water—a terrible state,

We gazed and we thought, as our eyes met that state,
Of all those good ships in that terrible plight,
There were British and Jerries, and Eyeties galore,
Oh the price that we pay when we are forced into war.

Now we sighted the Town which before us did lie,
And most of us then heaved a mighty big sigh,
For this was our home right down by the sea,
But none of us knew for how long it would be.

We walked through the streets 'twas a pitiful sight,
Each step in a turmoil just a ragman's delight,
Devastation lay round us where bombs had come down,
Man's folly had wrecked this once beautiful Town.

As weeks passed to months and the weather grew hot,
Each Mothers Son groused at his terrible lot,
With fags unobtainable and no hopes of beer,
We all cursed the man who had sent us out here.

We worked with a will and enjoyed all the fun,
For the Eyeties turned tail and started to run,
But we worked just as hard and didn't relax,
For our Troops reached Benghazi and stopped in their tracks,
They had fought a long way their strength was depleted.
For Jerry was strong and fresh in the fray.
We were vastly outnumbered that tragical day.

You've all heard the story of that thin long red line
Our coy rearguard action was equally fine,
But the sixth of April the bugle was sounded—
Alas and Alack—Tobruk was surrounded.
We wouldn't surrender, our morale was still high,
When suddenly there came a roar in the sky,
They machine gunned and bombed us and shelled us as we fell,
To be in Tobruk was like being in Hell.

We all now look forward to that glorious day,
When once more on a ship we shall sail out the bay,
And as we glide out, we shall take a last look
At the wreck, that was once the proud town of Tobruk.

Norman Hampson

Assault Convoy

How quietly they push the flat sea from them,
Shadows against the night that grow to meet us
And fade back slowly to our zig-zag rhythm—
The silent pattern dim destroyers weave.
The first light greets them friendly; pasteboard ships
Erect in lineless mists of sky and sea.
A low sun lingers on the well-known outlines
That take new beauty from this sombre war-paint;
Familiar names trail childish memories
Of peacetime ports and waving, gay departures.

Only at intervals the truth breaks on us
Like catspaws, ruffling these quiet waters.
Our future is unreal, a thing to read of
Later; a chapter in a history book.
We cannot see the beaches where the dead
Must fall before this waxing moon is full;
The tracer-vaulted sky, the guns' confusion,
Searchlights and shouted orders, sweaty fumbling
As landing craft are lowered; the holocaust
Grenade and bayonet will build upon these beaches.

We are dead, numbed, atrophied, sunk in the swamps of war.
Each of these thousands is a life entire.
No skilful simile can hide their sheer humanity.
Across the narrowing seas our enemies wait,
Each man the centre of his darkening world;
Bound, as we are, by humanity's traces of sorrow
To their anxious women, alone in the menacing night,
Where the rhythm of Europe is lost in their private fear
And El Dorado could not staunch their grief.

The Med., July 1943

Foreign Commission

November's anger flays all northern seas
And whips great weals across their slaty waste,
The sheering bows fling wide the broken water
It tumbles off the fo'c'sles, bitter spray
Knifes by the lively bridges bursting through
And low hulls welter in the marbled water.

On cabin panelling the pictures hold
Their balance in a world swung all awry,
On the damp mess decks now the lisping water
Slides with the restless hours, the cable bangs
Its slow mad rhythm in the navel pipes
And close-packed hammocks jostle all the night.

From heaving tables spins the inky thread
Leading from Theseus through the maze of time
To inland homes where seas are images;
These faded photographs hold frozen truth,
Quick smile, blown hair, in lines map-accurate,
The contour skeleton of living land.

Through all the shapeless months these minds support
Fading perspectives with their wishful dreams,
Assurance grows appeal, their letters scream,
Their own alarm makes fact of all their fear,
The woman's boredom stares between the lines;
And then the silence and the anxious faces.

These are your heroes, whom tomorrow's dawn
May find half-frozen in an oily sea;
They have their memories, their friends who were,
They know the shapes of death and dare forget,
But slow corrosion rusts their lives away
And etches grief on brows that should be young.

There are no killers here, whom crusted pride
Armours against their own humanity,
Or bigot's eyes can blind to bloody hands;
The quiet counties are their pedigree
Whose honest living asks no easy answer
Nor moves the goal to meet their straying ways.

Look for no tragic actors great in stature
Whose blazing hearts might kindle half a world,
These live obscure, only their sorrows vast
Winds of humanity that sigh by night
Through all the peopled earth; the men who bear
A fate acceptance cannot make less real.

Mediterranean. February 1944.

Hamish Henderson
Alamein, October 23, 1942

On this moon surface
of cracks, craters and depressions
the ant-hill stirs. The spring is compressed for the blow.
As we jib and jolt
in a shiver-shaken Dodge down the Springbok
road, the clouds muffle
the vast mobility: the clouds cloak
the continuous whirr and clatter of our
advancing armour, mustering for the thrust.

Only the pipes this night will match
the music of revving Shermans: with this name
we'll bring jubilee to the whiggish desert!
The hardy Highlanders
have trained hard: ten times over they
    have stormed and taken
the trial sangars, have sworn and sweated
by order of the laconic self-confident General.
And now the real thing. The Jocks greet it
for they know they are in good company:
the Aussies are here,
surest-footed in the desert, who captured
Tel el Eisa: there are Afrikaners,
the burly Jaapies[1], the Saray Marays,
now longest in the line: and the cool New Zealanders
well-acquainted with action—
together, the hard spear-head.
             And a moon to do us proud
enters into alliance.

Armour has foregathered, snuffling
through tourbillions of fine dust.
The crews don't speak much. They've had
last brew-up before battle. The tawny
deadland lies in a silence
not yet smashed by salvoes.
No sound reaches us
from the African constellations.
The low ridge too is quiet.
But no fear we're sleeping,
no need to remind us
that the nervous fingers of the searchlights
are nearly meeting and time is flickering
and this I think in a few minutes
while the whole power crouches for the spring.
X-20 in thirty seconds. Then begin

Let loose (rounds)
the exultant bounding hell-harrowing of sound.

---

[1]A nickname for the South Africans, also known as 'Saray Marays' from the title of the
Afrikaans song Sarie Marais they sang.

Break the batteries. Confound
the damnable domination. Slake
the crashing breakers-húrled rúbble of the guns.
Dithering darkness, we'll wake you! Héll's bélls
blind you. Be broken, bleed
deathshead blackness!
          The thongs of the livid
firelights lick you
          jagg'd splinters rend you
               underground
we'll bomb you, doom you, tomb you into grave's mound

Feu d'artifice!
Coloured tracer swerves over deadly illumination.
We watch it
this *auto da fe*, this show for lusty arch-angels.
End to end
of the western horizon it crackles, crepitates and lightens:
four hundred and eighty guns on a front of twelve kilometres
between Ruweisat ridge and the sea.
Our ears become indifferent
to the faceless din of ejaculation. Only our eyes
our eyes watch with eager elation
the jittering St Vitus dance
jabbing, jerking and quivering
from the middle distance into shivering jerryland;
bringing to the children of Wotan
wild blood-letting of witches sabbath
rough riotous road to Valhalla
Walpurgisnacht with a vengeance.

          The Jocks
move forward into no man's land, a vibrant sounding board.
          As they advance
the guns push further murderous music.
Is this all they will hear, this raucous apocalypse?
The spheres knocking in the night of Heaven?
The drummeling of overwhelming niagara?
No! For I can hear it! Or is it? . . . tell
me that I can hear it! Now—listen!
          Yes, hill and shieling
sea-loch and island, hear it, the yell

of your war-pipes, scaling sound's mountains
guns thunder drowning in their soaring
    swell!
—The barrage gulfs them: they're gulfed in the clumbering guns,
gulfed in gloom, gloom. Dumb in the blunderbuss black—
lost—gone in the anonymous cataract of noise.
Now again! The shrill war-song: it flaunts
aggression to the sullen desert. It mounts. Its scream
tops the valkyrie, tops the colossal
                    artillery

Meaning that many
German Fascists will not be going home
meaning that many
will die, doomed in their false dream

We'll *mak siccar*[2]!
Against the bashing cudgel
against the contemptuous triumphs of the big battalions
mak siccar
            against the monkish adepts
of total war against the oppressed oppressors
mak siccar
            against the leaching lies
against the worked out systems of sick perversion
mak siccar
            against the executioner
against the tyrannous myth and the real terror
mak siccar

Flowers of the forest: Alamein: this is what it means.
A boy of twenty, married nine months,
who died tonight among the first on Mitereiya.
The lament is for him, who will have
no more kisses from his pretty Jeannie
(and no more 'beeze'[3] in the Cameron barracks)
After nine hours
of deaths like his, the ridge is ours.

[2]Scots for 'make sure.'
[3]Spit and polish.

Quintin Hogg

Night Patrol

Muttered the sea, the hill
And silent wadis lay
Black in the moon, when we to kill
Went on our silent way.

Whispers of listless wind
Hissed in the drifting sand
And ancient names gaunt bushes signed
In a forgotten hand.

Menacing ill the wrack
Of last year's battle frowned
Grim in the dark, most like the mark
Of Cain upon the ground.

Silent, we came, we killed.
One blow, and quiet he lay.
One cry, and all was stilled:
Then silent we crept away.

John Jarmain

Embarkation, 1942

In undetected trains we left our land
At evening secretly, from wayside stations.
None knew our place of parting; no pale hand
Waved as we went, not one friend said farewell.
But grouped on weed-grown platforms
Only a few officials holding watches
Noted the stealthy hour of our departing,
And, as we went, turned back to their hotel.

With blinds drawn down we left the things we know,
The simple fields, the homely ricks and yards;
Passed willows greyly bunching to the moon
And English towns. But in our blindfold train
Already those were far and long ago,
Stored quiet pictures which the mind must keep:
We saw them not. Instead we played at cards,
Or strangely dropped asleep.

Then in a callow dawn we stood in lines
Like foreigners on bare and unknown quays,
Till someone bravely into the hollow of waiting
Cast a timid wisp of song;
It moved along the lines of patient soldiers
Like a secret passed from mouth to mouth
And slowly gave us ease;
In our whispered singing courage was set free,
We were banded once more and strong.
So we sang as our ship set sail,
Sang our own songs, and leaning on the rail
Waved to the workmen on the slipping quay
And they again to us for fellowship.

Ring Plover at El Alamein

Nothing grows on the sand-flats
Beside the salt lake at El Alamein,
The water is still and rust-pink
And the flat sand rim is crusted with salt.
Beyond the white dunes and the shallow beach
Is the brilliant tideless sea;
Behind is the endless sand.

Yet here at the dead lake's side
I saw a solitary ring plover—
Small and plump and coloured,
Black and white and red,
Surprising as a painted wooden toy.

He and I alone had the pale shore,
I still and watching him,
The bird busy as an absorbed small boy:
He ran importantly, bobbed and cocked his head,
Small and pre-occupied, always hurrying,
As if he were always a little behind.
So I have seen him on busy beaches of the North
Hunting with the dunlin, between the fishing-boats
And the nets hung on poles to dry
Along the shores of the Moray Firth.

But like memory the quick wings flickered,
Left momentarily a white arc in the air,
And he was over the dunes, out to sea.
I was alone on the sand-flats
Beside the rust-pink water.

El Alamein—El Daba,
October-November 1942.

L. K. Lawler

Fever

In blackness lit with an idiot spark
Slow fever traces memory, paints a face
Opens dead eyes, in this deep crimson dark
Weaves the old pattern of a yellowed lace.
So many fading hands which dance the black wall
A frescoed jig, pink-black and sickly white
Jerking informing stepping hands that maul
And fumble at my eyelids through the night.
Whispers in thick walls turning ceaselessly
In manus tuas silliness and grey
Worms that point and threaten, childishly;
Before the slim cold fingers of the day
Touch at the window, say the day is won
With the clean smile of the sun.

I Have Searched for a White Coat

All night down the dark street
I have searched for a white coat,
for the gleam of the flesh of a white throat
and hands and white coat in the dark street.
Still listening, listening
for the slow ring
of her feet on the stone of the street,
seeking her face in the faces that come—
with the beat of a drum
saying no . . . no . . . no—
in the faces, grey faces that waddle along
and belong to the dark and the dead;
with no sight of a white coat
and white hands and white throat,
pale and moon-clean in the dark street.

To drink in cafes where the glasses are dirty
and stainings of coffee on tables and floor,
where the glances are bright from the eyes without light
and the painted-on grins and the near-double chins
of the faces that sweat
and fever and fret
till the price of a drink sops them up;
while a band with accordions crashes and crawls
through the Saint Louis Blues—
got the Saint Louis Blues
and the whole bloody place goes round and round
to the Saint Louis Blues—
and nothing to lose—
only the keen clean edge of love,
only the lemon taste.

North Talpioth, April 1941.

Dennis McHarrie

A Desert Airman's Diary

Aug. 4 1943

Like Bob Hope and Bing Crosby—we're on the 'Road to Benghazi'. Our transport is a 10 ton R.A.S.C. truck, one of a convoy of nine, our seat is perched high on top of a load of spares. This way we see the country but there's no protection against sun, wind and sand. We've got 298 miles to go and it will take about three days, so we carry rations with us, cases of bully, milk, beans, tea and sugar.

We set off about 1000 hrs this morning and the day's travel was pretty dull, fast rolling on thru' mile on mile of desert, you get so used to battle wreckage it ceases to be of interest. At 1300 hrs we leaguered and each group made its own fire and meal. The 'shai' (tea) tasted good. We just put tea, sugar and milk into a can, added water and boiled it up. Our driver showed us how to make a cooking fire by soaking a tin of sand in petrol and lighting it—it lasts for ages.

Towards evening the desert started to give way to green scrub, and with all her showmanship nature suddenly produced the Derna Pass.

We came on it suddenly, a sheer drop to a small plain, where against the fragile blue of the sea the white buildings of Derna stood out in dazzling contrast. Guarding this small spot from the desert there stands an old wall near the bottom of the pass, puny against tank or aeroplane but I suppose a formidable obstacle to the raiding 'harka' of the past. Nature itself has provided the guard for Derna in this war—the Pass. The small plain on which it stands is approached from East or West by a road that winds down the side of the plateau in a series of breathtaking hairpin bends pretty shaky coming down in our 10 tonners—and exhilarating. And so tho' war has flowed backwards and forwards round this part in the last few years it has always by-passed Derna, and we found its buildings untouched, its streets tree lined and an air of peace lying over it.

We passed thru' the town and leaguered six kilos to westward of it. We've cooked our food, dug out our bedrolls and now to sleep under the stars.

Oct. 6 1943

Gosh! What a bloody useless mess this war is. Leros as well as Kos has been invaded and to have these two bits of rock for Britain lives are being thrown away freely. Truly may it be said of our lives that the High Command have a big Notice over our Names saying 'These are expendable'. In addition to the troops trapped there, the Navy have lost six destroyers, 252 Sqdn (Beaufighters) has lost over half its crews and we've caught a packet.

Oct. 17 1943

'Fish and bombs'—Rover patrol in the Aegean.

Found only one caique. Not worth bombing so attacked Syros Harbour low level. Intelligence told us to expect very light resistance—they hadn't a clue. We had the hottest reception we've met in these parts—at roof top height and in bright moonlight we were caught in a flak box—ruddy great walls of fire all round us and Jack on the inter-com saying 'Let's get to hell out of this'—we let our bombs go at a warehouse and I took his advice at a rate of knots.

J. G. Meddemmen

Al Bint az-Zar'a

Like a blue-purple viola,
Simple, silken, duskily passionate in appearance,
Like a sulky viola stuck on a dung heap
So sat in the rickety tram a girl from the South,
Sulkily passionate, silkily soignée,
Murderously beautiful and tigered with vice.
How express the sultriness of her,
The smoky blue-purple duskiness of her,
The lean thewed warm animal litheness of her?

Hot flower,
Dusky flower,
It is easy to see what will happen:

By the bronze-green Nile at midnight
A dusky flower will bloom with murderous beauty,
A tiger with vivid velvet petals.

6 July 1942.

William E. Morris

I Saw a Man Walking

I saw a man walking, slowly falteringly
clotted blood coursed slowly so that limbs were
hesitant
momentum was not of his volition
each step silent willing encouragement
gentle hands led him.
There was no gratitude in his eyes for their sure
support
no lightning or quickening of a glance
in pleasure of needful aid from a trusted helpmate.
Bandage and lint pressed close against his
forehead
a compelled gaze could not see beyond to
sightless sockets.
Firm capable fingers rested lightly on each side
to guide him
for his hands were multiple wrappings hiding
charred stumps.

Doughy features blue-mapped with powder
burns
punctured with particles of infinitesimal
shattered steel.
A cataleptic walk insensible to dolour of
those who watched
feeling behind an opaque wall the passage way
he must tread in slippered feet.

Yet, this was Man.
His garments loosely flapping about his
quiescent form.
A lath of skin and bone,
shroud of man wrapped in darkness,
shudderingly with shuffling steps he moves across
a shaft of sunlight—he would never see.

2nd. N.Z. Div., Egypt, 1941.

48

The Captured

Barrage silk cast shadows where we sat
on kit bags gas mask and tin hat embedded in a crusted sand.
We sat swatting Egypt's flies with a peaked hat.
Our R.T.O.[1] was having someone on the mat,
still we sat, watching rusted prows of
sunken ships—grim reminder this was war,
a harbour bombed a little while before—
now Tewfik slumbered, as we reclined
uncomfortably on an alien shore.

Marching four abreast in column array
Hitler's beaten army halted for transport in the Bay,
tired features creased by particles of desert dust
shabby uniforms infested by its all embracing crust,
dust—entrenched itself in ridges on head gear sadly worn,
irritated sweated forelocks closely shorn.
Down-at-heel boots made no imprint in sand
fringing polluted land—ugly born.

Bleak eyes had this sullen band
arrogant in their shifting sideways stare,
eyes that had witnessed swift victory in other lands—
then reluctant surrender chill despair
a valedictory to high hopes
to triumph that was never really there.
Where shifting dunes shimmer under Libya's molten sky
vultures cast shadows flying high
over rock cairned graves where comrades lie.
'Neath windswept desert's rim barb wire had hemmed them in;
between reaching fingers of twisted wire
threadbare prisoners huddled as cattle in a byre
their hearts racked with questioning doubt,
minds seared from barb's reality.
Beings filled with but one desire
to throw twigs on a home hearth fire.
Sentry go on sentry beat made mockery of a dream complete—
they scrambled for the 'cigs' we threw—
then cursed us 'cause there were so few.

[1]Railway Transport Officer   Egypt, 1941.

The Sound and the Fury

You crouched in a cacophonic world
where an orchestra of medieval hate
crashed out a symphony of discordant note
of chimera devoid of music;
quivering muzzles of guns purposefully
unfurled.

Terrain leaped and shuddered to sound,
sound battening itself on cotton-woolled eardrums,
mouthed words lacerated in vibrant chaos,
vast all embracing all obliterating fury
flinging itself into battle.

Kaleidoscope of colours of pink, purple and yellows
gun flashes as wadis erupt—
erupt into flame of rending fragmentation
tearing and mangling in frantic animation
red hot metal screaming above bedlam
crimson tongues licking heavens, dunes and desert
slashing enemy ramparts and mummified tree-trunks
truncated branches beckoning in ghostly frenzy . . .
midst a reeling world.
Blasted face shocked into comprehending surprise
that death's searching fingers should reach so far,
emblazoned day turned into everlasting night.

Alamein, 1942.

Jack Partridge

My El Alamein

Sundown, 23rd October, 1942. Two Battalions of 131 Brigade (The Queen's) of the 44th Home Counties Division, 13 Corps, under the direct command of General Harding's 7th Armoured Division (The Desert Rats) moved forward on foot through our minefields and the concentration of Royal Horse Artillery 25-pounders to a point fifty or so paces beyond the guns, there to lie prone until further orders. So commenced our part in the battle which Monty had told us 'would be one of the decisive battles of history . . . the turning point of the war . . . let us all pray that "The Lord, mighty in battle" will give us the victory.' For three years the British and their Allies had suffered the slings and arrows of outrageous fortune at the hands of the German Goliath, Hitler's invincible Wehrmacht. Monty said that, 'the eyes of the world are upon us . . . together, we will knock the enemy for six, right out of North Africa.' We believed him. Not blindly for there was a feeling in our bones that he was a 'Man of Destiny.'

The Free French were on our left flank to take Himeimat Ridge and 50 Div on our right. Our task was to breach two consecutive enemy minefields, code-named 'January' and 'February' and form bridgeheads for the armour to come through. Camouflage deception of a scale and quality previously unknown, had been practised during the weeks running up to the battle. Dummy petrol, water and ammo points and dumps. Many hundreds of 'Sunshields' i.e. hollow tank dummies on real lorries and vice-versa. Similar disguises named 'Cannibals' for the Artillery. The R.E.s built a 'water pipe-line' from the coast to the Southern sector, but it never conveyed any fluid!

At 2140 hours our guns commenced the barrage. The ground shook. It was fantastic . . . like hundreds of pneumatic-drills breaking up Piccadilly Circus while you lay, with Eros above you, in the middle! It went on for hours; one lost count. Then it ceased and we moved forward beneath 'Monty's Moon' which by then had risen.

Eventually we arrived at the Eastern Boundary of the February minefield and were strung out in line with about six feet between men. The ground rose gently to the West. Nearby to the North we could see the twin white tapes marking a path which our Scorpion tanks and Recce-Corps had cleared for the advance of the armour. Came the order and, hearts in mouths, we moved forward. To face an enemy with bomb, bullet and bayonet was a reciprocal situation, but to step on a land-mine and automatically bring about your own demise without being able to hit back seemed a poor way to go. But, our's not to reason why, and on we went, silently saying the Lord's Prayer or such invocations applicable. After the first two or three hundred feet, without mishap, it was obvious that a man's weight would be unlikely to detonate what must be exclusively vehicle mines and so our confidence returned, only to be shattered as we neared the top of the rise and the end of the minefield. Several explosions sounded left and forward. We froze. Anti-personnel mines, of course. Several of the lads were wounded, one screaming for his mother. Conscience-voices within our heads muttered, 'Forward, you cowards! Away and help them!' But we were rooted like trees. From our right, four stretcher-bearers broke from the taped path and ran across our front to succour the wounded, and the voice of our sergeant ordered us onto the path, where we proceeded in file to the 'plateau' between the minefields.

It stretched forward for about three hundred yards to the commencement of the February minefield, and, presented a welcome relief until, suddenly, our guns opened up again and the enemy artillery joined in reply. It was coming in low over the 'plateau'. You could see the shells glowing as they whizzed just overhead. Some were but waist high! Other even less. One landed close by. We didn't hear it at all. Some were killed, others knocked out, some wounded. We regained consciousness. The barrage had stopped. There were four of us. Two unscratched even. One sergeant with a shattered shoulder and a man with a leg all but blown off at the knee. We bound the sergeant's shoulder with first-aid dressings and tourniqued the other's leg above the knee before cutting the leg away. Inside my battle dress I had kept a tie. It was the tie I had taken to OCTU[1] in England to wear when I became a second lieutenant. But weeks before the end of the course there had been the urgent call for a draft to the Middle East. And that ended my officer's aspirations. But I still had that tie with me and in the middle of El Alamein I tied it as a tourniquet to stem the blood. There was a forward Aid Post in the vicinity, if it could be located. My companion was a big ex-docker from Bermondsey and he carried the man with the amputated leg. I managed the sergeant. A Bren-carrier appeared and took them both back to the Regimental Field-hospital. The sergeant lived, but the other man died there. Wounded and surrendering Italians streamed in during what remained of the night. An ammo truck was hit on the plateau. Better than Crystal Palace fireworks! The forward body of the two Queen's battalions negotiated the February minefield and tried to dig in to hold a bridgehead, but the ground was hard and the armour was unable to get through to them.

They suffered heavy casualties then and during the following day. Radio contact was lost almost as soon as they formed the bridgehead, so a recce-patrol was sent out to investigate at sundown on the 24th. We found only corpses of our comrades as we crawled along on our bellies to avoid the fixed-line machine-gun bullets which accounted for many of them. Such was our baptism of fire. Two of us survived from a section of ten.

---

[1]Officers Corps Training Unit

A KNOCKED OUT GERMAN "TIGER" TANK

BARBED-WIRE BY MOONLIGHT

Geoff Pearse

Morning Flap

Grey dim the mind
And grey the morning light
Maps, chutes and camera
The erks swarm round the kite
Briefing half remembered
Positions are all in doubt
Tea and sand for breakfast
What is it all about
Engines now are revving
Across the sand in a roar
Thank God we are up and flying
From the flap that went on before

1942.

Ivor Porter

The Briefing

After the ride in the Wimpy's[1] womb,
Your despatcher feeding you rum,
Senses walled in by the noise and vibration,
Oxygen-starved and numb,

Came the jump and the line was snapped
And you hung in the night without plane or crew,
The enemy ground swinging up,
The briefing deep-frozen within you.

[1]Wellington bomber

Enoch Powell

The Net

The net like a white vault, hung overhead
Dewy and glistening in the full moon's light,
Which cast a shadow-pattern of the thread
Over our face and arms, laid still and white
Like polished ivories on the dark bed.
The truck's low side concealed from us the sight
Of tents and bivouacs and track-torn sand
That lay without; only a distant sound
Of gunfire sometimes or, more close at hand,
A bomb, with dull concussion of the ground,
Pressed in upon our world, where, all else banned,
Our lonely souls eddied like echoing sound
Under the white cathedral of the net,
And like a skylark in captivity
Hung fluttering in the meshes of our fate,
With death at hand and, round, eternity.

M. Rawlinson

Mediterranean Song

There's some who say the Medi-
Terranean air is heady;
While others, who have stayed there
Are very much afraid there's
A lot more to be said
About the highly vaunted Med.

For instance there's malaria
In the Mare Nostrum area;
And pox in many a guise
Small and cow and otherwise
Can easily be caught
Doing things you didn't ought.

Then there's flies and fleas and
Lice and crabs, that tease and
Make themselves a pest
Always hanging around the test-
Icles; playing hide and seek
In the ballroom, so to speak.

And many more afflictions
That cause a lot of restrictions;
The brothers 'dyer' and 'gonner'
Are active winter and summer.
And dysentery's a damned in-
Convenience notwithstanding.

So I think that you'll agree,
That those who say the sea
Is nearly always blue,
(Which is nearly always true)
Are deliberately misleading
The folks who judge by reading
That the Med for sure and certain
Is the place to do some flirting.
But you and I know better,
And you can bet an old French letter-
Box, that when this war is over
I'll count myself in clover
As long as I've a bed,
And am nowhere near the Med.

R. M. Roberts

Troop Train

Dark has fallen on the crowded troop train
Lumbering slowly through the Egyptian night,
Cold as the smooth steel of the coaches.
We in our thin drill shorts huddle close
The thin ribbed wooden seats,

Wrapped each in his single blanket,
Staring unseeing with large pupiled eyes
Mirrored in the pool of black glass windows,
Drugged and heavy with the dust of Africa
And the sweet desire of sleep.
The broken rhythm of the jolting carriage wheels
Brings to the soldier a fitful slumber
And the lights that flare with the passing
Of each unknown clamorous station
Paint grotesque pictures of living light
Flickering on the shrouded waxen faces
And as the train in its relentless funeral pace
Slowly rumbles through the dim lit bays,
Arab shirted close cropped urchin hawkers
Shriek their wares with all the discord of the east,
Trailing the red glow of receding tail lamp
With fading high pitched half tone echoes
That shiver the sleepers and walk the skin
With the spiders icy feet.
Deep into the night and waste lands
The sleeping coaches roll,
With the firelit clanging monster
Probing one eyed its grinding way
Until the biting cold dew of the desert
Glistens on the swaying steel,
Etching the twin threads of railroad
Converging under a pale moon far to the west,
And the east breaks in a fan of brittle light
Flooding the lonely plain.
We the shrouded sleepers in a golden train
Wake, beard rough and dust red eyed,
Stamp the cold from stiffened limbs
And boisterous blood beats in shouting life
Chasing the phantoms of the spell ridden night,
While the train presses on to the west and the camps
To the unknown but rumoured future.

John Ropes

The Chars Look Back

The scene: Any office in B.T.E. (for the uninitiated, this means the headquarters of British
Troops in Egypt, situated in Cairo).
Three charladies of formidable but faded charm sing:

In the last war we were beautiful Russian spies,
   Now we're cleaners at the B.T.E.
In the last war we were full of intrigue and lies
   And subtle kisses on the strict Q.T.
      We lay around on divans
      A-working for the Cause,
      Dressed up in frilly you-know-whats
      And yards of lacy drawers.
      They come in handy nowadays
      For mopping up the floors,
Because we're cleaners at the B.T.E.
      Many's the time we used to have!
      We cut some fancy capers!
      The things we ladies had to do
      To look at secret papers!

The diplomats adored us,
And some of them were Hot.
They'd gaze at us with passion
As they turned a Bonny Mot.
The Soldiers, too, were fond of us,
Observed our lightest whim.
They loaded us with diamonds
As they leapt from limb to limb.
Now no-one gives us anything
Except a tin of Vim,
Because we're cleaners at the B.T.E.
In the last war we were beautiful Russian spies,
  Now we're cleaners at the B.T.E.
In the last war, we put blue stuff round our eyes
As we looked at men and said, 'Oui, oui,'
  We served our country faithfully,
  Three bogus British Blooms.
  In night-clubs and in restaurants,
  In bars and private rooms.
  It never got us anywhere
  But mucking round with brooms
Because we're cleaners at the B.T.E.

Note: This lyric will recall memories of Christmas 1941. It is taken from the Ropes-Tuckley 'Revue Order' of that year as performed at the Royal Opera House by the C.A.D.M.S.

Alf Sampson

The Siege of Tobruk — October 1941

When you're sucking at your pencil,
  And you don't know what to say,
When you wish the blooming censor
  Had ne'er seen light of day,
There's always one thing that's considered
  Pretty good to tell,
And it doesn't take much writing,
  'DEAR MUM, I'M SAFE AND WELL'.

When you've seen, oh, many funny things
     But mustn't say a word,
Where you've been, just name the place,
     Your letter gets the bird,
Your paper blank, time marches on
     Cor, blimey what a sell,
Well anyway just bung it down,
     'DEAR MUM, I'M SAFE AND WELL'.

When the water's pretty rotten,
     And the food is bloody rough,
If you can't sleep lying on the rocks,
     They say, look he's not tough,
The fleas if they'd stop biting,
     And leave you for a spell,
It won't take long to scribble it,
     'DEAR MUM, I'M SAFE AND WELL'.

If Hitler had a mother,
     I bet that she would frown,
At what her little Adolph
     Has done to London town,
And when at last they kill that guy,
     Why it'd be simply swell,
We'd write it down a dozen times
     'DEAR MUM, I'M SAFE AND WELL'.

Thomas Skelton

Inside the A.F.V.[1]

Start up. The whine of the gears
Penetrate my ears, inside the headphones.
Armoured plate shuts out all else as well as desert silence.
Rolling inside noise, not out,
Pushing in soft places, four powerful wheels
There through the desert onward.

[1]Armoured fighting vehicle

Rolling relentless forward to someplace and back again,
Not broken yet.
Heat shuts up with engine fumes
And noises sewed up in steel.
Man in a visor behind his subterfuge
Facing other iron casings.
The cogs grip for a turret turn, noises unite in noise.
In headphones a labyrinth of whistle and raucous noise,
Intent on being heard—and being heard—
In the revolving world of periscope
Naught thought about but noise and involvement.
Inside the rolling iron case
'Ahead is target', 'Guns Fire'.
Inside hot shell cases scald my back
Acrid smoke plucks nose and throat.
What safe hell hole is this, commander?

1943.

Finality

Is it good to die when you are hungry
Wanting a large slice of bread,
To fill up a stomach that's empty
Because in two twos you'll be dead?

M.E.F., 1943.

Gordon L. Smith

Salute to Summer

From Almanacs piled in profusion,
And Temperature Charts by the score,
Some expert has reached the conclusion
That Summer is with us once more.
     So clothing K.D.[1]
     Is le dernier cri,
It's time to select natty shirting;
     Take an icy-cold shower
     At an unearthly hour,
And arrange your Spring programme of flirting.

Stow Battle Dress into valises,
Emitting a nostalgic sigh
As you gaze on your trouser-leg creases,
And abandon your beautiful tie.
     But don't be dismayed—
     You can be bright-arrayed
For an akker, or hardly much dearer:
     Every dhobi[2] is keen
     To bestow a starched sheen
On your shirt for your walks round Gezira.

If you'd like to exhibit the beauty
Of your soldierly legs, gleaming bare,
You're allowed to wear shorts when off duty—
And it gives you much-needed fresh air.
     So doff, and be glad,
     Let your legs go unclad,
It's really a grand institution
     For your knobbly knees
     To be bared to the breeze—
And they MUST have a daily ablution.

[1]Khaki drill
[2]Local laundry

E. M. Spalding

Letters Home

1st September 1942

Jerry is trying to cut us off. I keep his positions marked on our map. He has now met our own tanks, who are covering us, so it cannot be long before we shall know many things. You'll be reading all this in the papers in a few days. I believe he will be held and badly battered. If so, I believe it will be his last thrust for Egypt and Suez. If the Russ ians can hold h im around Stal ingrad, I don't th ink it will be long before it will be over. Then home sometime next year!

Last night was unpleasant. Driving sand all night. Once I woke to hear the air throbbing with engines. I covered myself completely with blankets to shut out the din and the sand and slept until everything around opened up on a Jerry plane. Then I got up, for dawn was near although the moon was high.

December 25th '42 Christmas Day in the Desert

Sorry I had to leave your letter two days after starting it. I'm on night duty now, the only time one really has light and peace in which to write. We had a Christmas dinner after all. Pork, baked potatoes, peas, tinned fruit, 1½ bottles of beer, 4 rations of rum and an orange. I thought it really very good and so would you if you knew our position. All cooked and well cooked on a field kitchen. We sat around in a circle on empty tins. The officers made a speech or two. Then came a lucky dip for prizes and I was fortunate enough to draw 2 gallons of liquid gold (I believe you call it water). Tomorrow I get a day off in which I'm supposed to sleep, but I intend to use at least one gallon in which to wash clothes, hair, myself and anything else, in that order. In presenting me the water they said it was pure, unadulterated with chlorine and therefore not likely to injure the hair. I believe they intended to be rude, but it was Christmas Day so I let it pass. A few minutes later someone trod on my mug (not my face) and smashed it. Another few minutes and I was given a brand new one, which was being used to dole out rum. There was little work to do as Jerry was concerned mainly in sending Christmas greetings which have little operational value.

Recently we had to camp for the night in some damp, marshy ground, so I looked around for support for my stretcher bed and found 2 German metal water containers—like large beer barrels. I placed my bed between them and the result resembled a steam roller without the funnel. I got into bed and soon 3 officers passed. I heard a whisper about my bed and expected them to give the steam roller a push, as they were in jocular mood. Nothing happened, but in the morning I found out what they were planning. They had found a human skull and had the brainwave to leave it beside my bed.

December 27th '42

Once again I had to abandon this letter. During the night, as I was writing, the rain began to fall and the cable bringing the light from our power van developed a 'short' owing to the wet. I had to spend my time sitting in the dark, twiddling my thumbs and listening to the rain beating on the roof and the angry roar of the Mediterranean breakers. Could not even go outside and study the stars. That is my latest form of passing my time in the darkness. I found a German book lying about the desert, which the Germans with their usual care have prepared for their troops to read. It is called 'Das Sternen Buchlein' (the star booklet) and I've learned much from it. Now when I gaze up into the great star-strewn canopy which covers the eternal sands of Libya I see new friends as they wheel majestically through the darkness.

5.1.43

We've just emerged from 2 days unceasing sand storm, blown this time by a raging cold wind. Oh my Gawd! For lunch we had bully, pickles, treacle and bread. One slice blew off the plate, then the treacle got mixed up with the pickles. This mixture effectively attracted the flying sand and the result beggars description. One of the signallers described it pretty accurately but I wouldn't care to pass it on. I was reduced to an unwonted impurity of speech and, at night, as I crawled in the darkness into a sandy bed, I reflected that Italy's post-war punishment should be the return of her ruddy Empire. Little wonder that the children of Israel cried out in the wilderness. My eyes were streaming and the resultant mixture of tea and sand would have delighted Elizabeth Arden. The storm blew from Jerry's direction. Sometimes I think he must muse bitterly as he reads on the buckle of his belt 'Gott mit uns'.

Our present location is in an area favoured by rain at times. The sand bears numerous wild flowers and the scent at night brings memories of English gardens, so unlike the 'dead' desert of Egypt and Eastern Libya. I have hopes that the final crack at Jerry in Africa will soon be on. I often wonder what old Churchill told them when he came out here.

Today has been a day of cleaning up the ravages of the storm. All the kit, hair, ears, in fact everything is sand-ridden. Even the morning porridge takes on a darker hue. We've just taken unto ourselves a new cook; this time a man of fewer words but greater cooking ability. Now the bully takes on the dignity of a Hamburg steak and the second course (commonly known as dough pronounced 'duff') is richly disguised under chocolate sauce. The tea now has strength and joy in it and soon removes that 'hopeless dawn' feeling.

26.2.43

Your news in a recent letter that E. Croydon was machine-gunned reminds me of a little trouble that we had, although of course it was not so serious. In Croydon you simply would not expect such a thing and that to my mind, makes

it worse. I had spent the afternoon amongst the mysteries of —————
(censored) and decided to leave the van in search of food, well pleased with the
results of my labours. On the way I paused for a well earned wee-wee,
contemplating at the time the glorious serenity of all things around. In front of
me was a ridge which broke my view of the far horizon. Suddenly my reverie
was shattered by a colossal din over the ridge and within a few seconds 20 Italian
fighters roared into sight skimming the ridge. Their guns were blazing and
everyone on the ground who had a gun was blazing back. Pandemonium! I had
just time (not what you are thinking) to yell at the rest of the lads in the van, who
tumbled out en bloc. Then we scattered and flattened in the sand, whilst the
Italians roared over. There happened to be a Major in our van who had earned
special mention for his coolness when under fire in Greece or Crete. He was
next to me and so we lay, Major and Corporal, prone on the sands, praying hard,
whilst little spurts of sand hopped into the air around us. Nobody was hurt, no
damage was done, but no doubt Radio Roma reported the devastating effect of
their gallant pilots' ground strafe. It happened to be a day when the RAF was
grounded by a sand storm in the landing ground area whereas the enemy
'dromes were clear.

The old circus rolls on and my mind is quite well, thank you, as the job keeps it
well occupied. At times it is saddened by the sight of so many lonely graves as
we roll on mile after mile. Nearly all have the owner's tin hat hung on the little
wooden cross. Sacred tin hats which the most ardent souvenir hunter would
never dream of 'lifting'. On the German cross one reads 'Soldat Hans Bauer
died for Greater Germany'. On the British cross Pte. Bloggs merely died.
When this madness is over I hope to God it will have brought a reason to add a
still prouder inscription to Pte. Bloggs' wooden cross.

Jerry has fought and is still fighting a magnificent rearguard action. That
accounts for the time taken in pushing him back. I shall be thankful to see him
leave Africa, but I am afraid it will not be possible until you are reading this
letter.

N. J. Trapnell

Lament of a Desert Rat

I've learnt to wash in petrol tins, and shave myself in tea
Whilst balancing the fragments of a mirror on my knee
I've learnt to dodge the eighty-eights, and flying lumps of lead
And to keep a foot of sand between a Stuka and my head

I've learnt to keep my ration bag crammed full of buckshee food
And to take my Army ration, and to pinch what else I could
I've learnt to cook my bully-beef with candle-ends and string
In an empty petrol can, or any other thing
I've learnt to use my jack-knife for anything I please
A bread-knife, or a chopper, or a prong for toasting cheese
I've learnt to gather souvenirs, that home I hoped to send
And hump them round for months and months, and dump them in the end
But one day when this blooming war is just a memory
I'll laugh at all these troubles, when I'm drifting o'er the sea
But until that longed-for day arrives, I'll have to be content
With bully-beef and rice and prunes, and sleeping in a tent.

R. N. Walker

Tent

All day long
The tent cracked and flapped and slacked
As the wind battered and tugged it
All day long; and the sun
Who could do nothing, having heavy business of his own
Got nearer and nearer to the end of his course,
Whilst drooping, sagging
Tent like a paper mâché elephant blown awry.
Wind poured steady strength surprising
Tent fretted and whimpered
Wind cracked and flapped it, slacked it
Poured sand over and under it, through it
At night when the first star looked out
It saw the tent exhausted
Unable to turn even a baleful eye to heaven
Wanting sleep anywhere, straight away.

Thursday, 18 December 1941.

The Camel

As the camel
   Undulates
His bell
   Tintinnabulates.
The knock-kneed
Beastie
   Pays no heed
To any other
   Lesser breed;
But at least he
   Is no bother—
For he goes on undulating
   And his bell
   Well—
I guess it just goes right on tintinnabulating.

                    3 November 1941.

John Warry

First Impressions of Egypt

I hate this land of Egypt,
This land of thieves and flies,
Of sand and sun and sickness
And ceaseless, shameless lies.

The Pyramids of Pharaoh
Were the concept of a fool,
And these parts have changed little
Since Moses went to school.

Ah, Scripture says God's mercy
Some centuries ago
Delivered hence the Hebrews.
Would Heaven might save me so!

Second Thoughts on Egypt

I wasn't very happy
To step ashore at Suez
All dressed up as a soldier.
But then I ask you—who is?
And though I've cursed this country
From that day unto this,
Yet I'll say a word in favour
Of Heliopolis.
Ah, yes, it would surprise you,
The things that can be done
After the moon has risen
On this city of the sun!
So if in my impatience
I have been over hard on
This place and its good people,
Here and now I beg their pardon.

Anonymous

Camel's Crap

Crumbling clumps of camel's crap
Lay glistening in the sun
The camel smiled as he looked round
To see what he had done.
'To think' said he 'this stinking mess
Will one day soon be State Express.

PLAYER'S PLEASE!

Ann Noneemuss.

A Matelot's Farewell to Egypt

Land of heat and sweaty socks
Sun sand sin and blasted pox
Streets of sorrow streets of shame
Streets for which we have no name
Thieving pestering bloody wogs
Smelly dust and mangy dogs

Blistering heat and aching feet
Gippo guts and camel's meat
Clouds of choking dust that blinds
And drives a man out of his mind
The Arab's heaven—the Matelot's hell
So land of b------s fare thee well

Ode to a Gezira Lovely

They call me Venal Vera,
I'm a lovely from Gezira[1],
The Fuehrer pays me well for what I do,
The order of the battle,
I obtain from last night's rattle,
On the golf course with the Brigadier from 'Q'.

I often have to tarry,
In the back seat of a gharry,
It's part of my profession as a spy,
Whilst his mind's on fornication,
I'm extracting information,
From the senior G.S.O. or G.S.I.

When I yield to the caress,
Of the D.D.W.S.
I get from him the lowdown of the works,
And when sleeping in the raw,
With a Major from G.4.
I learn of Britain's bargain with the Turks.

[1]Island in the Nile, location of sports club.

69

On the point of his emission,
In the 26th. position,
While he quivers in exotic ecstasy,
I hear of the location,
Of a very secret station,
From an over-sexed S.C. from 02E.

So the Brigadiers and Majors,
And the whiskey soaked old stagers
Enjoy themselves away from Britain's shores,
Why should they bring Victory nearer,
When the ladies from Gezira,
Provide them with this lovely f------ War?

A Soldier's Ballad of the Nancy Astor

Out of the Old Dominion
Full of nigras and hominy grits
She fell on poor old Blighty
Like a Henry the Eighth with tits.

First she was Nancy Langhorne,
Next she was Nancy Shaw,
Then she was Nancy Astor,
Now thank God she's Nancy No More.

On her plantation at Cliveden
Dropping a no-no creed:
Christian Science, Blue Ribbon
And down with Bint, Booze and The Weed.

On her plantation at Cliveden
Chief of the 'Nannies know best':
'Give them more than they ask for'—
Her field-grey friends in the west.

'That darling little Mr. Hitler,
Well, he doesn't smoke, drink and the rest—
So give him still more than he asks for,
He's doing it all for the best.'

Her field-grey friends go goosestepping
Past Brussels, past gay Paree.
Is she lopsides down in some dungeon
Encrusted with leg irons? Not she!

She's up in those Parliament Houses
Distilling and shrilling out her spew:
'It's Blue Ribbons and tie up your p----s, boys,
And Mrs Eddy she'll see you all through.'

Now Nancy she swivels her beadies
At the boys becalmed over the Med:
'They're having it rather too cushy
While others do the fighting instead.'

Still she's got the ear of the nobboes
For Nancy she always is right:
Chief of the Nannies knows better
For if you can f--k, you can't fight.

'Now clap down those houses of passion
In the streets of the Birka and Sister,
I won't have them dunking their willies
Till they bring back an army of blisters.

Before they're demobbed and they marry
With salversan stuffed, mapacrine,
Like a bracelet of pus let them carry
Yellow arm bands that warn "We're unclean!".'

So sweat it out here with Mrs Eddy
And gnats' piss and Hamid and Co.
And when it's the year back to Blighty
We'll drop all our friggings and go.

O when we get back Lady Nancy
We'll thank you for all that you've said
In the five years we've romped here so cushy
In our nursery down by the Med.'

Edited by Ian Fletcher.

Benghazi Ballad

I will tell you a tale of Benghazi
    Where most of our fighting was done
It was there that a brave British soldier
    Was killed by an I-talian Gun.

As he fell to the floor mortally wounded
    The blood from his wounds, did flow red
He raised himself up on his elbow
    And to his comrades around him, he said

'You can bury me out in the desert
    Under the Libyan sun
You can bury me out in the blue'y
    For my duty to England is done.'

'My only true love was my mother
    No sweetheart have I ever known
There is no-one at home left to mourn me
    I will die as I lived all alone.'

Note: One of many versions, from all ranks, who produced daily variations sung to a maudlin tune.

II
North Africa

C. H. Bevan

Medjez-el-bab

Shell shattered tanks, seared hulls burned red with fire;
Steel helmets, broken rifles, coils of wire;
Beside the track, abandoned guns point blind at vanished targets;
Here's the cast down rind of yesterday's battle.
Only yesterday
This plain was loud with guns and all ablaze with our attack.
Now new men come to gaze
Uncomprehending.
How can we explain
the tension and the tumult and the pain
of yesterday?
Dulled voices ask
what came ye forth to seek?
Astonishment and drama here revealed?
There's nothing that's so rustily antique
as yesterday's battlefield.

1943

Hangover

With eyes like lumps of coal in virgin snow
Thus! in my head those blacksmith's hammers go,
Flattening my eyeballs glowing cherry red
To rivet iron bands about my head.
My tongue is arid as a country lane
Dry, dusty, parched, longing for summer rain.
My stomach heaves like the Atlantic swell
In short—as you have guessed—I'm far from well.
My breath is stale and fiery, comes in gasps
Scoring my brazen throat like steely rasps.
Peccavi! I will not exceed again
I swear it—Oh, relieve my aching brain.
Enough, the wise say, is itself a feast—
Will someone call a doctor—or a priest!

1943

J. K. Clark

Night Withdrawal

'The fighting during Ochsenkopf, though rather scrappy was often hard ... Matters did not at first go well for the British because they were elbowed out of El Ouana on 1st March, out of Sedjenane on the 4th and ...' ('History of the Second World War' Vol. IV Chapter XIII).

'That night transport came forward and took away all the surplus kit and the following night the Battalion started back down the road towards El Ouana, leaving in position a platoon from each of the rifle companies to keep the enemy ignorant of what was happening.' (Battalion History)

We packed and waited; the rest had gone at eight.
The shelling stopped.
The hills were black and smothering in the silence.
We stumbled down the goat track; thud of boots,
A belch, a fart and 'F! the f---- anti-tank!'

'Let's see if Company have left some loot!'
We crawled into their dug-out, struck a match
And found three bottles full of whiskey
Wrapped in tissue paper still.
'The f---ing Jerries won't get that!'
We swigged it as we walked back down the road.

An hour or two and someone was ahead—
'You eight platoon? We thought you'd had it!'
Down on the grass, feet up, my water bottle out—
then two boiled sweets
And all around the stink of steaming, sweating, khaki serge.

The Dead and the Wounded

'During the Sedjenane action the total casualties were 21 killed, 98 missing and 46 wounded'
(Battalion History)

The Dead

Wedged with their mates in two-man trenches:
some blue, some green, some bloated up;
and others white, immaculate, dignified;
Behind the matted hair or red-ringed in their khaki
                                                    battle dress
A neat and single bullet hole.

The padre picked the discs from in among their guts.
I couldn't.

The Wounded

Inside the tunnel-near the entrance—
our doctor and the German worked together:
two nodding heads with downturned mouths.
'Up on the table with him.' 'Rauf, schnell!'
Another shattered groin.
The testicles their covering gone
lay pink and bare and smooth
like pigeons' eggs.
They put a dressing on him
and then they left him in the group about to die.

'Next up!'
A jagged bloody scoop below the knee.
'Ja, amputieren. Man kann nichts anders.'
No anaesthetic so I gripped his hand
and watched.
He bit his lip—no cry;
the knife slipped slowly through the flesh;
with delicate respect they laid the leg
among the severed members
placed in the darkest corner.

H. Compton

To Carthage Then I Came

Gonzalo: This Tunis, sir, was Carthage.
Adrian: Carthage?
Gonzalo: I assure you, Carthage.
            —*The Tempest*, II, 1.

We know what it means, once in a man's life,
To march with Montgomery Africanus
To the conquest of an unknown city.
Descending from the sky-burdened Atlas,
Brown, sere, waste as the mountains of the moon,
We have seen in the valley before us
The slow Bagradas—that is, the Medjerdah—
Pointing vaguely towards our objective.
We have followed hope and fear to the valley
On tanks, on trucks, on chariots, on foot.
Apprehensive of raids by 'plane or horse,
We have known what it means to camp for months
By Bulla (never regal in our time)
In mud clogging the feet of withered hills.
We have known preparations for battle—
Have thought of home in cold fields starred with fires
And peered through night at the veiled face of dawn
Bringing the emergency of morning.
We have left friends where darkness detained them,
Met enemies where daylight revealed them
In the quick intimacy of combat.
Zama, Oued Zarga, awoke in us
Ecstasy eclipsing what came after:
The counting, enslaving, slaughter of captives,
The march to Tunis—or was it Carthage?—
The drinking, looting and drunken laughter
In the conquered city.

When we awoke
The light of memory fell on the past
From a quite different angle, picked out
Forgotten features and cast new shadows.
After the Byrsa, Casbah and brothels,
The suburban residences have changed.

Sere, waste and withered, mountains of the moon
Usurp the Apennine, the Pennine, sky.
Medjerdah merges with Tiber and Thames,
And Bagradas erodes the banks of Time.
It is hard to re-learn geography
And to see history overflowing
Text books and flooding unforeseen channels,
Which point vaguely to a fresh objective.
Nor is it easy to realise that
Zama, Oued Zarga, Carthage, Tunis,
Were places where we threw up dikes against
The current—digging, blasting, sandbagging,
Pile-driving, tipping, building, consolidating,
Sweating and swearing, pushing and straining,
Working blindly as a team, in the dark,
Until they said the job was finished and
We stumbled, dazed, nearly indifferent,
Towards the chill sobriety of dawn.

On a Soldier Playing the Piano

The Naafi much admires
The lucky, gifted man
Who, lacking thought or plan,
Incites these weary wires,
Like rivals hoarse for votes,
To argue over pitch.
With long-habitual twitch
His left hand dully quotes
A ready-made, staccato,
And smudgy ostinato.
Unhampered by notation,
He learned to play by ear.
This leaves his right hand free
To ramble languidly—
To roam his private sphere
By free association,

And with subconscious bonds
To bind up odds and ends:
Remembered gramophones
That mingle with his dreams,
And visions in a trance
Of girls he saw in trams,
Dim evenings drowned in bars,
Embraces on the stairs,
An impulse at the dance,
The body's vain expense.—
All these he now lays bare,
His wealth is here displayed.
O who will say he's hollow,
Whose drift we all can follow,
Or find in him a lack
Who, innocent of Bach,
Thus scatters on the air
The notes in which he's paid?

F. K. Forrester

A Song of the Airfield Autopatrols

In the construction of dirt aerodromes in the Mediterranean theatres of war, autopatrols—grotesque self-propelling mechanical graders interminably crossing and recrossing the landing strips, played a vital part. The advance would be held up until the air cover had been organised.

Nothing goes forward; tanks and guns are stay'd;
This is the war's siesta. Only we
Move on and on, like shuttles carelessly
About the landing field, weaving a braid
Of dust on dust. Or say, like mice afraid
We run from wall to wall, all witlessly,
Leaving our tracks behind. Yet you shall see
Swift eagles rising from these marks we made!
Then shall the war go forward. Then the pent
Impatient tanks and guns, finding release,
Roar on—
And we forgotten!

Tony Goldsmith

The I.G. at War

I'm Captain Blenkinsop, I.G.[1],
Sent by mistake across the sea,
To land upon this dismal shore
And find myself involved in war.
Sad is the tale I have to tell—
For a man like me this war is hell.
For how can anyone expect,
My fall of shot to prove correct,
When everything I tell the guns,
Is interfered with by the Huns?
When bombs are dropping down in rows
How can I make my traverse close.
Or take a bearing on the Pole
While cowering in a muddy hole?
It's plain that the opposing forces,
Have not been on the proper courses.
But, worst of all, the other day,
When I was checking someone's lay,
The Germans rushed the gun position
Without the Commandant's permission.
I had to meet them, man to man,
Armed only with a Tetley fan.
O send me back to Salisbury Plain
And never let me rove again!
Larkhill's the only place for me,
Where I could live at ease and free
And frame, with sharpened pencil stroke
A barrage of predicted smoke.
Worked out for sixteen different breezes,
With extra graphs, in case it freezes,
For non-rigidity corrected,
And on a Merton Grid projected!
O take me to the R.A. Mess,
To dwell in red brick happiness,
Enfold my body, leather chair,
And let me fight the War from there!

[1]Inspector of Gunnery

Spike Milligan

Tribute to Tony Goldsmith[1]

That April day
Seems far away
The day they decided to kill
Lt Tony Goldsmith RA
On the slopes of Longstop Hill

At Toukebir
The dawn lights stir
Who's blood to-day will spill?
To-day it's Tony Goldsmith's
Seeping out on Longstop Hill

One can't complain
Nor ease the pain
Or find someone to fill
The place of Tony Goldsmith
Lying dead on Longstop Hill

In Germany
There still could be
A Jochiem, Fritz or Will.
Who did for Tony Goldsmith
That day—on Longstop Hill.

[1]Killed Longstop Hill, April 22, 1943
(Tribute written post-war)

K. S. Grannell

Reminiscences in a Tap Room

I mind well the day that I joined, 'Sir.'
I'd come up from Base on a train.
It was hot and my kit, 'Sir,' was heavy.
Well thankee, 'Sir', yes same again.

I was sent to Battalion headquarters,
Who were up on a 'Djebel', it seems,
Now 'Djebels' a word, Sir,
I hadn't heard, Sir,
So I asks a bloke just what it means,

He looks at my badge, and then he looks at my boots.
Which were polished I am sorry to say.
And at last he replied.
And the words that he used,
Have stuck in my mind to this day.

If you ain't never heard of a 'Djebel',
Or a 'Ras', or a 'Kef', or a 'Bou',
Well you've come to the right 'Bloody' place chum,
Cos we breeds the 'Barstards' we do,

Now I thought at the time, that this bloke had a grudge,
Sort of bitter, he seemed like to me,
When I found that a 'Djebel' was only a hill,
Unreasoning like, don't you see?

But I fought with the 'Kents', Sir, for many a day,
And those 'Djebels' rose up like the sea, Sir,
And at times if I'd found,
A flat piece of Ground.
I'd have walked like the 'Tower of Pisa'.

There were green ones, and bald ones, and old Abrod too,
There was 'Bou-Diss', and longstop—the swine!
There were Wadis and gullys, and scarps and mules,
And trying to dig trenches, in rock, with no tools,
It was 'Djebel', Sir, time after time.

But they're memories now, Sir, of ten years ago,
And those trenches be long overgrowed,
But it's true what I tell,
There'll be 'Djebels' in, Hell,
Well Thankee, Sir, One for the road.

La Marsa, May 1943.

Alec Grant

Fallen Out of Convoy

Here in the deep cavern of a drifting ship,
The reckless heart of our universe—
A green crap table, and demanding dice.
Beyond that solitary downward light,
The watching, silent darkness.

Our engines cut; only the lapping waves
against the hull—
A brooding breathless shape across the stars.
And someone there, the listening U-boat
Also holds its breath.

Keep throwing that dice—who cares!
When dawn will take your money
And your life—
Unless that corvette comes.

Tunisia—Italy, 1943.

Note: An LST (Landing Ship—Tank) in transit from Bizerta to Taranto with 624 (Special Duty) Squadron (Halifaxes) heavy equipment had to drop out of convoy to return a severe case of peritonitis to Bizerta, then proceed on course alone. A U-Boat alert entailed most of those aboard (mainly U.S. Air Force and a handful of R.A.F.) standing silently all night, in stockinged feet, wearing life jackets, around a green baize table while bundles of dollars exchanged hands at the behest of the rolling dice. For the penurious watching R.A.F. men, the bizarre game ended when the corvette found us and began dropping depth charges. For the Americans, the game went on . . .

Return of the Bod

With metallic shivers, four propellors stop.
A pool of light on the dark tarmac
As the belly-hatch clicks open.
First out is the Bod,
Unwillingly safe on Algerian soil,
Not in some dark European field,
Black parachute buried,
Stealing towards a sinister dawn.

But here he stands, unshaven, hollow-eyed,
Two cigarettes clamped in still tense jaws,
Two matches flare together.
In sharp sucked breath jetting smoke,
The agony of the failed drop—
And the moonlit repeats to come,
Until, they too, light up their signal fires.

Blida, North Africa, 1943.

Military and civilian personnel (Liaison Officers, saboteurs etc.) parachuted to the Resistance
Movements in Europe were referred to as bods (bodies). Usually they were dropped by moon-
light, often with black parachutes, after recognition of a pre-arranged signal fire code.

W. G. Holloway

1st Army Soldier

He lies quiet on the desert,
Sun-bronzed legs shot through with lead;
The battle sounds still linger
But he does not hear—he's dead.

He was no prudent soldier,
Chose life's exit not with care
Valourous indeed he was
But 8th Army were not there.

His blood flows just as steady,
His sharp wound cut as deep,
The sand soaked just as crimson,
By booted, shattered feet.

But Praise's voice is muted,
Seek no record of his fame—
The poor boy died at Medjez
And not at Alamein.

These modest verses are prompted by the bitter remark of a 1st Army man when he said, 'You are no bloody hero unless you've been in the Monty mob (8th Army).' Perhaps, as with justice, there is not always enough fame to go round.

Ronald Lewin

Remembering Zion

Aloof as ghosts from the fireside world we cherished
And only in our daydreams revenants
We drain a brief and honeymoon delight
From the Remembered.

A tinsel trinket on a chain of brass,
A nibbled photograph, a threadbare letter
In the renewal of our milestone moments
Are Sesames sufficient.

And Memory, like some merciful reagent,
Planes from the past the bitter and the haggard,
Condensing into clear and rosy crystal
All we have treasured.

At night, at ease, even in the heart of tension,
Sudden as shells the revelation kindles:
Like liberty-men, to lost unhoped-for Edens
We take our furlough.

Observation Post, Enfidaville, 1943.

Lawrie Little

Sentry Duty, 7.15 a.m.

Morning grins in mud
But is too late
To mark the sleepy guard perform;
And wolfish, sulky dogs
Drowse now and ruminate
Like wrinkled logs
Which house gross, burning bees
Droning in furry hate
Before they swarm.

One fellah's eyes
Are cunning as a rabbit's,
Twitching wise:
He watches the soldiers at their making war
Who trundle in their khaki orbits,
Showing no black surprise.
They have interminable habits
And tell shifty lies
To miss the thought of their drab limits.

And under the feline velour of the skies
They sprinkle English catcalls,
Hum broken jazz,
And break the wet mud of a fellah's wall,
Grovelling round the few goods that he has,
For which he crawls.

Souk el Khemis, Christmas 1942.

Monastery Billets

Algerian night
And I can hear
Like a bell's tearing of the air
Their songs and chatter
The young barrel-makers
Bent by their dark benches among wines,

Vin rose and muscatel, fermenting skeins
Of red, of lambent amber.
Nothing is in slumber; slithering bats
Skate the tiled vats, the voluminous
Darkness of the cellars.

Soon the young men pass,
Soft, gazelle shadows on the path,
These young, curly and practical heads,
These plump mouths
And ingenuous gestures.

Robert, the handsome Tunisian,
Young go-between,
Silent weigher of plans, adroit
With his patron's francs, who frowns
Defensively, as though the nightsounds are too wayward,
And his snug ears not acute.

And the smiling Henri, the gentle Kabyle,
The small, slowmouthed barrelmaker
Who hammers his whispered humour into wood:
Hear how his drifting chuckles
Wander along the olive trees of the path
Like feathered rumours of amusement
Dozing in breeze.

The woodpecker clatter is Alexis,
The squeaking dwarf, shrewd
Buyer of soldier's food—and his clothes—
Who once, in a baby adventure
Fell from a vixenish bean tree;

Humped now, but humorously chic
With an infant's curious eyes
And startling anger when he is teased.

And scarred Baptiste, the clown
Who speaks the good Arabic, who knows
All the black marketeers, the shady
Untrustworthy merchants and makers of plots,
The sackcloth thieves, and Kasbah monied scoundrels,
And each lavish cafe.

Listen to the heathen chatter
Of your orphan children, White Fathers,
Pray for them.

Maison Carrée, November 1942.

From a Med. Diary

Wines of the Harrach Hills, Algeria. 15th December, 1942

Bottles of wine are brought from a suitcase under the bed. At one breath he drinks a bottle. We must follow, speaking with gestures, smiles, foreign accents. The air is thick with our gratitude and goodwill. If we are much more friendly we shall burst into tears. As we are leaving tomorrow we act like lifelong friends. We were never more sincere. Later when we crawl behind the one-roomed house to be sick, it's our sincerity makes us vomit; we'll blame the wine.

Arab Beggar, Souk el Khemis, Tunisia. January 1943

The man is thirsty and hungry. Dirt moves over his face like shadows. Perhaps he limps, or the track he walks along is filled with holes. What language does he speak? He has no tongue. He was designed to be seen in a poor light, to be bumped into blindly by drunks. His hand stretches out—so he begs . . . It is a hand quite light in colour. Clasp it!

(But I'm speaking to people across two seas.)

Soldier Writer, Cliffs at Monastir. Tunisia, July, 1943

He is sitting upon a hill overlooking the sea, his shirt open at the neck, the grass coiled under his thighs, a white pad on the ground between his shoulder and knee, his right hand resting in his pulsing groin. His pose suggests poems, his eyes self-love. He cannot forget that no-one noticed his potential glory. Now he denies he saw it once himself.

The dry movements of lizards waken him. Surrounded by orchards of tangled olives, he displays a very young indifference. The sun has scorched his thighs. Shade disappears prodigiously up cliffs. He stretches, shouts, has no wish to be interrupted. Love? There are no echoes. Comradeship? He knows what that is. So this day will join the others. Everything begins to gallop. Faster and faster. He is not alone. His laughter rings between ragged palms. But the world is flat. Flat. He will always be in the sun.

(He boasts that no-one loves him. He escapes our prisons of flesh or pure feeling. He is free to bore us, our minds chained to our thighs, our good wishes suspect, our arrangements never discarding a convenient bedroom. We are animals with one use for speech. Any mirror tells him he's not one of us.)

J. Neilson

Battle in Tunisia

This poem written on Blackwatch Hill while sheltering under my tank from enemy shellfire, gives an accurate and fairly detailed account of a few hours' typical tank battle.

Sleeping, blear-eyed, flaps furiously banging,
'Wakiee, wakiee, four a.m., get cracking!'
First light, faint Orange appears eastward
Rev. to fifteen hundred, let clutch in,
With clatter and clang of giant mowing machine
The masculine monsters move ponderously forward
Squadron sweeps line abreast across the plain,
Through fields of luscious green
Rustling wheat, ablaze with golden flowers
Tracks clang furiously over rocky outcrop,
And tank slithers to rest with broken track.
Spanners and sledges flung furiously down,
The sweating crew work swearing on the broken track,
Suddenly fling flat for screaming shell,
Twenty yards away freckled gunner kid
Dead, lies inertly in a bloody heap.

'Grab his rifle, he won't need it again!'

'Get that brew of tea on!'

Water quickly simmers on petrol fire.

'Throw the Compo[1] in, and make it strong!'
Ton and a half of broken track linked up
'Hey, we're moving; jump in!'
Scramble into tank swallowing scalding tea
Through lips sticky with four days' stubble,
Cram sardines and bully into mouth
Light up inevitable fag, eyes strain through visor
Speeding over fields spangled red with poppies
Flat out to hidden gully, slam on brakes,
Forty tons balance gently, see-saw over.
On skyline see Jerry Mark Four Tank
'Gunner, traverse left. Steady, yours on!'
Telescope cross wires quickly, swing central
'That's got him—Yahoo Mahommed!'[2]
Commander's cry of boyish glee
Quick rush to grab loot

Creep cautiously uphill to hull down position
Intently peering through periscope
At changing world of four by two
Over crest, screaming Stukas swoop
Gunners with Besas blaze furiously
Arid puff of bomb blast taps face,
Raid over, taut nerves relax.
'Let's get another brew on!'
And so the battle carries on.

10 April, 1943.

[1] Army tea, sugar and milk powder used for making tea.
[2] Originally the Battle Cry of the Paratroopers who were with 'C' Squadron at Sedjenane, passed from them to us, and so generally to the Royal Armoured Corps.

E. M. Spalding

Letters Home

18 April 1943

Yesterday we entered Sfax; maybe you remember the place from the news. The last but one important place before Tunis. Jerry had left the day before and emotion ran high. I had a good view of things from my usual lofty perch on top of the van (like the man from Maples.) Sfax is entered by a bridge, over a river which was almost dry. The thin stream flowing slowly through the middle of the bed was black with tadpoles. Jerry had naturally 'removed' the bridge before leaving and for a radius of 100 yards all was black, bent and twisted. The loss in tadpoles must have been terrific. So we had to make a detour through the public 'jardins'. They were hardly in a state to invite youthful play or aged relaxation, for yards of white tape told the old story. Mines! Overhanging branches and needle-sharp palm leaves made life difficult for me for some minutes and the blokes inside watched from out of the back door lest they should miss the sight of Tarzan among the branches. My tin hat had already fallen off as we swayed and rocked over a rough track a few miles back. The rear wheel had run over it, for when I collected it later from the following van it had become quite a cute poke bonnet. Somehow I must restore it to the shape expected by the Army. However, to continue. We left the 'jardins' and drove through the town or city and saw for the first time since Tripoli old men and boys, matrons, maids and babies, white in colour. How they must have suffered, for the place was badly damaged by air attacks. Then the riot began. Flags everywhere, Union Jacks, Tricolour, Stars and Stripes. The old men waved their sticks or crutches, the girls said 'Oh, lala'. On we drove, laughing, waving, giving the 'V' sign and many a 'Ca va bien?'

An elderly Frenchwoman rushed into the road and gave the driver of our cookhouse a bouquet, but he lacked gratitude for a little later, as we slowed down, he presented it to a Military Policeman on point duty. The M.P. was too surprised to return it and we passed him, a bouquet in one hand as he directed the traffic with the other. Suddenly another M.P. barred our way, waving his arms like a windmill, bearing a distressed countenance, so unlike M.P.s, so we stopped to humour him and then I could hear the sound of pipes drawing near. (Even as I write this my spine grows chilly in recollection of the scene which followed.) The M.P. made further frantic efforts to clear the route, thronged on both sides by people white and coloured, whilst vehicle after vehicle of H.M. glorious 8th Army passed through. But we stopped, all of us, at the frantic one's behest, whilst the pipes drew nearer, leading a procession. There were cars in it. To my surprise the first one was filled with flowers and amidst them, the red of his cap band more vivid than the flowers, sat General Montgomery. The crowd roared and clapped and waved flags as he passed. Military law is silent on my immediate problem. What does a man on top of a van do when the General passes? In my ignorance I gave a salute, sitting to attention. Monty looked up and acknowledged it. More cars, more red hats, whilst the pipes drowned every other sound and the drummers crashed their sticks from eye level to drum. The 51st Highland Division; kilts swinging, webbing white, metal gleaming, every rifle at the same angle, a triumph of military perfection.[1] In the Army we have a word, just one word to describe it. The crowd roared and clapped again, whilst the more agile ran with the pipes. It was a contest between sound and colour. White walls, red roofs, flags, trees, flowers, summer dresses, native wraps of all shades, brown skins and, not far away, the blue sea. It was a gala day and the man from Maples had one of the finest views, but also he could see the other side of the picture. Destruction and ruin, great holes, smashed buildings, wrecked homes, engines and coaches at all angles, bent iron, twisted rails, hanging wires and broken mains. In all, the inevitable result of the bombing of military objectives in a city. The objectives were truly hit, but . . . I wish we could have stayed awhile, but duty called and we passed through. Some way further on we stopped and took up our leaguer amidst an acre of olive trees. Meanwhile Tunis lies ahead where I hope soon to witness another gala day with the glorious 8th. I went to bed very tired at the end of the day, under a spreading old olive tree. I had passed the previous night on duty and should have been sleeping some part of the day, but the sights of the day were worth the lost sleep.

29.4.43

Tunisia is a land of earwigs. They infest everything. I am not greatly affected by the sight of them but one gets tired of shaking out showers of earwigs before putting on clothes. They are also fond of a damp towel and it is wise to flap the towel violently before drying the face. Just one of the penalties of the life close to nature. Parts of the country are beautiful; fairly hilly and covered by masses of wild flowers. The olive groves form a large part of the picture. Perfectly planted in avenues as far as the eye can reach.

---

[1] This, after six months fighting and pursuing Jerry from El Alamein, over 1,500 miles!

Alan White

Overseas

Here is the airgraph's destination,
nucleus of the guardian thoughts
from those at home who think of us.
This is the country which we might so easily
have visited as tourists,
but with a camera rather than a pistol,
rubbing on the thigh.
Here is where we must forget
the numb bewilderment of separation,
and begin to learn
appreciation of new things,
such as the elegant ellipse
of Spitfire wings,
tilting and glinting in the sun.
Here the ties of tenderness
are stronger and delve back
into a precious past.
Here upon the battlefield,
the pawn on war's gigantic chessboard
can become a queen.
But with each coming night
a simpler thought prevails,
when soldiers make their bivouacs
into a fragile, private shell
tuned in across the waves
to England and their vivid home.

Algeria.

German P.O.W. Camp

Here where the flies are thickest,
and the jagged strands of wire
enclose with coil and palisade
is a zoo grotesque,

where trained, potential killers
are without their fangs
and pace the cage in twos and threes,
dragging boredom with each step.
On the ground, baked hard as teak,
the motley bivouacs are strewn,
ground-sheet, silken parachute,
torn canvas, dusty blanket,
anything that serves
as parasol and parapluie.
Observe the prisoners,
blond arrogance of hair,
the athlete in their stance,
and hear their marching songs,
drum-like in cadence
and as mellow maudlin
as the feel of wine,
making an outlaw flag
wave in the heart,
hysteria its nationality.
These traits in time of war,
when all virility is at high price,
almost compel an urge to fraternise.
But then an inner voice recalls—
Dachau, the death, despair and darkness,
Rotterdam, rased flat by bombs,
Paris, festering with pompous uniforms
and the malignant swastika,
and England's scars.
In a trice I have become
the gaoler once again,
confident with hate
and quick to penalise.

Tunisia.

Anonymous

Song of the Irish Brigade

The Rifles, the Skins and the bold Fusiliers. (Sung to the tune of Master McGrath.)

They landed in Africa to clash with the Hun
And came out in good time to miss none of the fun,
They jumped into action with three hearty cheers
Did the Rifles, The Skins and the bold Fusiliers.

Lord Haw Haw is a liar of truth you'll admit
He said that our lads weren't doing their bit,
But they'll dash Hitler's hopes and they'll crown Goring's fears,
Did the Rifles, The Skins and the bold Fusiliers.

'Twas the week before Easter the enemy held
Great fighting positions north of Medjez-el-bab
But, without hesitation, and nothing to fear
Went the Rifles, The Skins and the bold Fusiliers.

On the hill called Tangoncha they opened their Show
And soon from the hill Jerry quickly did go.
They hoisted the White Flag and surrendered in tears
To the Rifles, The Skins and the bold Fusiliers.

When Longstop had fallen we knew we'd have fun
To the plains with our rifles we followed the Hun
When we marched into Tunis the French gave three cheers
To the Rifles, The Skins and the bold Fusiliers.

As we marched in through Tunis heading straight for Cap Bon
The French in their thousands said: 'Irelandais tres bon'.
To see the Rifles, The Skins and the bold Fusiliers.

Lieutenant General Kenneth Anderson, Commander, First Army, North Africa

III
Italy

Introduction

The Troops and the Arts

It is certainly a widely held view that the armed services are no haven for artists and intellectuals. Even graduates in the humanities are rare birds in both peacetime and wartime armies, so much so that having an MA, I was often known as 'Prof.' to brother officers as well as the the other ranks in my battery, but as I hope to show this is not entirely correct.[1]

Those who had spent months and months in the North African campaign with either the Eighth or the First Army (the latter's a much shorter spell) had spent much of that time in desert or near-desert conditions, under canvas, a long way from any library or concert hall or theatre. For the luckier ones in the Eighth Army there was the occasional leave in Cairo, and there the artistically- and intellectually-inclined sought each other out and clustered together. But unless they were stationed in or near the capital, visits were rare and Muslim culture, fascinating though it might be in other respects, was alien to the main cultural forms of Europe.

So the descent on Italy in 1943, whatever its dangers and discomforts, was also a liberation. One was back in Europe, in Western civilisation, and in a country particularly rich in reminders of that heritage. It was a heady homecoming. The British have always tended to have love affairs with Italy (look only at the line from Browning to Forster). There had never before been such a mass love-affair by so many in a whole generation. Many of them are still in love today.

And, again writers, artists and intellectuals sought each other out, spotted the 'ironic points of light' flashing out their messages. Luck played its part. In the gun battery next to my own in the early days after reaching Naples, I met a man of about my age, similarly given to comic criticisms of some of the habits of regulars and ex-Territorial Army types. We became friends and remained so through all our time in Italy and then on until his death. That was Andrew Shonfield. Nearly thirty years later we gave the Reith Lectures in successive years. That conjunction also tickled his acute fancy. I spoke at his funeral one bitter winter day in 1981, up in the wastes of North London.

Much more widely than in such individual contacts, Italy affected servicemen of all ranks. She did so especially through her opera. That

---

[1] Sir John Hackett pointed out that in his regiment in Egypt in 1935 there were some twenty-four officers, excluding a couple away on other duties, with arts degrees. Forty percent of today's regular officers have university degrees and the proportion is rising.

flourished throughout, though standards of performance could be wobbly and production and properties odd. I more than once saw Mimi breathe her last at the San Carlo Opera House in Naples on a US Army blanket. The San Carlo attracted servicemen by the hundreds and week after week, many of whom had never before seen opera. It would be wrong, though, to assume that its music came to all of them as something entirely unknown. In the Leeds working-class where I was brought up we knew and loved many of the great operatic arias. We knew them above all from the visits of the San Carlo Opera Company. I imagine its standards would today seem very low but, as the Italians say, it 'had heart'; and we responded to it. The oratorio tradition in the local nonconformist chapels ensured that we had a good range of local 'principals' and they loved to give us gems from the opera at Saturday night concerts. And there was the radio.

So, many people knew something before they set foot in Italy. That land, by providing opera cheaply night after night, allowed those able to get into the towns to wallow. And wallow they did. I knew one Cockney private soldier who fell in love with opera, went round the back to tell the prima donna how much he was affected by her and became her boy friend. She was of Neapolitan working-class stock (potential opera singers were winkled out of those huddled apartments as effectively as potential footballers were winkled out of the back streets of Manchester ... the arts ran with the grain of the two cities as a whole). So the soldier regularly went to huge pasta meals in her home. He remarked acutely that the atmosphere was much like Sunday dinner with a roast and two veg at his own home.

I'd met him because he had become a habitué of the Three Arts Club, just off the Via Roma in the heart of Naples. That was started by a handful of us as a haven for any serviceman or woman from any of the Allied Forces with an interest in any art. It became a classless and rankless honey-pot, a continuous swirl of painters and writers and musicians and lovers of these things. Peter Lanyon, prematurely killed in a gliding accident fifteen or twenty years ago, did a magnificently dotty mural across the whole back wall of the main room. I've no doubt the owners, when they got possession again, obliterated it. It would have been worth a fortune now.

The place was a watering-place, an airhole for those wanting some escape from the not very literate life of tents or for that matter of most army offices. It published a handful of collections of services' writing, some of which appears in this volume. The old philosopher Benedetto Croce, who lived near by, smiled on it and its authors. So did some more unexpected people. It needed friends, for how could such an enterprise take out—for example—a lease? The solution to the problem was found by a major in the Army Education Corps, Ben Baxter. He saw the point and the drift; he rented the premises on our behalf, squared the operation with someone higher up and left us alone as promised. He wrote well himself and could have been a straighforward member. But he knew that might be misunderstood and so stayed away unless we urged him to come and reassured him that he was welcome as, and for, himself and not only because he was our secret patron.

He too—and since I have never written about this period before I now realise for the first time how many of the participants are dead, almost all of them cruelly too soon— Ben Baxter too was lost; in a yachting accident on the Thames not long after the war. Others survive, and I see the names of some of them from time to time in newspapers and journals or get messages from them at second hand. Revisiting Naples for the first time in the late Sixties, to lecture at the university again (I had done that in my last months before demobilisation in 1946), I passed the end of the street on the Via Roma in which the Three Arts Club had stood. I felt no wish to go down and look at the building. The world it nourished was an internal world and bricks and mortar could do nothing to bring it back.

RICHARD HOGGART

J. Cutliffe Aldridge

Red Beach

Leading to the beach is a lane,
White powdered, rutted, and confined by walls
Of drystone. Laden almond trees hang down,
and the peasants tend the melon-plants below.
There was a sniper in those woods two months ago,
And burnt-out tanks were half across the way;
But now a donkey cart, lurching in clouds of dust,
Is all that passes with its load of hay.

In the woods the birds are singing
Where the bullets sang then. The green crickets cry
Where the bull-dozers churned, and the dry
Lane was spattered with wet, crimson flowers
When the Stukas dived.

Night Wind in Italy

Sitting and brooding as the night glides by,
Dully remembering things that are gone,
Longing with twisting fibres to be with you again,
I hear the night wind.
Softly this evening it is crawling round the roof-tops,
Idly slicing the day-warmth from high gables,
And scything the cold streets below.
Smoothly, ignoring the enemy's guns, volplaning onwards,
It will chill their square helmets
As they gleam in the olive groves.
Over the fretting land it will wander,
Skirting moon-silvered Alpine peaks.
And briefly embracing the dispassionate snow
It will glide onwards, over a thousand tiled tower tops,
'Til it probes icily through wooden windmill-sails
And sees the sparse sandy grass of the Channel coast.
As it spears along over the salted wave-tops
Lopping their vacillating surface with a cold indifference
It will see, with disinterested frostiness,
Those good shores of respectable chalk
That I remember achingly.

Drummond Allison

Verity

In memory of Captain Hedley Verity, injured in Sicily. Taken P.O.W., buried at Caserta.
Pre-war, Yorkshire and England slow left arm bowler.

The ruth and truth you taught have come full circle
On that fell island all whose history lies,
Far now from Bramhall Lane and far from Scarborough
You recollect how foolish are the wise.

On this great ground more marvellous than Lords
—Time takes more spin than nineteen thirty four—
You face at last that vast that Bradman-shaming
Batsman whose cuts obey no natural law.

Run up again, as gravely smile as ever,
Veer without fear your left unlucky arm
In His so dark direction, but no length
However lovely can disturb the harm
That is His style, defer the winning drive
Or shake the crowd from their uproarious calm.

T. I. F. Armstong[1]

Encounter

What do you do here, soldier?
It seems I know your face;
On the pampas you were with me:
I was well served by your race.
Who am I? my bronzen stripling,
Well, your grandfather would know.
I am the shade of Garibaldi.
I was a soldier long ago.

I fought once upon this island,
Calatafimi was my field.
Then, as now, the sabred Austrians
Held Italy, and would not yield.
I am the shade of Garibaldi:
Before my blows they reeled.

[1]Better known as John Gawsworth.

Ah, by old Etna, there above us,
Those were such days as the Gods send:
Poncho-warmed nights and frays to prove us,
And with Freedom our aimed end!
I, the grey shade of Garibaldi,
Wish you no worse, my friend.

Victory, peace and ease to limber
War-taut thighs before your hearth
When oppression has fled blanching
Before your ever-advancing path:
These I wish, too, who was farmer.
Fight for the soil that you would till!
Says an old eagle, Garibaldi,
With whose shadow you now kill.

H. E. Bell

Night Op. 1945 Italy

Beneath a pyramid of searchlight beams
The runway lies, mapped out in points of light.
All is prepared; the routine of the day
Reaches its climax in the marshalled regiment.
Flares gleam at planes, planes glitter back.
Amber.   Green.   Red.
With throaty roar the giant hosts advance,
Yellow-rimmed circles of gossamer on their wings,
And so are launched into the still dark blue.
With stern intent they mount and make for—(where?)
The ground lights dance more merrily now.
The stars wink mockingly, serene spectators.
Stars, did you say? One moved, another stirs,
And soon the sky teems with floodlit angels of death.

Addio

Mud, rain and mud;
An endless squelching from the clogged-up tyres.
    Searing hot sun,
    And dust-dry camp sites with a few bright flowers.
Cobalt-blue seas;
The long hours lazing on the scorching sand.
    Glorious days
    Among the ruins of an ancient land.
What memories
Are stored in my mind confusedly!
    I will remember
    Italy.

Robin Benn

On Hearing the News in C.M.F.[1]

The major issues are too large;
this universal war enwraps
the details of a bayonet charge
in parcels of discarded maps.

The news at six and eight and ten
leaves little time for sorrow;
the Army's on the move again—
where shall we be tomorrow?

For Patton, Hodges, Tolbukhin
may take this town, that city;
the uninvited thought creeps in
that shell-wounds are not pretty.

[1]Central Mediterranean Forces

As common thoughts obtrude themselves
to make the edge of sense more blunt;
each one the bigger picture shelves
and gazes, anxious, to his front.

The War is going well.—Enough!
The end is any date you choose;
and, while the soldier does his stuff,
the public will not lack for news.

J. Bevan

Killed in Action in Italy

'Calabri rapuere, tenet nunc Parthenope . . .' *Virgil*.

A small, tin-hatted grave, and you,
Invisible you I've come to see.
It's hard to meet you and try to greet you
Under the leaves of a mulberry tree.

Is this your horizontal length?
Is this your great biography?
Is this your permanent address?
The scene is all soliloquy.

This not-replying and non-smoking,
This losing of half your thirteen stones
Has turned you into a gloomy fellow;
The damp is getting inside your bones.

Leave off loving, leave off living,
You can't jump into my dancing jeep;
Learn to do nothing for ever and ever.
Goodbye, and try to get some sleep.

Italy, Evening on the Gun Position

The time is slack, the evening cocoa's up;
Cordite and cookhouse scent the cooling air.
A mess-tin chinks; I take my metal cup
And pause from plotting on the gridded square.
A squeeze-box wheezes down on Number One,
And Sergeant Harris mutters to his crew
Of Alex. Florence, hot from her feast of sun,
Arno and Fiesole curtained from our view.
On Number Four they stagger up with shells
And stack each hundred pounds inside the pit
(Tonight's ten rounds an hour is theirs). The bells
Faintly intone for Vespers, and bats flit.

Ubique

(Motto of the Royal Artillery)

The long barrel of the past is pointing towards me;
I peer down its spiral rifling, reflecting those times
so many mortgages, lectures, removals,
so many bombards, ranging rounds ago.
I can see those long five-fives with the vertical horns,
and the stencilled hundred-pounders we posted each day
from our cluttered dens in tents or farmhouse kitchens
to destinations we thought we knew,
a few thousand yards, years away in our future:
Forcoli, Campi Bizenzio, Astra Signa
swim through the donkey's ears;
that time with the guns straddling the Serchio
deeply snowed where David made a suspension footbridge,
and all those fireplans at two or three hundred hours
on Monte Rumici, Monte Caprara, Sole,
ringed in crayon on the talc, names of fear;
HEN (it is marked in red) when the Guards
ran into fixed-line fire on a night attack

and the casual company commander who had a look-see
beforehand from the O.P., dumped his valise there
and never came back to unroll it; that
premature on the hilltop
position at snug Bombiana, the gun-barrel peeled
back like a steel banana skin, circular saws
of jagged bits, plummeting down whining thousands of minutes later;
that first barrage in the Gothic Line
when everything suddenly blazed round the pivot gun,
haystack, boxes of cordite, and Gunner Lea
(who is it walking up with a mug of tea?
I wish I remembered the Number One's name who is pulling
his clothes off and kicking away the charges
and burning hay while the rest of the crew
lie about dazed in the scorched grass. The strong men
are all nameless in history);
and the night-move over to Castelfiorentino
where we lost a gun-tower on a mine;
I remember the goggled D.R.[1] on his motorbike
(squarehead concealed by crash-helmet)
who directed me into a minefield with the guns
and vanished without so
much as a Leben Sie wohl;
Those winters of deep ruts and wheels
spinning the trucks lop-sided, world of wires and phones,
a crazed polyphony of dozens of frequencies
marking the F.D.Ls[2]; the always arriving,
always changing Meteor; slewing the grid, and shells coming up
from the wagon lines (strange
Nineteenth century name from horse-drawn days),
havens of sleek non-combatants three miles back,
with constant brews and pick of all the perks.
Where are all those thousands of indestructible metal
charge boxes, some in junk shops on Merseyside still?
Some under the curtained bunks on Appenine
farms; one in the garage at my last address;
and the summers, the scissor sharpeners busy all night in the quincunx
olive ranks; musk smell of the dusk,
and sudden flash-bang of the high-velocity

---

[1]Despatch Rider
[2]Forward Defence Lines

guns, dragged on the edge of dark over the ridges to fire
quick rounds with open sights from the forward slopes,
then limbered up and away before we could say Take Post;
the morning mist thinning at the feet
of Santa Maria, and black crosses on the grey
shapes I looked steeply down on, turning on tracks and
rumbling away to the cemetery (I hear
the drone of their lumbering exit);
shouting to the mike, hearing the battery, neat
miniature toys hidden in the next valley,
orders going out to the guns, the tiny
reduced voices of the Number Ones, then
Ready: No time for range tables, time of flight?
thirty seconds.
Fire! (and Fire! and, fainter, Fire!);
then waiting,
the shells already posted, for them to fly
over my head like whistling kettles, magnificent
loving response;
then below, four hundred yards away, land in a clump of
(puffs first) crumps;
and one tank, hated, like a rat in a wainscot,
stop and turn round and round and round
concussed
by a hit, then judder like a compass needle
and follow the others away with seeming unhaste.

Ah, those ithyphallic barrels, always exactly parallel,
pointing where someone's right and glory led us
through two long winters, over the Appenines,
across the Arno and beyond Verona
to the great plains and the lakes
(peregrino labore fessi), Garda and Como
where we fired our final rounds for ever and ever.
Can a few tree trunks, sawn and sloped to the sky
in a field on the eve of Good Friday, decades later
still fire such long-range salvos?
The soul saves what it needs
from the waste, halts time at its will.
Those gun positions, those faces, those parallel pieces
are ranging on me still.

Reverie by the Mare Nostro

The summer folds me in its heat,
its languor wraps me, soul and sense.
The voice grows faint. I have no time
for glory's timeless recompense.

Far off and near they toil and die
while near and near death sighs and sings.
No vision clothes his entrance now.
There is no sound of viewless wings.

Earth with its gutted villages
lies scarred and maimed. Parthenope
bleeds as I bleed, she feels my hurt,
cut by this steel-tracked panoply.

One who was dear to life as life
has vanished in a printed phrase,
pulped by an airburst, braised and gutted
out of the sequence of his days.

Here where the Mare Nostro coils
beneath me like a picture sea,
the air still tender with his life
lip-reads my anguished reverie.

This is the place fate requisitioned;
his number, name, and rank, and he.
All that remains of him is here
at the roots of a fruiting gelsi tree.

Hilltop Gun Position at Bombiana

When I was green as grass,
Cadet-new, bright as paint,
The passing-out parade
Loomed as the last constraint.

But now I'm old as rust.
The road to Zocca looms
For recce, white with dust,
Mined with a thousand dooms.

Counter-Battery Fire

The sun is gone, the convent bells bring
their dolorous single ringing in the dales.
Subalterns flick their frequencies in gin
and gunners wash themselves in canvas pails.
The voices in the olive groves grow still;
silence and sadness with the dark descend,
drawing the moon up from the shadow hill
into a realm of stars that has no end.

Sleep folds us tranquil through the changing night
under the turning of the watchful Plough,
in army blankets, out of mind and sight.
The thinning darkness shatters. 'What's the row?'
'Getting it heavy over on the right'.
Telephone chinks: 'Bombard H.20. Now!'

Dennis Birch

Gunflashes — Castelfrentano

The night is a dark tinder
Touched off by the matches of the guns
Into a finger and thumb of flash and flame
Snapped full in the watching faces
Dark night and click of bursting light
As though the fist of darkness flew straining open
And closed as fiercely on the prize again
Light and dark flicking over like the flying pages of a book
Falling from a mild and uninterested thumb
That halts momentarily on the dark pages
And lets the bright page flash and be gone
In a whittled splinter of a second—
Clean light under the crushing, smothering body of the darkness
Darkness with arms bowed widely from horizon to horizon
Straining down to force the gleam white and vivid body
Into the inert and slobbering mud—
Fiercely and hastily he throws about its struggling
Cords and muffling clothes
Uneasy, with head turned over shoulder—
But the blazing white will not be made null
And tears free a limb—a hand—a foot
To flare, for a moment, clear of the swaddlings and the bonds
And hearten hope, and pride, and conscience—
If we may see in this the dead—the new, the warm blood dead
Making their protest against future forgetfulness
Setting rebel matches to the tindery night
And living in mad struggle
Under the hulking, crushing body of the dark
Then so, too, has truth lived
Lived longer and under fiercer torment
And is she dead?—And forgotten?

H. Brennan

Bitter Weather

There is no man—no soldier
Though his heart beat with the great tones of a bell booming
And his body is his own rich blood flowering
But rain and earth—mere mud
Will put lips to him and suck away his strength
And wind set on his little thimbleful of fury
With enough of shrieking, slashing madness
To set the full moon guttering;
Cold—the quiet and velvet-mannered cold
Bringing the warm and friendly air.
To be, in living fact, the piercing, chilling stare
Of that wide isolation, icy and passionless
Which makes the cold stars embedded there
Seem each a blazing fire;
Cold will stare down at him.
The moistened lips of rain and earth set their mouth to him
And the wind break upon him like stupendous surf
Upon soldiers, in battle and in hazard
Who have other enemies, more direct and foresworn;
Let them use prayers—or use twisted, rage-wetted curses
To buttress them—to steel defiance in themselves
Whose duty makes them stay abroad in bitter weather;
For the strengths are masterless
And yet, though no man's enemy
Are merely crushing strength, blinded and unheeding, reasonless
And we dare not be cowed by that—or its mortal like.

Forward Defence Lines, Cassino

Sleep I remember;
It came like a moth-dusted mist

That in its own looms became floating, fold-rich veils:

And the mist was in my breath
Tip-toeing through mind and body
Dimming their flaring lights:

And the veils were woven into walls:

And a strong door closed softly—and was barred.

But here beat the Spandau knuckles
A tattoo on the door we dare not close
The mortars fists pound solidly
And the great, double-handed crash of 88's.

If sleep but paused for a moment
Then death smiles—and sleep must reel on:

Someone has stolen our soul away in pity
And we watch the darkened body
Drunk and debauched by wakefulness
In its dull pretence of life:

Oh, everything that orders and directs
Keep thirst, keep hunger, keep love and friendship,
Keep happiness and all contentment
Keep all those souls of ours,
But let us have their worth in sleep.

A. L. Burrell
Crossing the Sangro, 1943

You who have crossed the river, shed no tear
   For us who made the crossing so secure.
Our work is over in that vale of fear;
   Our mouths breathed curses, but our hearts were pure.

Press bravely forward, we are not behind
   But go before you on the farther side,
Having fulfilled the task to us assigned,
   To cross the river and to be your guide.

C. Carter
Naples

The autumnal city in decay
With whitening rain soft on the darkening street,
Moves in a slow withdrawing way
Into the muddled turmoil of defeat.

No longer Ethiopian kings,
Those Eritrean dreams, and Libyan sand,
Distract her hand from humbler things,
Like bread and houses in a crumbling land.

For now the shoeless children brood
In sodden coats beneath some dripping arch,
And lift their unwashed hands for food
To alien armies pausing on their march.

The armies pass, and evening falls,
On un-sexed women and pride-broken men,
While crumbling mortar from the halls
Of outgrown power breaks loosely, now and then.

W. Nelson Cheesman

In an Italian Field

Who has not lain down
In a field of wheat?
And heard the whisper
Of crushed stem speak
Or the answering hush
Of the winds' running feet?

Picked and gripped the sugary stems
With tooth and tongue,
Like the lion rends
As with agonised cry,
His victim, his last breath expends.

Looked to the blue—
Through the olives' wide spread—
Tied to the sky like a Gorgon's head,
Nurtured by grey and pocked
Hands of the dead.

Who has not spied
The poppies' flushed face?
Peeping from sheathes and
Thistles green lace;
Or succumbed and plucked
Her virginal grace,
Watching the crimson vein
and deface.

Stretched on his back and
Closed his eyes,
Aware of the sparrows and
Hearing their cries,
Sleeping content who cares
If one dies?
Even under Italian skies.

Bert Cole

Toilers in the Vineyard

Mars turned Bacchus stripping the vine,
Caterpillar tracks treading the wine,
Pushing through tendrils and bines.

The mastodon's muzzle sniffing the air,
Thrusting the clusters of fruit hanging there.
These toilers in the vineyard somehow akin,

Soft, vulnerable inside their skin.
Not a good year forty-three,
For wine, for pity, for Italy.

Edward Cope

Letter to Fiancée

Sgt. E. Cope, MM,
The Rifle Brigade,
C.M.F.,
26th September, 1944.

Well my darling,

Here's another month nearly at an end, and I'm thinking that I haven't written very often this month.

Still you can blame the Gothic Line for that. But now that we are resting there's no excuse.

The weather is steadily changing and becoming almost English in its steady rainstorms. Whilst we were up the hills, at about 2–3000 ft., mist and rain surrounded us nearly the whole time and things were very 'umpty (if that conveys anything to you!).

Add to that the fact that we were using mules to bring up any kit and rations, and carrying the rest ourselves, and you will have a small picture of our little sector.

Still everything comes to an end, and when the sun returned and Jerry pulled out there we were with nothing to do but climb down the hill. And, after climbing up, it was a bit of cake!

So now we are resting and cleaning up and I hope soon to have a day in Florence. When I do I'll let you know what it's like.

So far I'm doing very well for letters and have just received letter 106. Both 105 and 106 were rather special letters and they certainly make me bless the day when I first met you. You've been wonderful all along and oh! how I long to see you again and be with you.

This latest scheme gives great hopes anyway, and according to that I should be one of the first out. But, of course, the war has to be finished first.

Out here there has been a great swing forward when the Gothic Line gave way, and it shows great promise.

In Holland too the struggle is reaching a new high level, and I can only see it ending one way. But one mustn't be over optimistic—there's still a lot to be done.

When you speak in your letter of the meal you cooked, when the neighbour came in, it seemed almost as if you were speaking of our home and that I was away and you had been looking after our next door neighbour! How I wished it were our home!

I'll bet you've already decided on the colour scheme of the rooms. Have you? Or does your fancy change with every shop window. Still, no doubt, you have quite a lot of furniture lined up in your mind's eye for the great day when we can approve it together.

Shops must be pretty normal nowadays, apart from prices of course. It will be a treat to go round gazing in all the biggest shops until we find just the thing we've been looking for.

Fred will be quite invaluable in those days, for he must have gained quite an experience where he is working. Still, so will your mother in that respect also.

You ask in your letter if there is anything I should like for Christmas, besides yourself—No, honestly there is nothing I want except your darling self, and I'd rather wait till I return than risk having such a valuable parcel damaged in transit, or even lost!!!

Give my love to all the family and I hope they are all keeping well.

Cheerio my darling for now, I am longing for you night and day.

All my love, and kisses unlimited

Ted

XXXXX

A. W. Crowther

Wayside Crucifix

A tank lies gutted in the ditch beneath . . .
English or German? That's no matter now;
The pinioned Man with thorns upon His brow
Looks down upon a grave that bears no wreath,
Beside the wrecked and blackened iron sheath.
The toil-bent peasant leaves his healing plough
To gaze upon the Sacrifice and bow
His head, pond'ring the gift that guns bequeath
Unto his ravaged soil: the human clay
Moulded from other dust—and hither brought
To jest and suffer for a space, to slay
And mingle with an alien earth, blood-bought.
The slain will guard the slain till Rising Day
When he shall know the End for which he fought.

Ronald Cox

Operation 'Husky'

A bright blue sky . . . a wind blown sea,
Great white-capped horses bearing down,
As convoy . . . fully fifty ships
Goes zigging here and zagging there,
Bound for the Isle of Sicily.
Soldiers sit shorted and shirt-sleeved,
Smoking, coughing, laughing, cursing;
Peering at maps and oiling guns,
As all the while big ships steam on
To what some know as Destiny.
    A recce aircraft drones on high,
God alone knows what he may spy,
While slit-eyes peer through brilliant light
And firearms spew their hail of lead,
As guns crash out their welcome blast.

The sneaking sod . . . he scents our blood;
But only days and three nights more
Till landing's made on hostile shore,
Where lies there death and mad furore,
Till we know who then is Master.
   Depthcharges clang throughout the ships
Gonging their frightsome knell of death,
While tracers . . . skipping o'er the waves
Search for the peering periscope.
Or cleanly-run tin fishes.
Hunt Class destroyers gallop in,
DUMFRIES—BERKELEY—ZETLAND—WARWICK,
NORTH COTSWOLD—FERNIE—BEDALE—QUORN,
Scenting 'death' as on op'ning morn,
While nostrils quiver . . . Asdics ping.

Trefor Davies

On Seeing Men Going to the Front

   They would die now
could they rape with their childlike stares
despair draped above their eyes;
the curtains conceal the contorted bodies
of men dying in blood: futures clotted
in one destiny's knot.

They bolt into uncertain clouds
that hold no promise, no despair before the
     actual meeting;
their thoughts are curled protectively about
     their loved images;
gold that has lost its lustre
dims the eyes staring backwards
through the greyness to pale yellowness.

And one thought is vagrant, racing always
to the naked pool of blood:
the wish weaves a web over that vision,
precludes unnaturally the withheld deathbreath.

The Clerk

The thin line of an uninspired brain's thought
traces itself with slow inevitability
straight and black on a long white page
where white ordered neophytes drawing their flat cloaks about them
stand in the choirstalls, unwhispering, behaving unnaturally.
The flat limited stone floor of the soul
panders to the regular tread of a day's heartbeats:
lacking emotion, beauty, the irregular rhythms
that charm; and an underbreath muttering
slinks like a slimy snake innoculating ache into the fat bloodless arm.
Living surrounded by false reasonable walls,
straight, high, built by the expert concentrating each thought's
energy
into the bloodless structure—grey, cold
sitting heavily on each thought that would escape
errant to seek a novel texture where to thrive.
Ah! could the heart beat through the heavy lifeless cloak,
spin vitally through new blood and breathe the natural airs of
varying moods!
and the white dress be stained with a virgin's blood:
breathing heavily under unmasked experience;
sense the beauty of loving life, free from the close entanglements
that breed forced torpor on the mind;
be thrilled with each new instant;
drawing more than life-blood
from veins that lie outside—to be reached with eager arms
from a mistress' breast where lie the confusing charms
relevant to the instinctive base;
catch the sunlight's tempting hand and resting on ambitious wings
travel new flimsy surfaces, risking the pitfalls,
unheeding the grown-old plaints from the stained window.

Rain

Impressions in a Dining Tent.

Whispered a dark-browed day a secret to the night:
long fingers darted from the sky,
like darting arrows stung our cheeks
and the gay gentleman's cloak
slipped to the mudding earth.
The faces lifted scornfully to a wet breeze,
laughing in calm caprices
above the trees and on into the light.

Rain trickled through, hard spots on a poor floor
and a hundred faces turned, two hundred eyes
stared at an inevitable conclusion, and thoughts
hid their heads in moods, hiding below an armour
against the wet idea: threatening unfavourable results.
Boots squelched; a laugh here; a curse there;
and a dozen faces echoed each other's form above the door,
Staring through a rain-swept hole in their safety.

The eyes alone on a table stare into a blue daydream
of a less grey mood: the yellow angels set against a red sky,
and the brown children of earth merry:
all in a channel of soporific thought
secluded above his mind's blue sky
beyond the complaining lark.

The good-natured traveller hastens westward
leaving the stage to an old veteran in a bad mood
singing his weary joints to anguished pain
and the tears of his bloodthirsty heart
close a primary lid over eyes
staring through a rain-swept hole in their safety.

Erik de Mauny
From an Italian Notebook

Rimini, October 17th, 1944

Why Rimini? I don't know, except that it is the next town of any size, going south, and it was near here (at Viserba), that I found the Divisional Intelligence Section.

For the moment, there are only odd things I want to jot down: some I might forget—others I shall not. I shan't forget the devastation just north of Pesaro. That was the Adriatic Coast end of the Gothic Line. And from there on, by the coast road, the landscape was predominantly one of half-shattered farms, the house walls pitted in villages that saw heavy street engagements. Many shell-holes. Ragged tree stumps staggered drunkenly in every direction. The colour of the water in shell-holes is curious—chemical green and grey and purple, with a sheen both evil and fascinating. We saw people pushing carts heavily laden with furniture, and old women with rag-wrapped feet trudging the roads.

Sometimes a poplar stood clear and slender green in the pale light. So these are the plains . . .

At Viserba a Hygience Section bloke turned on a fearsome apparatus one evening and gave two of us a much-needed shower. The hot water was good, but I was afraid of being blasted naked out of the building. The machine spluttered so angrily!

. . . Just before we crossed the Uso River, our own artillery opened up with deafening din, just behind us. A little further on, we saw a dog in a field, a black and white dog. The others said he was a pointer: I shouldn't be surprised. Every time one of the 'heavies' went off, he raced round in a small, bewildered circle, looking for something to 'point' at! It was very amusing.

. . . I can smell a German prisoner smell everywhere, especially on myself. Not too pleasant! I have already interrogated about 40. Some of them haven't washed for ages. They are all sorts—including many Poles, Alsatians, Luxembourgers, etc. The latter in general are very glad to be at last P.W. The Reichsdeutsche have fair morale generally, still seem to believe in the Führer, the Secret Weapon (especially that!), ultimate victory and so on. How utterly fed up I really am with the whole business!

October 20th

Last night we were in Gatteo: now tonight in Ruffio: so goes this very mobile war. This morning at G. we took an old Mauser and had potshots against a green door propped against a tree.

We have had about 30 P.W. today. Someone—possibly a partisan—sent a message through to us in Russian, via a German soldier and an Italian soldier.

I translated it, very, very roughly, with the aid of two Turcomans. Neither spoke good German, so we made do mostly with Italian and many wide gesticulations.

October 24th

... How many strange lodgings we've had. In a small village called Fabrona, it was a storeroom-cum-stables, still full of bales of pressed tobacco leaves, standing near a huge country mansion, lately occupied, I believe, by our friends, 29th Panzergrenadier Division. The whole set among beautiful beech trees.

At Gatteo, an ordinary farmhouse: but I had a fine room for interrogating (what a luxury, after squatting in a windy field, my maps and papers fluttering about, continually threatening to disappear over a hedge).

The things I remember about Ruffio are several: the bombed church where some of our blokes had put their beds, and a slim girl in a red dress and a peasant-style kerchief headdress, kneeling in prayer before one of the few undamaged Stations of the Cross. One afternoon, the old man brought in a box of grapes on his head to the farmhouse, but they weren't up to much— all wizened, or muddy and mushy. He shrugged and said, '*Tutti spoliati—le grenate!*' I understand why the whole tragedy of war for such people is summed up by the ruined, broken vines.

But it is funny to see the very tame rabbits bobbing about under the withered rows of vines: pretty, stupid creatures— quite friendly really.

November 10th

Matelica (in the Marches: the Division rested there for several weeks).

But what a changed Matelica! This morning, when I awoke, snow lay thickly over the landscape. The village square looked charmingly Christmassy: and the hills and fields, further off, under a pearl-grey sky, with only the dark walls of houses, stone hedges and an occasional haystack, so like that Dutch winter landscape of Peter Breughel. But oh, how cold when you go out for a walk! Feet frozen, nose blue and smarting! ...

November 12th

Sunday is the social day of the week in Italian villages. This afternoon, all Matelica wandered sedately up and down the main street, or loitered by the fountain in the square, in the thin autumn sunlight. I went for a stroll with a friend, but we didn't get far. In a tiny grocer's shop we found a bar, and sat on packing-cases sipping anisette.

A very fragile old lady in black, with grey hair piled up to a bun on top, sat behind the counter, crouched over the till. She had a croupy, thin cough, and a querulous voice; but her face was surprisingly unlined, a pleasant gleaming red like an apple: only the eyes were sunk in deep pools of shadow—as though a bird had pecked deep holes in the fragrant old apple of a face.

November 17th

Spent the whole day inspecting the countryside from a jeep. At Macerata, we found one or two excellent bookshops, and I managed to acquire editions of Dante, Cervantes, Leopardi, Boccaccio, etc. The excitement gave me a headache. We had a 'brew-up' high in the mountains, and drank raw new wine at a farmhouse, under a big, iron crucifix.

On the way home, we stopped at the *Castello della Rancia* and climbed to the top of one of the towers. One room was glorious—a huge fireplace, big enough to hide half a regiment in, small windows looking down over the moat, and tremendous rafters losing themselves in the smoky heights of the sloping roof.

At Camerino, we stopped at a bend of the precipitous road to watch the sunset over the snow-capped peaks of the Appenines. In the attractive little university town itself, slogans rejecting the monarchy were daubed on the walls—most vivid, a gallows with *'Per i Savoia.*[1]'

November 28th

Back into action! . . .

The 6th Brigade is in a farm, just north of Route 9. If I had any illusions about swiftly and easily making contact with partisans, they have been dispelled. It has been raining steadily since I arrived, and the yard is a cold, watery expanse, islanded with mud, more suitable for amphibians than jeeps and 3-tonners. The hardiest rebel would surely have his ardour dampened by such uncompromising weather.

In the stable, a touching sight: a wounded bull, flanked by two of his harem, munching with a gentle, far-away look. But the poor old bull is not feeling very happy. He nods his great head up and down sadly. The stump of one hind leg is bound up in rag . . .

I tapped one of the civilians at the back of the building for news: he agreed there were plenty of partisans in the district—but I don't think he can give me any specific information. However, we exchanged vino for cigarettes.

Major C. rang to ask, could a partisan get across the river into Faenza: but according to battalion patrols which went out last night, there is a wide and nasty water barrier, with Jerry firmly entrenched behind it.

The big guns are going off occasionally, with a sullen crump . . . A white rain mist hides the fields from view . . .

December 7th

. . . So we're still sitting behind the Lamone, but 46 Div. put in an attack south of Faenza a couple of days ago, and are now approaching the town along the northern bank. Meanwhile, I've had little enough to do—only customers, one or two suspicious civilians (one Italian carrying primary charges and

---

[1]Reference to the Italian Royal House.

detonators in his pocket) and a mysterious P.W. from a G.A.F. *Marcschbattalion* who arrived in mufti with a weird story of having been sent on a wine-procuring mission in Faenza, entering a house alone, being hit on the head and losing his uniform, coming to in his underwear, and after snaffling some old clothes, making his way in error into our own lines, along the railway track!

Jerry shells Route 9 spasmodically, and the crumps sound all too close! The other night, a single plane came and dropped a few bombs . . . The whole 'I' Section has now acquired fur caps, and looks like a detachment of Don Cossacks!

December 8th

Slang provides excellent raw material when writing dialogue, but it's very tricky to handle. Here are only a few the New Zealanders use:

Wouldn't it root you!
To get a burst into someone.
A stonk. (Artillery or air barrage.)
Wouldn't that Farouk you!
You've had it.
To have a snort. (A drink.)
To wipe someone. (Dismiss them cursorily.)
Time to munga-up. (To eat.)
He did us over. (A German artillery concentration.)
Trigger-happy.

And, originating from that nefarious character S., who allegedly sold everything he could lay hands on to the locals (including a pile of firewood laboriously collected by the M.P.'s!), an apocryphal sentence, which, in the way such chance expressions do, became 'good for a laugh' at all times among Brigade 'I' Section: 'Going up the *montagna* (mountain) for some *uova* (eggs).'

December 28th

The 6th Brigade H.Q. is now installed on the northern edge of the town (Faenza), just past the very fine Imolese Gate, now only a pile of rubble, as 'Ted' (short for *tedeschi*, the Italian word for Germans) blew it to make a road block. (Ineffectually: bull-dozers cleared it in under an hour.)

The Italian family with whom we are billeted have a shaggy dog called 'Muri'—a pedigree truffle-hound. They swear that the best *tartuffe* (as they are called in Italian) in the country come from around Faenza, principally from Celle, just north-west . . . Christmas was a curiously dull festival.

I spent Christmas Eve with P. of Partisan Liaison. We were just starting on the old brandy, at about 6.30 p.m., when there was a Godalmighty crash, windows tinkled, plaster came down and a few odd vicious flakes of shrapnel. Our Italian guests rushed round in circles crying *mamma* (and so did I), while P. kept monotonoulsy reiterating, 'The *bastards*! Oh, the *bastards*!' Our lights were out. Going into the street, we found lurid red smoke and flames mounting the sky from a burning truck, some 50 yards away. Then a tin-hatted voice called out: 'Give us an 'and with this 'ere bloke, chum!' We had to rescue a poor wretch who'd been blown five yards off a latrine seat. He had shrapnel wounds in arm and leg, and his pants were round his ankles: he was letting out blood and profanity in equal proportions.

The little girl of the house had a nasty cut in the head from a stray fragment, and we had to run her down to the nearest dressing station in the jeep. However, when we finally returned home, the party went quite well, with Neopolitan choruses, etc. We were bombed twice more before midnight.

December 29th

I find that in the process of retracing my steps, I've forgotten all about Christmas Eve with that sinister-looking libertine P. (the Bolognese) in Forli. After dancing and drinking with Dental Corps people (of all things!) at the Countess's, we went into the slums to arouse some dubious friend of P.'s called Nella, by throwing stones at her window, 3.30 a.m. Nothing doing: so we had to break into another house (whose fame was no doubt in as sickly a condition!—P. knows only these places), which seemed deserted. Only think of us, creeping round the first floor landing lighting matches, looking of course very grotesque and fearsome and probably like a drawing by Boz, when out trots an old dear in a nightcap, frightened to death; and started to scream hysterically in dialect. It took P.'s heaviest, silkiest eloquence to calm her, but she finally let us stay: slept between two mattresses in my underwear and overcoat...

Spent the morning at the half-ruined Faenza library with G. *fils*. He showed me an illuminated parchment of the 1400's of church plain-song and chorales...

January 4th

...A trick they played on New Year's Eve. A party went up to one of the battalions to get a pig. When they arrived back, they put the bloody corpse on a stretcher, covered it with a blanket, and carried it solemnly into the M.I. Room. The M.O. apparently took it in good part...

January 9th

Looks as if we may spend the whole winter here...I have no ideals left, nothing: feel completely burnt out, lie in bed at night and cough, with my head empty of all but vaguely obscene hallucinations and fears.

But just now, in the quiet of my own room, in front of a blazing fire (why does that suggest convalescence?), I feel reasonably cheerful: it seems possible now, in this mood, to make a fresh start, enough of being...('Hell is the incapacity to be any other than the person one ordinarily behaves as')...a shadow of myself, lust and nostalgia...

De Lautrémont says that poetry springs from a sense of wonder.

C. P. S. Denholm-Young

Cassino

A million tons of wreckage piled high
Upon the streets and pathways of the town,
Which only yesterday was teeming with
A multitude of people in their home.
A flock of happy children played their games
In alleyways which now are merely dust
And heaps of rubble left there by
The passing of the Allies' powered host
Of aircraft, blotting out the sky
Till all of it seemed overcast
With shadows of their wings in great array.
A day or so ago, the chickens ran
Squawking when motor-cars approached,
Dogs barked, and women stood around
And gossiped, or they merely watched
Their offspring playing on the ground.
And now, what is there left to tell the tale
Of all these centuries of rural lore?
A mass of ruins, left there in the trail
Of total war.

January 1944.

F. K. Forrester

Lire — Sicily 1943

It would have been all right if they hadn't issued a G.R.O.[1] saying the men must be paid in lire.

The Major said, you can do anything provided you don't touch a soldier's pay. Once you do that, he is entitled to demand your Court Martial.

Sergeant Inkwell said he thought it was his own Court Martial, not yours, that he was entitled to demand.

---

[1]General Routine Order.

C₂Q.M.S. Payroll said, you can send a man to Russia in tropical kit, you can lose his rations, you can delay his mail, you can call him anything you like, but you mustn't touch his pay.

Pte. Holdall said 'This is a democratic army, ain't it, and if a man can't be sure of his pay, what's he ---- well fighting for?'

Cpl. Dishwash, who is an expert on economics, said it was inflation, pure and simple. The Italians would fly to sterling, and we should all be left holding lire when the latter crashed. Which proved what he had always maintained, namely that the politicians would lose the peace for us.

Two American sergeants who had dropped in in the middle of the discussion said they had always been paid in dollars, they always would be paid in dollars, and if anyone paid them in anything else America would inevitably get embroiled in Europe after the war, which would upset the Monroe doctrine.

I said, well there's the G.R.O. and we've got to abide by it. I can see troubles coming out of it on all sides, but I don't believe in meeting them half way.

Lt. Boxfile said, how does that fit in with your lecture yesterday on attack being the best means of defence?

L.A.C. Wavelength, the attached R.A.F. Wireless Operator, said G.R.O.s didn't apply to the R.A.F., so we would have to pay him in sterling.

Sergeant Pullthrough said it wasn't patriotic to pay men in lire anyway.

The Major said, Orders are Orders, and we shall have to obey them whatever the consequences. Captain Messtin will conduct the pay parade next week.

Which observation had the double effect of clinching the argument and passing the buck to me.

The first Friday I paid out in lire the atmosphere was as tense as a violin string and pregnant with possibility, as Boxfile put it in the Mess afterwards. Sgt. Pullthrough said he didn't want to draw his pay this week, thank you Sir. Cpl. Dishwash said he wanted his credit paid to his wife in England, *in sterling*, and muttered something about 'getting her to send it out in postal orders'.

The next on the roll was L.A.C. Wavelength, and I sensed a major crisis. However C.S.M. Damnit said he had ordered him to the sick-bay that morning, because he looked pale. I asked no further questions. C.S.M. Damnit is a man of tact. In an emergency he will do anything.

It was in this atmosphere that Pte. Afterthought announced that he wished to draw out all his credit. A gasp of horror ran through the serried ranks before the pay table. Sgt. Pullthrough opened his mouth and shut it again. Tears of pity welled into Cpl. Dishwash's eyes. C.S.M. Damnit looked as though he might do anything. Pte. Afterthought was not one of the most promising men in the unit. True, his conduct sheet was clean. But he did strange things at times. The Major said he was mental, and would have sent him to the trick-cyclist long ago, if he hadn't been a batman. As Afterthought was *my* batman I never quite saw the logic of this last piece of reasoning.

C.Q.M.S. Payroll hastily totted up Afterthought's credits. Afterthought usually drew very little pay, and had £26 to come. At 400 lire to the pound, this meant 10,400 lire. The sight of so much money shook the onlookers visibly. Damnit perceptibly wilted. Pullthrough said he hadn't realised the exchange rate was so much in our favour. It was obviously patriotic to take advantage of the Italians when we could, so might he draw his pay after all, Sir? Dishwash said he never did believe in trusting his old woman with money anyway. Wavelength suddenly appeared from the sick-bay and sidled along to the end of the queue.

After that the pay parade was an outstanding success. Unfortunately there was a spot of bother when we came to check up at the end of it. Lire don't add up like £.s.d. Most of the columns are full of noughts, and the number of columns used seems to be purely arbitrary. Perhaps it was our unfamiliarity with the technique involved which led us to three separate conclusions—Boxfile that we were 3,000 lire down, Payroll that we were 15,727 lire up, and myself that we were 251,002 lire down. However Boxfile pointed out that, although the majority vote was in favour of our being down, we might be up in the morning if the rate of exchange altered overnight, and with that consoling thought we decided to call it a day.

The second week we paid in lire went much more smoothly, except that the Cash Office made us take half the pay in 1,000-lire notes, because they had a surfeit of them. We had to give them all to the N.C.Os, since they were the only people who normally drew as much as £2-10s-0d while in the field. Unfortunately a note for £2-10s-0d is not an easy thing to change—indeed the only man in the unit who could change any of them was Pte. Afterthought, who suddenly became extremely popular in the Sergeants Mess and charged 5% on each transaction. Even so he could not save the situation completely, and a number of N.C.Os were virtually broke, in spite of their token paper wealth. By the end of the week three Sergeants and five Corporals were on charges for borrowing money from private soldiers. The Major said he believed there was something in King's Regulations which said they would have to be tried by Court Martial, but as Sergeant Inkwell, who was one of them, was the only person who knew where the unit copy of King's Regs. was kept, and the only person anyway who knew how to find anything in it even if we did know where it was, he would have to remand the cases for further investigation—by which time the debts would, he hoped, have been repaid and the whole matter forgotten.

On the third pay day the Cash Office went to the other extreme and informed me that they had absolutely nothing but one-lira notes. These, they said, were extremely convenient, as a bundle of 100 could be paid out as the equivalent of 5/-. Moreover they were all packed up in boxes so that I needn't count them. C.Q.M.S. Payroll and I walked the two miles back to camp under a pile of boxes (clearly labelled 'Lire') that reminded us of the days when our wives used to take us out Christmas shopping and made us feel horribly vulnerable to any smash-and-grab types who might be passing!

Admittedly the one-lira notes settled the problem of change in the unit once and for all. But some people are never satisfied. The look C.S.M. Damnit gave me when I handed him 30 packets of 100 one-lira notes wasn't dirty—it was positively insanitary! I was vastly relieved when pay parade ended without any major incident.

On Saturdays we draw our N.A.A.F.I. rations. I pay for them out of regimental funds, and then sell them to the men. I had foreseen that I might be inundated with the one-lira notes I had issued the day before. But I had overlooked the fact that they would no longer be in neat little packets of 100, value 5/- each, which did not need counting because they had been checked by the Cash Office. Instead they came in bundles of 7 and 23 and 39—anything but 50 or 100—dirty, torn, dog-eared, almost impossible to count. It was a relief to come across and 'unbroken' packet amongst this maze of tiny slips of paper—until Payroll discovered that most of the 'unbroken' packets I had accepted unchecked as 100 lire varied in contents between 83 and 97!

Eventually I put my foot down. Every note must be counted, and I would do it personally, even if the sale of N.A.A.F.I. rations had to continue all night in consequence. I packed each hundred notes into a separate pile and lined them up along the table. Even the biggest difficulties, I said (for the benefit of the N.C.Os in general and of Payroll in particular), can be overcome by efficient organization based on common sense.

Just at that moment the afternoon breeze got up. The afternoon breeze in the Mediterranean is as violent as it is sudden, and it blows towards the cookhouse.

'It just goes to show, Sir', said Cpl. Dishwash, as he fished the five hundredth one-lira note out of the tea dixie. 'It just goes to show, like what I said, that it's all a matter of inflation . . .'

E. D. Forster

A View of the Sea

Italy's a fine country. It rained and snowed a lot, but what a spring! The signorinas were a bit upstage—except those who were so downstage anyway that it was nobody's business—I'd rather have a nice, hot cup of tea myself. I was driving up from Taranto to the Adriatic coast, and I stayed with a small unit that was billeted in a crumbling castle on a little hill. There were only two or three blokes in the mess, and though it was still early in the year, we sat outside after dinner on a little piazza of broken brick. There was plenty of plonk, and there was a thread of moon. The war had moved beyond the mountains to the north, and we felt the more secure and peaceful just by knowing it was there, like an armchair by the fire at home, when the rain is painting out the windows.

Next day I drove along the ridge—the old I5 was running smoothly, and the surface was not too bad, though the road didn't look much on the I/500,000. The sun was shining, there were fields with some sort of crop, and by the roadside a few late flowers were attending to business in a conscientious manner. I felt full of joie-de-vivre and what-have-you-there, as it might be Bertie Wooster spinning down to Blandings for the weekend—and I was in fact impelled to sing.

Annie Laurie goes a bit high, I grant you, and a bit low if you pitch it wrong, but it's a fine song when you're driving. Then suddenly my song was cut off in mid-bar, for my road ran out to the end of the ridge, and about a thousand miles below me I saw the sea. It seemed hard to imagine how the road might reach it, but there it was, a complicated pattern of hairpin bends. This was one of the things I liked about Italy, the little roads that somehow scaled the most incredible ravines and cliffs, at least as spectacular as the big Dolomite passes, though the surface was often bad.

The sea looked like a blue pavement, and I could see a border of cream ribbon where the waves were breaking. Yet behind the screen of mountains to the north, men were trying to kill each other, and that beautiful ballroom floor was a thing of storms and tin fish and chaps adrift in open boats, without food or water, no pity or favour shown.

There I was philosophising away, yet all the while I was dropping through the steep hairpins, and counting engine revs, by ear, as I changed down for the loops. And then I saw Ackack begin to flower in front of my nose. A few fighters were diving on a tanker in the bay, and some of the little white splashes were fairly close. But they failed to touch her off, and as they pulled out of their dive they came drifting up the hill towards me like leaves on a high wind.

One of them flicked right past my radiator, and I must have filled his gunsight as full as a tick with pi-dog's blood. He had a few pellets left, and he pressed the doings, and let me have the unexpired portion with all his heart. Nothing hit me, but he must have got a wheel or the steering, for the old girl turned sharp left like a guardsman, and dived over the drop. Things started whirling round a bit, and there was a godalmighty crash.

I must have been knocked out, and when I woke up the sun was declined, and the sea a dull purple. My faithful steed had rolled down the hill, and was kneeling on her forehead on the next section of the road. I stretched myself cautiously, but nothing seemed to give or waggle in the wrong place; and I felt fine, not even a headache. And I felt even better when I found Dicky Roberts sitting on a rock beside me.

'Gosh, that's a bit of luck, now I shan't have to walk. My I5's been scrambled by a 109. But I'm O.K.'

'Oh, yes, you would be.'

'Why, what d'you mean, and what the hell are you doing here, anyway? The last time I saw you was at Keren'—but then I stopped and felt *very* peculiar.

'Dicky,' I said 'you were killed on the ridge. 'Dicky,' I said 'you're dead!'

He sat quietly looking down the hill. An ambulance had panted up to my poor old truck, and some medics had jumped out and were fiddling round the ruins.

'So are you,' he said.

And, blow me down, if we didn't both sit there, and watch them load me into the ambulance! It was a dream, all right, all right, and I woke up to a nice, hot Cairo morning, which was no laughing matter, either.

But it was dam' queer, wasn't it?

Autumn 1943

Robert Garioch

Kriegy[1] *Ballad*

Note: This is somewhat nearer to being a definitive edition than previous definitive editions have been. In fact, it is the definitive edition to end definitive editions in the meantime, under the circumstances.

CHORUS:
　　Toorally Oorally addy etc.
　　Here's hoping we're not here to stay.

Yes, this is the place we were took, sir,
And landed right into the bag,
Right outside the town of Tobruk, sir,
So now for some bloody stalag.

There was plenty of water in Derna,
But that camp was not very well kept,
For either you slept in the piss-hole,
Or pissed in the place where you slept.

And then we went on to Benghazi,
We had plenty of room, what a treat!
But I wish that the guard was a Nazi,
He might find us something to eat.

We sailed on the good ship Revalo,
She carried us over the sea,
You climbed up a forty-foot ladder
Whenever you wanted a pee.

And then we went on to Brindisi
With free melons in fields on the way,
Parades there were quite free and easy,
Except that they went on all day.

In transit-camp at Benevento
We stayed a long time, truth to tell,
It was there that we all got the shivers
And were all bloody lousy as well.

[1]German slang for P.O.W.

133

The sun it grew hotter and hotter,
The shit-trench was streaked red and brown,
The stew it was like maiden's water,
With gnatspiss to wash it all down.

With hunger we're nearly demented,
You can see it at once by our looks,
The only ones really contented
Are the greasy fat bastards of cooks.

And then we went on to Capua,
On hard ground we mostly did snooze,
The bedboards got fewer and fewer
As we smashed them up to make brews.

It was there that we got Red Cross parcels
With bully and packets of tea
Would you swop it for . . .
For want of some brew-wood? Not me!

And now it was late in the Autumn
And our clothes they were only a farce,
For torn K.D.² shorts with no bottom
Send a helluva draught up your arse.

In Musso's fine box-cars we're riding,
All fitted with wheels that are square,
They park us all night in a siding,
But somehow we bloody get there.

At Musso's show-camp at Vetralla
They gave us beds, blankets and sheets,
They'd even got chains in the shit-house,
But still they had no bloody seats.

We were promised a treat for our Christmas
Of thick pasta-shoota, all hot,
But somehow the cooks got a transfer
And shot out of sight with the lot.

²Khaki Drill

So somewhere they wish us good wishes
That we're not all feeling too queer,
And while they are guzzling our pasta
They wish us a happy New Year.

The Presoner's Dream

In Italie, in strang presoun,
on Christmas nicht I beddit suin
    on my wee sack of strae.
Cauld gained on me: I couried doun
and happit me my greatcoat roun,
    wi puirshous blankets twae.
Thon day in special we had dined
on pastashoota biled wi rind
    of kebbuck, I daursay.
I'd hained a supper of a kind,
a big raw ingan, as I mind,
    or wes it Hogmanay?
It's queer hou memory gaes dim;
I ken ma stammick wesnae tuim:
    it wes some special day.
But, fir aa that, the Christmas cauld
nippit me, fir ma bluid wes thin,
    altho I wesnae auld.
Thaim that hauf-stairve their presoners
are no exactly murderers;
    whan the taen sodger dees
they scrieve wi sooth in registers
    some orthodox disease.
There arenae monie sophisters
    wad prieve sic truths are lees.
Our sentry, sloungin at his post,
kechlit outbye wi Christmas hoast,
his rusty rifle white wi frost
    frae whilk reid fire micht flee.

Aye frae the village campanell'
I never saw, I hear'd the bell
cancel ma hours ... eleeven ... twal ...
    sleep wadnae come to me.
The New Guaird cam, het frae their fire;
I hear'd his fuit outbye the wire,
I hear'd his kechlan mate retire,
    I hear'd his Moorie sang,
a belly-sang of luvers' stour
like Baudrons in the midnicht hour.
The kindly cauld brocht me succour:
    he didnae sing owre lang.
The presoner's friens are sleep and time;
I cuidnae sleep, I hear'd the chime,
fu lang I lay, forspent wi care;
the saft seduction of despair
forset me till I gied-up, syne
intill her slouch I sank faur hyne
    and fand some easement thair.
I dream'd as I wes waukan yet
in Edinbrugh, in Canogait,
    aye heidin wast, uphill.
I saw the dial of the Tron
and read the time: hauf efter ane,
    the swevyn seemed that real.
I luikit owre the Nor Brig,
I saw the Auld Toun on its rig,
    and, in the tither airt,
Lord Nelson on the Calton Hill
raxt for the Embro Muin, but still
    she keepit weill apairt.
The Embro ambience curled roun,
    like haar, about ma hairt.
The bite of inwit shairpt on sin
nirlt me like the east wind.
Whit I had duin I didnae ken,
    binna that it wes wrang,
wi glowran wemen and sour men
    the causey wes that thrang.
Fechtin ma life's ain pressure, chokin,
I hear'd a sang, and I wes waukan
    intill yon presoun strang.

It wes our sentry's Moorie sang
whilk in ma lugs like music rang;
   wi joy I hear'd him singing.
But whitna bogle wes't thon nicht
gied me in dreams sae fell a fricht?
Nou, luikin back, I think I'm richt:
   It maun hae been the ingan.

A P.O.W. in Italy[1]

The bath-parade having been duly counted out of the gate, we filed past the wood, lifting our quota of sticks as we passed. The important thing was to get pieces thin enough to break easily. The sticks were five or six feet long, and could hardly be concealed unless they were broken into smaller pieces. We used to jockey for position to get near the thinner sticks, which caused some delay. 'Giorgio!' the guards would shout (all the prisoners were George to the guards), and point at the big logs, while we pulled away at the sticks which we had carefully selected from afar off. The parade proceeded on its way, to the sound of cracking wood. If we got a nice dry piece, we could break it easily as we went along, and stow the pieces beneath our greatcoats, which we had prepared for the purpose with inside pockets, Sometimes, however, you would see a man struggling with a green sapling which he had grabbed in his haste, twisting it into hoops, and cursing, having abandoned any attempt at surreptitiousness. The guards' chief worry was lest this should be seen by the Carabinieri: so far as the guards themselves were concerned, we could have the lot, especially when a few cigarettes found their way into their hands. When we had a specially tough consignment of wood to deal with, the air used to be filled with plaintive shouts of 'Giorgio!' from the guards, whose heads would swivel in all directions till they seemed in danger of coming loose altogether. The most awkward part was climbing up the bank, when long pieces of wood thrust down trouser-legs and almost protruding from the greatcoat collar made it impossible for us to bend our knees. We generally had everything under control by the time we reached the bath-house. The larger pieces would be passed to friends coming back from the previous squad, and the short sticks were safely stowed away. When we arrived, we went through a solemn ritual of each laying a nominal load of wood on the pile, and went inside, as soon as the dressing room was empty.

---

[1] From 'Two Men in a Blanket'.

There was always a great scramble. We dumped our clothes on any ledge that would keep them off the muddy floor. Only the very quick could manage to get a share of a form to sit on. There had at one time been wooden pegs, but these had been stolen long ago for purposes of brewing-up. Then we would crowd into a warm, dark and very steamy cavern, full of wet people competing for their share of the hot shower, soaping away, and rinsing, and washing one another's inaccessible backs, in a maty sort of way. We had to work fast, in case the water might go off and leave us still soapy. The Italians provided towels of the same material as our thin bed-sheets, one between two; and with these we dried ourselves as well as possible. The luckier ones might have a sheet each, having shared with someone who had received a towel in a personal parcel. Then we dressed, trying to keep our feet out of the mud, and emerged into the very cold air outside.

There was usually some time to wait until the squad was gathered together and counted; and during that time a further opportunity presented itself of scrounging some brewing-material. It was the custom in this camp to tip out the contents of the Red Cross parcels into blankets, when they were issued; so that the Italians might keep the cardboard boxes for salvage. These boxes were very useful to us, as well as the paper shavings in which the tins were packed. As it happened, the boxes and shavings were stored in a shed next to the bath-house; and it was our purpose during the waiting period to collect as much of this stuff as possible: and if we could get a piece of string with which the parcels had been wrapped, so much the better. So we used to pad out any spaces between the sticks under our greatcoats with shavings and cardboard, and walk very cautiously back to the camp. On successful days, when the guards were good-natured, or less scared than usual of the Carabinieri, or well primed with cigarettes, the road back to the camp used to be so strewn with shavings as to look like a stretch of country over which a paper-chase has recently passed. It was not usually difficult to get through the gate with our spoils, as the guards on the gate were mainly worried about getting their numbers right; and there was a peculiar satisfaction in reporting back to one's mate with a good haul of brewing-material!

Engineering. At this time, I was in a combine of three. We pooled our parcel-and-a-half, and brewed up together; two of us usually doing the brew, and taking turns to be the odd man, who waited in the hut for the brew to be served, and complained if it took too long. Unfortunately most of our brewing was very long a-doing; and our difficulties increased as the weather became worse. It settled down to rain every day, and all day; sometimes the rain changed to soft snow, but that was about the only variety it gave us. When the time came to brew up, we used to put on our greatcoats, and sometimes we would manage to borrow a topee from a South African who had fetched it from the Desert. It looked out of place, but kept the rain off very well.

We tried to keep our brew-wood dry on the way to the brewing-ground, which happened to be at the other end of the camp from our hut. If possible, we would find a space under the roof of the wash-place. We laid our primitive stove on the mud, and our box of fuel, and proceeded to light the fire. If we could get the embers from the stove belonging to someone who had just finished, the job was much easier; otherwise we had to get a light from somewhere and start from the beginning. We crouched and blew and wafted, our coat-tails trailing in the mud. We coaxed our little fire, and the rain tried to put it out. It took a long time to make a three-man brew in this fashion, especially if the wind happened to be cold; for it would cool the dixie almost as fast as the fire heated it. We had to pile on the fuel, and to blow hard all the time. We could not help remarking that it took about ten times as long to brew the tea as to drink it; and it was doubtful whether the heating properties of the tea were sufficient to compensate for the state of cold we had got into, in preparing it.

During especially bad weather we used to argue about whether or not the brew must go on; the most emphatic of the Ayes being the man whose turn it was to stay in the hut. He would remind the other two that on the last occasion he had brewed in a blizzard, and had not raised a word of complaint. We became quite ill-tempered over this sort of thing. Also when the two men on duty returned with the steaming dixie, they were inclined to regard themselves as having done something wonderful, and the sight of the third man, who was dry, and comparatively not so cold, reclining on his bunk and accepting it all as a matter of course, used to be very irritating. The solution was obvious: we must make a blower. How we were to manage it was another matter.

For several weeks, we had made a habit of collecting anything that might possibly be useful. Our best find had been a nail about five inches long: a quite priceless nail; also we had a stock of tins which we had opened and trimmed to make sheets of tin plate, and a large number of odds and ends. We had been studying different types of blowers, also, with an eye for ease of construction rather than efficiency: but even the easiest of them looked hard enough to make.

It was in the course of preparing one particular dixie-ful of porridge that we decided that something must be done. The weather was particularly bad that day, and our wood was green, and everything was against us. We wafted with our piece of cardboard till it grew limp, we blew, and we stirred, for three-quarters of an hour in a wet blizzard; and then the third man (I forget whose turn it was that day, but we were all alike) came all the way from the hut, not so much to help us, as to ask whether we were ever coming back with the porridge at all. Then the three of us joined in the struggle, so that we were all wet. The porridge was still half-raw when we finally ate it. We started making a blower the very next day.

We began by taking a bedboard out of one of our bunks, and then proceeded to examine the ceiling above it, this being regarded as coming within our tenants' rights; we removed thence a nice spar of wood, about an inch square and a yard long, from which to make a spindle, and all the small nails that held it to the cardboard panel, which now sagged badly, but we couldn't help that. We made the spindle by sawing a piece off this spar, using a strip of tin, the edge of which was just as a tin-opener had left it; this took a long time, but it was quite a neat cut when it was finished. I had managed to bring my Army jack-knife-cum-tin-opener through all the searches so far, and we used it to round off a couple of inches at one end of the spindle, where the belt was to run in a V-groove. The rest of it was left square, so that we could nail eight fan-blades to the four sides, the idea being that in a small drum we needed more than the usual four blades. We had some arguments about this, not having any engineering books to prove us right or wrong, though we searched diligently in the library for information on the Theory of Blowers.

For the fan-drum we had to use a Klim-tin, which was not as big as we should have liked, but the best for our purpose that came in the parcels.

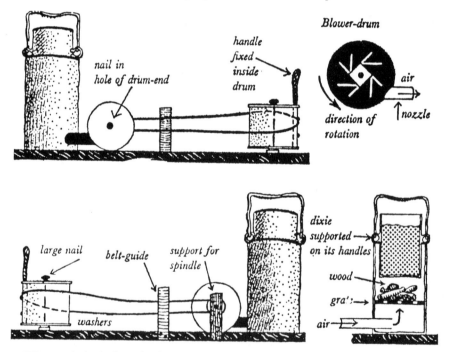

handle fixed inside drum

nail in hole of drum-end

Blower-drum

air

direction of rotation

nozzle

large nail

belt-guide

support for spindle

washers

dixie supported on its handles

wood

gra':

air

We needed a belt and a driving-wheel. The belt would have to be the string of a salami, but it should have been none the worse for that: some of those salamis took a good string to hold them down. This business of engineering, without either the skill or the tools required to make anything run true, was bad for the temper; it rained all the time, and we still brewed up on our non-mechanised stove, so that those days did not pass very smoothly. There were objections to borrowing other people's blowers: we had to make one for ourselves. So far, we had adopted standard practice, for plenty of people were using Klim-tin drums with good enough results. Now we tried a new idea that was easy to carry out. We made a driving-wheel out of two Klim-tin lids, which happened to fit over a pudding-tin from which the top and bottom had been removed. We punched holes with some success in the centre of each lid, this feat being made easier by our managing to borrow a pair of compasses; we fixed a wooden handle with two small nails inside the rim of the wheel (which might be more accurately called a drum), making a hole in one of the lids to let it pass through: we pushed the very large nail, our most treasured bit of engineering equipment right through the centre of this wheel, or drum, with a washer or two, and knocked it into the base-board at the other end from the blower-drum, so that the wheel rotated on a vertical axis. So we avoided having to make a wheel running true on a horizontal axis, with the very strong supports required to stand the twisting forces set up by turning the handle: rather a difficult job.

People laughed at this, and asked where the belt was supposed to go: but we fixed the fan-drum at an angle on the base-board, so as to make the groove on its spindle lie in line with a tangent drawn to the circumference of the driving-wheel. (We found a book which explained that two pulleys whose axles are at right-angles to each other should not be arranged just as we did it: but somehow we could not get the correct arrangement to work, so far as we understood it, at least.) We ran the belt from the groove in the spindle round the driving-wheel, with the slack part running back over a piece of tin that we fixed as a guide, and so to the spindle. We turned the handle and the fan revolved. The wind blew out of the hole provided for the purpose, and the belt stayed where it was meant to.

We made a firebox without much trouble, and fixed it on, and the results were pretty good. The contraption looked rather queer, especially because the base was a whole bedboard, but we had kept it that length so as to have a longer belt and consequently less acute angles for it to go round. Also, if we ever had to go to another camp, and had to account for our bedboards, the base of our blower could go back in its place, none the worse except for a little singeing; and we should thereby avoid having to pay a fine for having removed it.

Michael Hamburger

For the Dead

I

What is it that cries in the silence? not
where the dead are only, the crippled
towns, Cassino's stubble of stone where a child
waits for the train, the engine potent as hope,
bread in the trucks, the salute of handkerchiefs,
to the survivors stranded on dead soil;
not only in the trampled fields where wrecks
of tanks lie rusted, nor in the docks of Naples
clogged with bulk of ships that shall float no more—
but on oceans at night and in the valleys
richly remote, the courtyards of Venice;
louder far where the living work and piers
are patched for their pleasure and shops unshuttered—
shrill when the voices cease in clubs, the drummer
goes home and the dancers linger subdued.

II

The crosses tell us nothing of the minds
whose common negative is history,
nor what last thought kicked at the blunted nerves
of those who left no relics to record,
who lie unmarked in deserts of sand or sea.

O the cheated dead, uncounted, unseen
as the winds of the world cry out; for the words
that drove them left merging echoes behind,
the flimsy frontiers they died for are changed,
and, though the guns are draped, there is no peace.

J. H. Harding

Letter to Next of Kin

Lt. J. H. Harding,
c/o Chief Base Censor,
C.M.F.
January 29th, 1945.

Dear Mr. Gregg,
        I am very sorry to have to write and tell you about the tragic
death of your son, and I hope you will accept my deepest sympathy.
        He was in my Troop at the time, and was proving himself
invaluable when the blow came.
        It may help if I tell you that he could have felt no pain, as it was
a piece of shrapnel from shell fire that hit him at the base of the neck. He
was taken to a Regimental Aid Post and treated immediately.
        I arrived 10 minutes later and he was asleep then, and passed
away while still asleep.
        His personal effects were sent back, and are being forwarded
through military channels.
        Please accept my deepest sympathy, and I hope the knowledge
that he felt no pain helps to soften the blow a bit.

                        Yours,
                                (signed) J. H. Harding.

Hamish Henderson

Anzio April

Headlines at home. The gangrel season varies,
And Spring has gained a beach-head with our blood.
I've half a mind to kiss the blooming Jerries
And then just beat it while the going's good.
I'll bed down where deserters live on berries . . .
I'll play at possum in yon cork-oak wood . . .
    Machine-guns prate, but dannert flowers, this Spring.
    Over the grave all creatures dance and sing.

Phil shows the latest snap of his bambino.
The new mail's brought a great big box of tricks
For Donny, lucky bastard,—but for me no
Reminders: not a sausage—naethin—nix!
We hear of 'heavy fighting by Cassino'
But still no sign of jeeps on Highway Six . . .
  In Rome the fascists lie between soft sheets
  And numskull death his little tabor beats.

The watching Jerries sight a convoy's funnels:
It's coming into range now, Anzio-bound.
Their railway gun emerges from a tunnel's
Commodious depth, and plonks a single round
A hundred yards beyond one mucker's gunwales.
I bet they'd feel much safer underground!
    This fight one's better off inside the ring.
    Over the grave all creatures dance and sing.

Last night we got a bash from Fritz's 'arty'
And then his mucking jabos[1] gave us hell.
Our mediums up and joined the mucking party.
At last our mucking planes appeared as well.
Now thirteen Jocks are dead as Bonaparty.
(Yon Heinie in the tank's begun to smell).
  Lilac in bloom: the cold's White Guard retreats
  And numskull death his little tabor beats.

Kenny's bomb-happy: I think I'm a poet.
By Christ, my case is worse and that's a fact.
Maybe I'm nuts. Maybe I'll start to show it.
Sometimes I think that all the rest are cracked.
They're on the spot, and hell they hardly know it
. . . Or so you'd think, the damfool way they act.
  Spud's writing home, and Eddie thinks he's Bing.
  Over the grave all creatures dance and sing.

Snap out of that. Brigades of battered swaddies
Have got to stay and shoot—or lose their pants;
While strange to say our Jocks (the muckle cuddies)
Have still an inclination to advance.

[1]German Fighter Bombers

Down Dead-end Road, and west among the wadis
They'll pipe and make the Jerries do the dance.
    Next month the race. To-day we run the heats
    And numskull death his little tabor beats.

Red Neil, whom last I saw at lifting tatties
Pulls-through his rifle, whistles *Tulach Gorm.*
. . . Two drops of rain. We know whose warning *that* is.
A plum-hued cloud presents in proper form
(The old court-holy-water diplomat) his
Most courteous declaration of the storm.
    The dance is on. Strike up a Highland fling!
    Over the grave all creatures dance and sing

    (*And numskull death his little tabor beats*).

Victory Hey-Down

6th (Banffshire) battalion of the Gordon Highlanders, celebrating the German surrender in
Italy, dancing a reel to the tune *Kate Dalrymple*

Hey for the tall
horned shadows on the wall
and the beer-cans bouncing in the crazy Corso.
Hey for a hoor
for a meenit or an 'oor
and a tanner for a taigle wi' her sonsy torso.
Banffies hustle
through the randy reel-rawl;
lowpin' like a mawkin[1] see oor dames fae hell[2] go.
Bang
through the steer
they advance
tae the rear
and the ankles jiggin' like a fiddler's elbow.

[1]Leaping like a hare
[2]Kilted Highlanders (translation of German soldiers slang)

Slash o' a dirk
bleeds the guts o' the mirk
wi' the glentin' cramassies, the greens and yellows.
Wind cracks the cheeks
o' the dudelsack's breeks
like twa damn poltergeists at wark wi' the bellows.
Tae hell wi' your oboes
and your douce violas—
your flutes and your cellos and your concertinas.
Oor pipes
and oor reeds
they supply
a' the needs
o' oor dear wee silly little signorinas.

Slap in the pan
fae a billy tae a dan—
o we'll pound aul' Musso tae a weel-tanned tyke's hide.
We'll beery soon
yon melancholy loon
an' we'll ding doon Kesselring tae dee in the dykeside.
Plums we'll pree 'em
wi' the *partigiani*—
they bluid-reid billyboys, the rantin'-rory.
Ye mean
crood o' bams
gie's anither
twal drams
an' we'll reel auld Hornie an' his gang tae glory.

Italy, April 1945.

Peter R. Hopkinson

Neapolitan Interlude

My mail has just caught up with me
And that's about time too.
I'll soon find out what England thinks
And what is fresh and new.
'Soft under belly of the Axis
This won't take us long.'
This cutting says. Now there's a thought.
Could Winston have it wrong?

A letter from my Auntie Gwen,
She's on the coast near Dover.
There's German guns at Calais and
The shells could hurtle over.
They're aiming straight at her front door
She's paralysed with fright.
They haven't fired for months now but
You never know, they might.

My Uncle George at number 6
Acacia Road, Kings Lynn
Writes, 'Every night the R.A.F.
Sets off to bomb Berlin.
They wait until he's gone upstairs
And tucked himself in bed
Then thirty thousand aeroplanes
Fly nine feet o'er his head.

My cousin Egbert, though 'Reserved'
Finds life extremely hard
For twice and sometimes thrice a week
He serves in the Home Guard
A parachutist they did catch
His letter does declare
But this bloke proved to be a Pole
So 'War' he says, 'ain't fair.'

The Stukas as they often do
Purr sweetly overhead.
The eighty eights play lullabies
As I climb into bed.
How proud I am of all my folk
At home who bear the brunt.
While I hide out in Napoli
To dodge the second front.

Michael Howard

Rejoining the Battalion
Extracts from letter July 1944

It was Sunday morning and church bells were ringing in Greve.[1] The town was not much destroyed. The first AMG[2] proclamations had just been posted, and little groups were gathered round them. The 'liberation' was new enough for the Italians to cheer us as we went past, but soon there weren't any more Italians. A sinister notice said: 'Drive slowly. Dust is Death!' and we peered rather nervously towards the hills the Germans held. At length we came to a farmhouse on a hillside, and in the field behind it was all the battalion transport—F echelon. Battalion Headquarters were five hundred yards away up the hill, just below the crest. We got out, collected out belongings, and got dressed.

. . . As I entered the house an enormous drill sergeant called all Christendom to attention in strident terms. I was flattered at this unusual attention and was about to return it when I realised that the compliment was not intended for me, but for the Brigadier, who was at that moment coming out. I unloaded the kit which dangled around me like a Christmas tree, compounded of a pack, a satchel with writing material and books, a water-bottle, a '38 pistol, a shovel, a steel helmet, grenade pouches and a Schmeizer machine pistol—the German equivalent of our tommy-gun—and went into a small stone room, furnished with a table, a chair and a moth-eaten couch. The Adjutant, Paul Bowman, was sitting at the table, immaculate and shining, talking to the artillery liaison officer. In the next room a harassed Guardsman sat at the telephone exchange,

---

[1]In the Chianti Hills north of Arezzo   [2]Allied Military Government.

with an even more harassed Guardsman who was pacifying a large and ferocious wireless set with the mystic runic incantations signallers often use. 'Barbecue, barbecue, barbecue, barbecue, barbecue, barbecue, barbecue,' he chanted. 'Tuning call ends, hear netting call. Net now.' On the couch sat George Montagu, who in Colonel George's absence was commanding the battalion.

Paul greeted me soberly and rang up Christopher Janson, ordering a guide to be sent down to fetch me. Looking at the map I gathered that Christopher's company, No. 3, was about five hundred yards to the right, farther up the hill crest. Two companies were forward of the hill, in the next valley, and one was in reserve. The situation was that the Germans, around the village of Strada three miles ahead, 'strongly resented', as the intelligence summary put it, any attempt to advance into the valley. Our forward companies were kept in check by heavy shelling, and there were enough Tiger tanks around to make our armour very unwilling to go by themselves. They had tried and a few charred wrecks on the opposite side showed the result. For the moment the battalion was taking things quietly while the artillery hammered away at the enemy positions.

Then my guide arrived with the officer I was relieving. Gerald Legge looked very well. 'Oh, Sgt. Smith's all right,' he mumbled. 'Sgt. Casey's all right. They're all more or less all right. No, we haven't done much. An attack or two.' I took his binoculars and his compass and his map, loaded my equipment on again, and started off. My guide was considerably more talkative. At the first opportunity he opened a blood-curdling account of the company's past history and present position which made my hair stand on end. 'It's terrible, sir,' he said. 'Shelled all day—five men killed in No. 2 Company last night— can't show your head without bringing dirt down on top of you . . .' and so on. I made noises which tried to be sympathetic but at the same time encouraging, resulting merely in strangled grunts. Muffett, my servant, was horribly impressed. 'Cor!' he said. 'Bad as that, is it? Cor!' Muffett was not one to say ha ha! among the trumpets.

After about fifteen minutes our track, which had twisted and turned to keep below the hill crest, brought us to a large white villa, behind which was clustered a collection of jeeps, Bren carriers and store piles. There were a lot of people there, not only Guardsmen but gunners and mortar men manning their OPs[3] and signallers working the wireless set and maintaining the telephones. Water cans, ammunition boxes and mortar bomb containers were heaped against the walls; broken flowers and creepers trailed on the paths. The place was in that state of messy untidyness which is inseparable from war, and is far more typical of it than any amount of horror. Think always of that when you try to visualise conditions at the front: the debris of a civilian house as it might be

---

[3]Observation Posts.

your own, dusty and looted; and superimposed on that the disorder of the army—weapons and ammunition, piles of web equipment, washing and writing materials hanging out of packs, maps and mess-tins and tins of rations; mattresses dragged from beds and carried to the safe rooms dowstairs; drawers hanging open; windows barricaded with washstands; men sleeping on the floor under dirty mosquito nets; a strange mixture of papers—the *Daily Mirror*, the *Volkischer Beobachter, Il Popolo, Eighth Army News*—scattered around, and perhaps a *Spectator* or an *Horizon* which not long ago lay on the table in your sitting-room in London; and flies, flies, flies. That is war in comfort, indoors, in summer. What it is like in a slit trench in winter I will tell you next year.

Christopher Janson met me at the door—tall, thin, and dark. The company had tried to advance a few nights before, he told me, to a hill about eight hundred yards ahead, and found rather a lot of Germans there, which they had not expected. We had withdrawn successfully but it had done morale no good at all. Then a frightful crash shook the house. 'That happens, too,' he remarked. 'It's a 15-cm. mortar a long way back, and it sends one over just when you don't want it.' Then we went upstairs, and he told me rather more about my platoon. 'We aren't really in defensive positions. I've got them all on the reverse slope behind the house, dug-in in the orchard. At night we occupy sentry-posts on the forward slope in case he sends a patrol up, but it's unlikely. One of your sections I brought into the house after the shelling this morning. The rest are outside.'

There was a fighting patrol going out under the other platoon commander, Dermott Magill. Dermott had been at Mons Barracks, Aldershot, with me and he is now considered one of the best platoon commanders in the battalion. After lunch Christopher took me up to the company OP to look at the ground. This, of course, was on the forward slope. While the reverse slope was open orchard, the forward slope was covered with scrub; and across it ran, most conveniently, a sunken track which easily accommodated on its banks not only our OP—two men with binoculars and a Bren gun—but the forward observers for the gunners, medium mortars and heavy mortars, each with a telephone back to the battery.

We crawled cautiously up the track and pulled ourselves up about five yards from our sentry, peering gingerly over the edge of the bank into the valley below. There were pine needles and ants, which reduced my efficiency a lot. But the view was magnificent. Directly in front was a valley some five miles wide, green and cultivated, flanked on the left by spurs of heathery hills and on the right by the prolongation of our own mountain. Three miles away were the red roofs of Strada, beyond which the road ran up to a crest on which stood the next village, Impruneta. In the background, startlingly near, were the blue mountains of the Gothic line; and in the haze at their foot you could just see, through glasses, the white suburbs of Florence. That was very exciting. On a little hill half a mile in front they showed me a farmhouse which was the nearest

1. **George Meddemmen:** *228 Bty R.A., Command Post, Villa Salvini near Arezzo, Italy, July 1944*

2. **Ronald Cox:** *Night Raid on Komiza, Yugoslav coast, 1944*

RAID KOMIZA HARBOUR. FEBY44
HIT - COXADT NOT HURT - E·M·E· WOUNDED IN HEAD

"PARTISANNES" TYPES

3. **Ronald Cox:** *Three Tito Partisannes, 1944. Women served as combat soldiers and as cooks/orderlies (better looking reserved for HQ); chastity enforced in two ways: women tried and executed men who seduced their comrades; pregnant women also went on trial.*

"ANZIO PORT" 1944

4. **Ronald Cox:** *Anzio Port, Italy, 1944*

German position. That also was very exciting. It was Dermott's objective for the night.

We shelled that hill either that afternoon or the next day, I forget which. It is most stimulating being in a gunner OP when a shoot is going on. And the gunner officer murmurs strange arabic formulae down the telephone. Then he says, 'Fire!' There is a silence. The leaves rustle peacefully and a bird twitters. You strain your ears to catch the bang of the gun among the miscellaneous, continual bangs which puncture time through the afternoon. Probably you miss it and hear only the strange swift sighing of the shell rushing overhead. Then comes a great brown mushroom of smoke and dust on the green hill opposite, two seconds before the crash of the explosion. The gunner repeats figures into the telephone, and you wait again. The next mushroom is behind the hill and you only see the smoke curling up after the explosion. Then perhaps the third shot hits the target and the house disappears in a cloud of yellow dust. The human element is quite remote, but you may as well get what pleasure you can out of shelling other people, as there is so very little in being shelled yourself. It is almost disappointing, when the dust clears away, to see how little the house is damaged. But the gunner has been busy, and at once mushroom grows out of mushroom in the house and the crashes are continuous. It will be a quarter of an hour before the smoke clears now, and you can see the damage. Before then the Germans will have retaliated, and you duck unhappily at the cresendo whistle of a shell which pitches a quarter of a mile down the hill, shaking the ground and the air with blast. Sometimes you know there is another company there and watch helplessly as your own position disappears in smoke. Yet the casualties are always astonishingly small.

... Next morning Muffett woke me for dawn stand-to. Dawn is a horrible thing and don't let anyone tell you otherwise. A grey, leprous, sluglike, creeping, corpse-cold, hostile thing. As soon as it was light and we could stand down I went back to the house and dozed in an armchair until breakfast time. Dermott was there, asleep, and I wondered how many Germans he had killed the night before. We woke him for breakfast, and he drowsily informed us that he had surprised a German working party and killed about five of them. Then he went straight to sleep again.

I washed and shaved, changed my shirt and went out of the house to visit my platoon. Five minutes later the first shell arrived. Where it landed I am not quite sure. There was just a sudden whistle and a crash so loud and so near that I was not conscious of it as noise at all, but as force, as violence, as air suddenly expanding in a great annihilating wave. Everything was dark with dust and cordite fumes, and there followed that sinister silence when all the world is still and you feel suddenly released from the panic-stricken fluttering inside your ribs which a second before was stilled, grasped in a hand of stupified paralysis.

'That was a near one,' said Sgt. Smith.

I was in my platoon headquartes, fifty yards up the hill from the house, and I got with what I hope was dignity into the nearest slit trench. It was horribly shallow, but there was a good stout wall beside it which helped a lot. Things were quiet for a moment, and I looked around. The shell must have pitched behind the house, from the dust of it. There were no cries, so all was well from *that* point of view. To shout to people to get in their trenches was absurdly unnecessary. There was nothing for me to do but to stay where I was. Then came another whistle, growing louder, horribly quickly, culminating again in the crash that could be felt and not heard, in that instant of blind, personal paralysis when all thought and feeling, even fear, is frozen, blotted out as vision is momentarily eclipsed by a wink. Then the release of breathing, the release of fear, the release of the bird under the ribs. That one must have been nearer the house itself, but I saw no object in going to make sure. As I debated the question I recognised in the distance the bang of our particular gun, and pressed closer, impossibly closer, to the ground, fixing my eyes on some silly little detail— a blade of grass, a stone, a struggling ant—concentrating desperately on that until the paralysis, the shutter descended and reduced me to something out of all semblance of a man.

There were about a dozen shells altogether, though I didn't count them at the time. In the intervals I lay still and thought how pleasant it would be when it was finished and we could get up and walk about in the sun again. After a quarter of an hour no more came; and cautiously I went round checking my platoon. There, at any rate, no damage was done. In the rest of the company, Dermott was scratched slightly and a signaller had a wound in the leg. That was all, by the providence of God. Christopher had had a fantastic escape. He was lying on his bed, on the ground floor of the house, with his head against the outside wall, when a shell struck that wall two feet above where he was lying. It exploded, knocking a hole three feet square and covering him with rubble and bricks. He was dug out, laughing as usual and white with dust, and took everyone off to the cellar where we had had the service the night before. The next shell bounced on the edge of the roof and crashed down on top of a jeep which was standing just outside the door of the cellar. The remains of that jeep and the one beside it were fascinating; it took me a long time to realise that the strange bits of charred metal where the shell had struck had once been a large and complete wireless set. A third shell had not exploded, and remained as a witness and example of the size of the things they had been throwing at us; and a fourth exploded upstairs, totalling destroying the staircase and the bedroom where I had washed—and left, I suddenly realised, all my belongings. All that was left was a great mound of rubbish on the floor of the room below; and everywhere there was the powdered plaster, the presence and smell of which always accompany ruin.

John Jarmain

Prisoners of War

Like shabby ghosts down dried-up river beds
The tired procession slowly leaves the field;
Dazed and abandoned, just a count of heads,
They file away, these who have done their last,
To that grey safety where the days are sealed,
Where no word enters, and the urgent past
Is relieved day by day against the clock
Whose hours are meaningless, whose measured rate
Brings nearer nothing, only serves to mock.

It is ended now. There's no more need to choose,
To fend and think and act: no need to hate.
Now all their will is worthless, none will lose
And none will suffer though their courage fail.
The tension in the brain is loosened now,
Its taut decisions slack: no more alone
—How I and each of us has been alone
Like lone trees which the lightnings all assail—
They are herded now and have no more to give.
Even fear is past. And death, so long so near,
Has suddenly receded to its station
In the misty end of life. For these will live,
They are quit of killing and sudden mutilation;
They no longer cower at the sound of a shell in the air,
They are safe. And in the glimmer at time's end
They will return—old, worn maybe, but sure—
And gather their bits of broken lives to mend.

Sicily. August-October, 1943.

153

B. G. J. Johnston

Cassino

The shattered walls, that stand half-masted to the sky,
The tangled thread of war, the blast-torn wire
    that twists o'er rubble and desecrates the graves
Of those that rest beneath a common funeral pyre
The myriad craters, laid to some inhuman plan
    to form a devil's links of countless holes,
The empty cans and cartridge cases spent in wanton waste.
All flotsam on a sea of mud
The riddled hulls, half buried in a pile of brick or sunken in
    some shell-shot slimy pond
The whole close grouped, impressive yet o'ershadowed by the hills
    and monastery ghosts beyond.
Mark this a resting place of men who conquered fear
Build them no Cenotaph, they sleep forever here.

Peter Kneebone

See Naples

No motion and no future.
The only now of which one is aware
is the open tomb's delayed exposure.
Behind a crescent tourist pamphlet,
flashy sea-reflection, lies the split.
Behind the exquisite mosaic
the tenement.
Behind the orange grove
the sewer.
Behind the warm smile
the sickness.

... Street-corner Midas whose touch turns to dross,
his cult is the Sterling, the market his Mass.
... She parodies sex and her grossness blurred
in a mask, hollow-eyed, she seeks the reward.
... With threadbare eagerness, trembling hands
grope in the crowd for what they can find.
... The theme spills gratingly from barrel organs
(the present primitive—once charming pagan):
the faultless notes are faltering and jerk,
the thick-lipped tenor now a sensuous bark.
From their cracked and peeling cardboard casing
the apprehensive notes are rising
along the gutter to a final ceiling
of dust and heat and fear and wailing.

J. S. L.

Italian Morning

Now it is morning,
The beginning of light in the mountains
And work in the vineyards. The darkness
Seeping insensibly from the fields;
And the sun coming up to a clangour
Of crimson gongs; and the singing
Of the women, the cattle-bells; and the farms
Startlingly white against the dark green hills;
And incessantly in the distance,
Beyond the dark green hills and the gentle river,
The blank unanswerable statement of the guns.

There is no meaning behind the distant guns,
Only a moron's formula. We are all caught in the river,
Whirled to a booming twilight distance,
Lost and deserted on the deserted hills.

Not being fools or saints digging in the white farms
For nirvana, nor hopeless pilgrims questing for a singing
Country, we can only accept the ridiculous clangour
Of this war, and be thankful for the sun on the fields—
Knowing that there is no change in the real, the human darkness
Because of the sun's abandoned gesture to the mountains,
Or because it is morning.

Lawrie Little

From a Med Diary

Beach at Baja, Naples. Summer, 1944

Frowsy umbrella shade naked ladies. The wild boy puts an unfastidious foot to their bottoms; they are not amused; bells ring, they doze. He keeps an eye on the church but sees used towels on the terraces, the hairy disappearance of a thigh, that's nothing fresh. Stale beach and peal of bells. He throws a pebble at the sexless sky.

Island of Nisida. Summer, 1944

The island is alive with prisoners; they watch the sea, the causeway, the leisurely traffic, women, children. Their theatre begins outside the castle walls. They offer provocations. Their hot breath excites the shamefaced players. Every woman is raped, every child indelicately fondled. Old men deliver tobacco, young men clenched kisses. Screams shuttle between the sun and the sea. The guards grunt their enormous pleasure. It's all done for them.

Mother and Daughter, Trieste. Summer, 1945

She bit his neck with passion. That was her motherly feeling for him. The sourness of her breath shook him like a fresh disaster. His shoulders quivered childishly against the wall. Whatever happened was in her hands. She had kicked his shins when he winked at her daughter across the table. The virgin's guardian. This was more horribly painful, a question of ages.

H. R. H. Lyster

Cassino Diary

From notes made by Captain H. R. H. Lyster of the Seaforth Highlanders.

9th May 1944

We all know that the events of the next few weeks will decide the end of the war, and so I'm scribbling down my daily impressions in the hope that they may prove of interest to you.

Today's date is May 9th and I start by being three miles behind the line at Cassino.

On our arrival at Naples we adopted a rear position, some twenty miles south of Cassino. Then the guns took over a small sector for a week to enable them to get familiar with the landmarks. We were then withdrawn while other people were allowed a look in. Meanwhile thousands of troops have gathered in their final position—ourselves included, all awaiting the order to start. We all realise that it is timed to coincide with a push from Anzio and the second front in Europe. Word has also been passed that we shall hear full orders two days before the start.

My own position is in the reserve lines, two miles behind the guns, and three miles behind the infantry.

Owing to the Cassino defence line, we are actually facing west—as the line runs N–S along the Rapido and Gari rivers. This means that we fire in the morning when the sun is in the eyes of the enemy, and they fire back in the afternoon. Both teams let themselves go at night, but naturally we restrict ours as we do not wish to give away our full strength.

I believe that there are 1100 guns here—nearly twice as many as at Alamein so there should be plenty of noise to indicate the start.

I'm well situated near a road, so that I can make a quick move forward when necessary. Just behind me lies the form of Mignano, now reduced to a heap of rubble, south west lie the French Forces, while directly ahead lie the Indians (Gurkhas, Mahrattas, Sikhs) and their heavy guns are 100 yards away, so they make conversation a lot difficult. Away to the north are the Black Watch, R. West Kents, the Guards Brigade and the Irish Brigade the latter actually in part of Cassino itself. Air co-operation is excellent, we have our own aircraft for fun work; but the sky is filled with our bombers pounding communications and fighters clearing the skies of enemy spotters.

We have got photos of the famed Hitler line, some 15 miles nearer to Rome, but we have assembled so many troops that we obviously intend to crack this country for good. It will mean about a week of heavy fighting and then I hope to be in the mad dash for the north. I feel that our greatest danger is not enemy fire, but enemy mines. They have had six months in which to plant the areas and it will mean tricky going for the tanks—especially our own Shermans which are manned by Derby Yeomanry, the Lothian and Border Horse; 17/21 Lancers and 16/5 Lancers—all in the famous 6th Armoured Division of which I am a part.

That about covers all the preliminaries.

18.00 hours same day

Just moved my boys a little closer under the shadow of the ridge because of one bunch of German shells, called a *Stonk* fell direct on the HQ of India Division killing a Brigadier—this was only half a mile from us, but I always thought that their position was too exposed. The accuracy seems to indicate the presence of enemy agents.

Received preliminary orders tonight and they were as I expected. I stay here while the Gurkhas force the Rapido and Gari rivers. Barrage starts at 11 p.m.—position to be consolidated before daybreak. Poles to isolate Cassino, Canadians to advance from the south. I move to Mount Trocchio, and then advance through the gaps alongside the Liri river. Final objective—Florence and Rimini—what an optimist.

Just heard about the pamphlets to be showered on Cassino and Monastery. They say 'You are surrounded by Poles—we advise you to surrender because of what you did to their people—you are now further away from Berlin than are the Russians'. Pretty good I thought.

Went up to a position this afternoon with the New Zealanders two miles from Cassino. They have erected a great sign over a graveyard of shattered vehicles (British) saying, 'The Results of American Precision bombing'.

I had heard before that the bombing of Cassino had been very bad. Apart from the death of many of our own troops, it was obvious that total destruction of the town would not make it any easier to enter. Now we hold part of the town, but general destruction makes the arrival of all supplies very difficult. Mules by night is the only way. Germans had expected bombing, and had dug in so well that a few loads of rubble on top did not worry them unduly.

10th May

Last night was nearly my last. I heard by wireless that one of my tanks was firing badly on one engine so I told him to report back to me by night as he was well forward and to return meant crossing a ridge in full view of the monastery. At 1 a.m. I was dragged out of bed to hear that he was in trouble on the ridge. I drove out there, without lights of course and found him stuck in the most exposed spot. Luckily the moon was clouded and he hadn't been spotted. He had got his tracks entangled in some battered steel mesh which we use for making roads in bad weather. We were too exposed to use oxy-acelytene so we had to use hands, wire cutters, crowbars and hack saws. All the time we could hear British and German shells whizzing over our heads. Very unpleasant.

Eventually got on the move and arrived at the end of the 'road'—this is really a railway but the rails have been removed. When we were 300 yards from the end an enemy aircraft—the first I've seen for a hell of a time, dropped a full load of anti-personel bombs—presumably at the Indian heavy gun positions. If I had been a little earlier it would have been a bit close. Anyway we steamed in and went to bed 4 a.m. all black with Diesel fumes and white with chalk dust.

Up at 8 a.m. to receive orders from the Colonel. Pretty well as I had guessed, except that it is the French on our left. They are called C.E.F. which I thought was Canadian Expeditionary Force, but I was wrong. Everybody very offended about last night's solitary 'plane. According to the press the enemy haven't got any here—perhaps the Germans don't get the papers. It looks as though tomorrow night will see the start.

May 11th

Yes, the party starts tonight at 11 p.m. This is written at 6 p.m. and I'm going to get a few hours sleep. I heard the tanks of 26 Brigade moving up last night. Today has been sunny, a fair breeze, slight haze, no clouds, so it should be clear for tonight. Guns quiet today, but it will be hell let loose in a few hours. Elsie's letter dated 6 April arrived this afternoon, just the tonic I required. Spoke a few words to the troops today—a much better speech than Henry V at Harfleur.

May 12th (9.30 a.m.)

Got a lot of sleep yesterday evening during an ominous lull, but 11 p.m. brought the opening chorus. All the mountains were silhouetted in the flashes which made the area quite bright. Moon had not yet risen. Every time the 8″ guns went off I was flung out of bed and I watched the fireworks until 1 a.m. Slept a little longer, wireless message at 4 a.m. to report a direct hit on one of my mobile guns. Drove out without lights along the railway track, passing a Jeep in a shell hole, a lorry upside down and a tank on its side. Gun position was like Dantés Inferno, but louder. Hit was on the front of one of Phillip Rooke's battery, no casualties and only slight damage. Stayed up there till daybreak, when we stopped the battle to have a cup of tea. Now back in caravan having finished a tin of beans for breakfast. Germans putting in a serious counterattack below Cassino. Poles are on top of Monastery Hill and doing well. No news of the French. Indians have two brigades across the Gari river, also elements of the Surrey and West Kents. Position not too good, we are behind schedule, and this counterattack will threaten our hold on the river crossings.

Bully beef lunch and two hours rest, wireless message reveals that the gun is in a worse state than I had expected, and my chaps are going to bring it out of the line tonight. They must not reveal the gun position by movement in daylight. It is now 8.30 p.m. and I'm going to bed. Rumours everywhere, but all unconfirmed. The only certainty is that we are well behind schedule otherwise the guns would have moved to their second positions on Mt. Trocchio. We shall know more tomorrow. Very tired.

Monday 15th May 9 a.m.

We had a bad day yesterday and I was too tired last night to write. The first news in the morning revealed that our two attacks had been unsuccessful, but the French had made good progress. Saw one of our spotter planes brought down but the pilot got out by parachute. Capt. Bob Massey operating as observation officer west of the Liri was reported hit so I went up to the gun positions again for further details. Enemy counterattacked and overan his tank. Last heard that he and his crew of two were all wounded, but safe in the Dressing Station. Tank written off.

Heavy casualties with Lothian and Border Horse. Second observation officer Capt. Williams reported a direct hit on his tank, no damage and carrying on. Third observation Capt. Bagnall reported fired on by a sniper whom he blew to pieces with a 75 mm shell from his tank.

A heavy rain of shells on the gun positions at 4 p.m. One man killed, one injured (our first death after four days of action). Direct hit on an armoured scout car—no injuries and very little damage. Vehicle withdrawn at daybreak. Today Major Middleton's tank withdrawn with engine trouble. We shall be getting short of tanks if we are not careful.

Inspected some guns before the light failed. Managed to buy some wine from a farm in the gun area. Wonderful show of fireflies at night. Drove back with the empty ammunition convoy, along a track I didn't know, without lights, very nerveracking—tanks still moving up—looks like 26 Independent Tank Brigade. Tremendous congestion by the river bridge. Thank heavens we have air superiority.

Many rumours about second front but nothing confirmed. Everybody quite pleased that we are having a battle on this line. It means that we are drawing Jerry from his mountain strongholds, and it will be all the easier later on.

Same day 9 p.m.

Just off to bed: wrote to Son tonight. Had a quiet day, but will have to visit the guns at daybreak. I believe that the 78 Div—our fresh troops—are going in tonight. This seems to be a good move, because Jerry must be pretty tired by now. By tomorrow night we should have joined up with the Poles and French.

2,000 prisoners so far—but a pretty poor lot.

Hope the batteries don't cross the Liri tonight. I'm so tired.

May 16th 9 p.m.

A bad day. French doing well, but we are still held up south of Cassino. The armour pushed ahead but at great expense. 78 Division now moving up for another attack at daybreak. We can see Bob Massey's tank but too exposed to recover it. Capt. Pine had a shell hit his tank, two killed, two injured. Capt. Bagnall hit by incendiary grenades—tank burned out—no casualties. Major Middleton developed engine trouble so back I went to the gun positions.

Another tank hit in the radiator, and they have managed to limp back to the Rapido river. Two of my fitters just going up with spares to try and repair two of them. Trouble also developing on the record system on the guns. Hope this doesn't get worse.

May 18th

Found many old German guns and lovely dug-outs. Horrible smell of death everywhere—made more noticeable by the contrast of poppies and ripening corn. You would trace the smell rather hesitantly, and find a horse, a sheep, a German or a British soldier—often unburied in the hot sun for four days. All very horrible. We identified as far as possible, covered the bodies and stuck up a reverse rifle to mark the spot. Found my own padre busy burying—chiefly Royal West Kent Regt. and Germans.

May 19th

My guns had moved forward three miles to north of Piumarola, which is 3 miles due south of Piedmonte. Still firing NNE. I moved up to the new gun positions as soon as possible (I always do this in case I have to find my way by night) and found that a D battery gun was badly scored—not surprising with the shells they have fired recently. On the way I passed five German tanks and one of ours all blown to pieces. Also passed about 50 unburied dead, chiefly shell casualties which were not pretty. Much equipment and many weapons scattered wholesale, showed that they went in a hurry. Among our prisoners were boys of 13 and 14. Unbelievable isn't it, but they are fanatically pro-Hitler and probably are volunteers from their boys' associations. They were brought in by the Black Watch who said they hadn't got the heart to shoot them. A shower of rain delayed my return to my own area, made it very difficult driving. Tired out again, but had a good meal and saw the men settled for the night.

Expecting my reserve tanks to come up tonight. Really very quiet here. I expect the sound of the guns is muffled by the hills. Poles now reported in area Piedmonte, but the hills between that place and Cassino are not yet clear, and mopping up is still going on.

Heard a strange story today—how a dead German killed one of the Hampshires. The German was shot dead as he drew a hand grenade. Later as a group of Hampshires were passing the body just as rigor mortis was setting in, this released the catch and caused a casualty. Even dead Germans can be dangerous.

20th May 9 p.m.

Awoke after a pleasant night, only slightly disturbed by the big guns (5.5 inch) which have followed us up. Slight drizzle which has made the temporary roads terrible. Vehicles streaming over the Rapido. 6 Armd. Div. coming up in force. Spent the morning burning the two horses. My replacement tanks

161

arrived also the replacement gun. We are taking full advantage of the lull to inspect all guns and check all tanks. Big attack on Hitler lines starts tomorrow night. During the afternoon I searched the battlefield for my two lost tanks and found one—the one in which two men had been killed. Direct hit through the turret by a 75 mm shell—very lucky that three men are still alive. Not worth saving the tank, so removed a few parts I wanted such as gun sights. Found two more tanks (Lothian and Border Horse). Still with bodies inside. Hadn't got the stomach to bury them—it is five days since they died, but reported the location to the people concerned. Spotted several more tank casualties, but in too dangerous ground to investigate. The wrecked monastery looks very dismal on its lonely height.

A. M. Bell MacDonald

Extracts from Diary

May 8th, Capri

Another leisurely morning shopping. I nearly bought some Capriot sandals, roped soled affairs most suitable for the cobbly lanes and beach wear generally. I was much tempted but forbore as it only means more to carry. We met Malaparte again, also with string bag doing his daily shopping. With him another old friend of mine Prince Parente, the last time I was on the Island we had passed the time of day at the 'Gaudeamus'. I had not known then that the person I was addressing so familiarly was a Prince, but apparently he is, a different type from Caracciolo. Parente is young, about 35, a great big cheerful man with a wide smile and probably a good many brains. Wears the latest in beach clothes, beige linen trousers and red sandals, a yellow shirt and a blue coat, that was roughly it. We saw him several times and he was usually dressed differently, that was just one example. He knew everybody on the Island and pinched the girl's cheeks with great charm and gallantry.

We also met an old friend of J's, an attractive dark girl with a slow smile and a way of standing that said a lot. She and another (whom J. familiarly and I think unfairly called the sexual maniac) lived at the Villa Olivia and with them were staying some Yank officers, why or in what capacity must remain a mystery as we never saw either the S.M. or friend again. This was, in view of the short time we had on the Island—probably as well. We agreed though that given a clear week matters might have developed. J's account of the S.M. were, even allowing for his natural gift for exaggeration, most invigorating and drew a splendid picture of a woman who gave freely of her beauty and charm. But, alas, for me she remains L'Inconnue.

After shopping we went down to the beach again and bathed. Few there, the odd loving couple and some Americans. It was lovely, we lazed in the sun and watched the impossibly blue and clear Mediterranean surge and wash across the pebbly beach. The whole scene was far too like a picture postcard to describe.

Lunch at the Villa, rather too much and what with the wine and morning exercise, I felt intolerably sleepy. We had, however, made a date with the Baroness to go round San Michele, Munthe's Villa. If it hadn't been the Baroness who was showing us round we wouldn't have gone. Such snobs have we become. It seems she is a very old friend of Munthe and has translated some of his books into German and when he left the Island he asked her to keep an eye on it for him. She is a German from the Baltic States, Esthonia way. The name is Von Uexküll-Schwerin, a slight, rather pale woman with white hair, but very lively and despite her age which must be considerable, very active physically and mentally. She spoke wonderful English.

We called for her at her house near the German Church, where we sat a little and talked. The house was cool and deliciously scented, rather like the smell of good China tea. I was fascinated by her and her house and the thought that she and her husband are our enemies, and that as far as I know her sons or grandsons may be fighting against us. Here we were being entertained by her and talking of the war in a detached way as though it were happening on another planet. Her husband was a biologist (Marine) and had studied fishes and what not most of his life. He writes learned books which she translates into various languages. Before the last war they were very wealthy and travelled extensively, he indulging his hobby and she bringing up his children. She must have some interesting stories to tell of pre first war Europe. The Russian Revolution affected Esthonia rather seriously, and they found themselves very poor. They sold what little land the Esthonian Govt. had allowed them to keep but retained the old family Island where the house stood, and there they lived only travelling occasionally till he landed up in Naples and founded an aquarium, which is still going.

David I. Masson

Rites of Passage

Grain and a half of morphia he received.
    He died in fifty minutes through his bowels.
MEs' H.E.[1] his charming wife bereaved;
    His corpse the rich Campanian soil befouls.
    Such a death calls for the extravagant howls
Of Webster's *Malfi*[2]: we just barely grieved
    When he gave out his last sub-human vowels.
His pay-book and his photos were retrieved.

Why is it, horrible world, we've grown so numb?
    Even as witnesses we hardly feel
    The full blast of the things we know are real:
       The wives that make the bombs can never know
       Just how obscene a fate they have let go.
The press and microphone, of course, are dumb.

Near Sparanise, Appian Way, Campania, November 1943.

[1]Messerschmitts' high explosive.

Kevin McHale

Com-bloody-parisons

Butman, founder of Melbourne, is quoted as saying, as he looked at the *Yarra Yarra river*:
'This is the place for a village.'

If you stand beside the Tiber
Where it splashes on the rocks
You can feel the ancient history
Come soaking through your socks
But I'm no man to give a damn
For others' rape and pillage
The bloody muddy Yarra is
The place I'd build my 'village'.

Have you seen the Coliseum
Where the plebs would get a treat
Watching hungry bloody Christians
Being given lions to eat?
But for me the Melbourne Cricket Ground
Is calling calling calling
With all those blokes from Pommieland
Their bloody wickets falling.

The plains of bloody Lombardy
We're led to understand
Are famous for their poplar trees
So tall and straight and grand
That's dinkum for the Ities
The tree for me, old chum,
A dirty great big sticky
Aussie eucalyptus gum.

There's quite a lot of beautiful
Ragazzas here in Rome
Attractive till they start to talk
Just like the birds at home
I dunno what they're saying
And I do not bloody care
I guess a sheila is a sheila
Any bloody where.

N. T. Morris

Sicilian Town: August 1943

What was your crime, you little mountain town?
Why is that mother picking through those stones?
The entrails of the church stare to the sky;
The Military Police say: 'Out of Bounds,'

'No halting on the Road': the people stare
Blank-eyed and vacant, hollow-eyed and numb.
You do not seem to hate us: we are they
Who blew your town to dust with shell and bomb.

'Water not drinkable'; 'One Way Street';
The road machine runts rubble from the track.
Was this a house, home of two lovers' joys,
Reduced by chemists' blast to pristine rock?

The moody mountain frowns, aloof, detached.
What was your crime, you little mountain town?
Just that you lay upon the Armies' route;
Two tracks met here by whim in ancient time.

Sonnet

The army lorry pulls into the square;
The wan and hungry townsfolk gather round,
In every eye a searching look profound;
'Biscotto,' 'Cigarette'—a dope for care.
Behind the town the orchards teem with pear,
With orange, apple, grape, with peaches sound,
While Nature's harvest sees the peasant bound
To beg for 'Carne,' 'Pane,' food too rare.
    This was a people subject to the yoke
    Who had to bow the neck to fascist greed;
    Simple and pious, pale illiterate folk,
    How could they hope a cancerous state to feed?
    In plenty are they famished, spirit broke,
    Though vanquished by the invaders, yet are freed.

Malaria Mozzie

Malaria Mozzie,
Tenuous, hairy,
Flit on the water,
Light as a fairy.
Locked in the bottle,
Flimsy, mysterious.
Deadly anopheles
Mozzie malarious.
    Sing a song of mozzie nets, of pills and mepacrine,
    Bells a-ringing in the ear from boosting with quinine.
    Spray the tents with flysol, face and hands well greased.
    What an awful lot of dope to thwart the little beast.
Bred in the waterways,
Starting life's little term,
Biting the native folk,
Getting the deadly germ.
Hiding in huts by day.
Nightly on prowl they go;
Noiseless they soldiers bite.
Laying an army low.
    Sing a song of shivering of going hot and cold;
    Of temperatures that jump about, of feeling tired and old,
    Sick parade at six o'clock; sweating, yet you're froze,
    Go and pack your small kit up and off the blood-box goes.

Molise 1943

The abbot speaks: the painter hears his task.
The Virgin is adoring, posture so:
The Infant earthly, as a human child,
Some common touch, but always, always God.
Composition . . . well, I leave to you;
A triangle is sound, so strong, so good,
Solid like our holy Catholic Church.

The background? Not important; what you will;
Something that's you, your village, if you wish.
Yes. True. The plain is washed in wat'rish light.
Oh, colours? Spare no cost. And time? Two months?

Through airless room the heavy footsteps pad:
The guide takes up the theme. And now this next,
The Virgin and the Child, in normal pose.
Please note the birds: robin and chaffinch, wren—
A human touch—the Infant Christ at play
With homely creatures; that is something new.
Another point: the background, to the right,
Is mediæval—some Italian town
Posed on a hill-top. Note the cypress-trees,
The artist painting what he sees and loves.
The light is exquisite, so wet, so fresh,
And yet the piece is near six centuries old.
And here we have another . . .

We breast the top and gain another view.
The lorries turn and twine their falling way,
And we can scan the pattern of the land.
I've seen the village on that hill before,
The wall about it, and its very towers,
The way it hangs upon its beetling slope.
Oh, where? Not here. The first time sounds a chord.
Another life, incarnate in far time?
But, no . . . That picture, whose? By Perugin?
I know not, but my mind can see it now;
What gallery? The Louvre? That placid light
Pours on the banks to silhouette the trees,
Cypress, and guardians of the plain. The painter?
My brain will fidget till I call his name,
Some limb of the Renaissance . . .

The front rolls on. The gunners and the tanks
Have all passed through. The hill-top town is dead.
Its wall is pock-marked: there a door is smeared
By flame-thrower. The houses naked lie,
Truncated by the artifice of war;
The towers I knew, unpinned and like to fall.

This place is dead, save for a dozen birds
Picking for bits amid a ruined house:
Robin and chaffinch, wren. This ancient quiet
Is full of ghosts . . .

William E. Morris

Imprint of War

Land desolate as a lone sheep
lost from flock in snow-storm's hazing,
olive trees walk as grey ghosts hand in
hand
denuded as sparse rock strata'd land.
Land winter clutching at its
throat
manacled by a steel encircled
moat.

A daub in artist's dingy scene
child figure tends a twig-fire green,
sketchy garments rent in every seam cling
dejectedly,
misery oozing from every pore
crouching on feet ridged and raw,
his legs as pea-sticks after you had plucked
pods
and left sticks to weather's unruly
nods.

Hands chapped from Appenine's breath-taking
chill
fingers rent from hunger's hopeless questing
drill.
Stomach distended to famine's compelling
pattern.

A stamp of hunger on child body pregnant
in its import of need—
all about war's greed.
Wise eyes that stare apathetically
through
an alien in narrow soul destroying life
he always knew.
Across curl of coiling smoky haze
a pleading cretin looks with
pleading gaze,
hope tinged in the thrust of a wizened
chin,
an old man mask creased in merest
grin,
embittered tread of war's rough shod
chariot,
firmly imprinted on features pigmented
in certain death.

Italy, 1943.

Sam Morse-Brown

Portraits at Sea

My unit was transported to Taranto, on the south coast of Italy, in a tank-landing-craft—L.S.T. 402, and it was on this ship that I did the portraits of the ship's Captain, his First Lieutenant D. F. Clarke and Petty Officer Wallace together with a study of a seaman on duty as a submarine watch.

Engrossed in portraying Lieutenant Clarke as a typical British Naval Officer, I did not notice that the sea had become rough until my Colonel, in search of me, appeared at the door of the cabin. His face, normally a bucolic pink, was green. He gave a quick glance at my subject, rising and falling before his eyes, exclaimed 'Good God . . . how can you do it?' and then slammed the door again. We heard him getting sick in the companion way.

I had never been sea-sick in my ife, but I became conscious at once that my model was sometimes above my eye-level and sometimes below, which was a

170

strange experience for me. However, it was not as difficult as it may seem to make allowance for this change in persepective because I too was rising and falling and Lieutenant Clarke and myself were, more often than not, in correct visual relationship with each other.

I can recommend concentration on a job as a remedy for sea-sickness; or, as the army would put it, 'maintenance of the objective!' The objective in this case was to get the portrait done at all costs.

The same conditions prevailed when I did the study of Petty Officer Wallace as a typical Naval rating, but by that time my Colonel could not care less what his Adjutant was doing. He was lying in his bunk, no doubt going through the three stages of sea-sickness—

1. Fearing that the ship *might* go down.
2. Convinced that it *would* go down.
3. Fearing that it would *not* go down.

So I was left alone to add these naval portraits to my collection, and also the drawing of the Capt. at the chart table checking his position in the invasion fleet.

Capt. Sprigge must have had a charmed life because he had served in thirty one ships and most of them had been sunk. Among these thirty one ships, the names of which he wrote down for me, was the cruiser Exeter that had been so heavily damaged by the German battleship Graf Spee in the Battle of the River Plate.

General Montgomery

The army teleprint passed to me by my Area Commander at Tunis, and reproduced here, reads:-

'Following received from Tactical Headquaters EIGHTH ARMY (.) quote (.) SECRET (.) deliver following message Capt. MORSE-BROWN HQ 3 A.C.G. (1) from Gen. MONTGOMERY 8TH ARMY (.) very glad if you will come my H.Q. at once to make PORTRAIT (.) unquote (.) arrange air passage and notify this H.Q. time of departure.'

This was the first intimation I received that I was to do the portrait of 'Monty', the Commander of the Eighth Army. He was at Vasto in Italy, at the time, at his advanced headquarters, eighty miles forward of Eighth Army Main Headquarters near Foggia on the east coast.

The flight from Tunis to Foggia, with a short stop at Malta, was uneventful. At Foggia, I was met by an A.D.C. in a jeep, and driven to Vasto through towns and villages bearing awesome evidence of the passage of the Eighth Army in its advance northwards. Mile after mile of cratered road was lined with abandoned trucks bull-dozed to the side and lying on their backs. An occasional German plane with broken wings and torn swastikas protruded from the mud in the fields. Trees had no branches.

As we approached our destination it became clear that General Montgomery's 'advanced headquarters' was indeed close to the firing lines, as it was reputed to be. The continuous rumbling of heavy guns grew louder and soon became punctured by intermittent bursts of automatic weapons. 'Warming up for the Sangro battle,' said my companion. I did not reply.

Suddenly the driver of the jeep turned down what was evidently once a winding lane, and braked in front of a farm house which miraculously seemed to have escaped the fate of all other buildings in the area.

Not having seen any sentries, or armed patrols, I was astounded to find myself face to face with the legendary 'Monty', immediately I entered the building.

His cold blue eyes were like gimlets, but his greeting was affable enough. 'You had better have something to eat' he said, 'before we discuss work.'

In the half-light of the passage in which we stood, I could see that Monty was dressed in a grey-pullover and wearing slacks. I was glad of his thoughtfulness over the matter of food, because not only was I feeling hungry after the long drive, but I was also cold. For the first time since I had been in the army, I seemed to be running a temperature.

An M.O. confirmed this, after I had had a quick meal. 'You've probably picked up a bug, somewhere,' he said. 'Bug or no bug,' I implored, 'get me fit again for tomorrow. *I have to do Monty's portrait.*'

The M.O. certainly tacked on to the urgency of the situation. I don't know what it was that he gave me, but it did the trick. I had an anxious night, full of visions of battered buildings and lorries lying on their backs like so many dead cockroaches, but I awoke feeling fighting fit.

'Thanks Doc', I said to the M.O. at breakfast. 'You don't know how much I owe you!'

Monty was now dressed in his battledress and wearing his famous beret with its two badges. 'You look cold,' he said. 'Feeling all right?' 'Yes, Sir,' I replied, 'never felt better.'

By the time my two hour sitting with Monty was half-way through, I could more truthfully say that I never felt better. In fact, I had completely shaken off the bug that had tried to sabotage my war effort.

Monty seemed very pleased with the study that I had made and suggested that one of his A.D.C.s should put on his battledress and beret to give me an opportunity of carrying the portrait to a greater degree of finish. He also asked me to do another portrait of him so that he could keep one of them if the other went to the Imperial War Museum.

But I had to tell the Army Commander that I had only been able to bring one sheet of paper with me . . . my last sheet of good paper.

This surprised and, I think, impressed him! 'So, you didn't anticipate failure in your first attempt?' he asked. 'No, Sir.' 'Good for you' he replied. 'I will get someone to fly over to Naples and bring back a fresh supply of paper; because I want you, not only to do my second portrait but also to go back to Eighth Army Main H.Q. and do the portraits of all my Division Commanders.'

In three days time, I was able to do my second portrait of Monty, on 'desert colour paper'. He signed and preserved this. After the war, I saw in a magazine, showing the interior of Monty's house, that he had placed it on a wall among other War mementos.

When the time came for me to leave Vasto, I asked Monty if I could send a teleprint to my long-suffering Colonel to tell him where I was.

'You are under my orders' was his curt reply.

The road journey back to Foggia was an unforgettable one, because the road was now teeming with trucks full of laughing, sun-tanned troops, heavy and light tanks, scout cars and ambulances, all going in the opposite direction to mine . . . re-inforcements moving up for the Sangro battle. Mile after mile stretched the huge convoy—each separate vehicle making its own kind of noise. There was the swish, swish, swish of the light cars passing me. Then came the clatter and rumble of the armoured divisions and guns, and finally the ominous silence of the ambulances.

The sounds of a powerful mechanised army on the move, heard against the background rumble of the guns, would have been too emotional an experience to withstand for long—but the mounting tension was fortunately relieved by the wit and laughter of the human element in the convoy.

'Hey! mate . . . you're going the wrong way!'

'Ever 'eard of the Eighth Army? We are it.'

'Forgotten something, 'ave you? See you later.'

One wag pointed to a lorry-load of Indian troops, evidently part of the 4th Indian Division — 'Them's not blacks! Them's white men browned off!'

A sobering thought was that so many of these laughing, jesting young men were going to their death.

But they knew that Monty was there, up in the front line, ahead of them, and Monty had led them all the way from Alamein. Victory was in the air.

As I said goodbye to the young A.D.C. on our arrival at Foggia, I asked him how it was that I saw no sentries at Monty's headquarters, so close to the fighting area.

'Sentries wouldn't be much use if you could see them,' he replied. 'They were there all right . . . Prowling sentries.'

At Eighth Army Main Headquarters, I had the honour of being accommodated in the fly-proof caravan once used by General Auchinleck. It had been brought all the way from Alamein as a memento of Monty's popular predecessor. If the 'Auk' couldn't be with his men in their triumphal advance from Alamein to Tunis and then through Sicily to Italy, at least his caravan could accompany them.

But it was not in the 'Auk's' caravan that I did the portraits of Monty's Chief-of-Staff — General de Guingand and the Division Commanders of the Eighth Army. Most of these sat for me in their own caravans or in the requisitioned buildings that served as their headquarters.

Outstanding among these brilliant leaders whom Monty had chosen to serve under him was General 'Freddie' de Guingand, his Chief of Staff. It was said that he was the military brain behind Monty's successes. My portrait of him (reproduced here) is said to be one of my best.

After the war General de Guingand wrote to me from South Africa asking if he might purchase the popular portrait which I had done of him. I could do no more than offer him a good reproduction, as the original, together with other portraits done at Eighth Army Main headquarters, was in the Imperial War Museum.

It was General de Guingand who got me to do the study of Sgt. Dickson — 'Old Bill of the Eighth Army'. This typical old soldier had fought under Wavell, O'Connor, Auchinleck and Monty, and had survived all the retreats as well as the advances.

At the conclusion of my three weeks stay at Eighth Army Main H.Q., I was flown back to my unit in La Marsa, near Tunis where my Colonel greeted me with the expected 'Sam, where the HELL have you been?!'

The flight to Africa in a D.C. 3 was this time not devoid of incident. While still in the 'fighter-zone', as it was called, a small plane was spotted rising from the ground, and climbing fast. The D.C. 3 was unarmed and flying at about twenty thousand feet, so perhaps I may be forgiven for thinking 'Well . . . this is it.'

But the imagined Messerschmidt turned out to be a sleek incredibly fast Spitfire. The pilot flew in from the rear and came up on the starboard side. He then dived and appeared again to port, evidently taking a good look at us, and flying alongside. The next moment he was waggling his wings in greeting and diving away out of sight into cloud-cover.

It didn't take much imagination to picture what would have happened if we had been a Heinkel bomber on the receiving end of a Spitfire attack. Perhaps the Spitfire pilot was one of those whose portraits are included in this book?

To my Colonel's greeting — 'Sam, where the HELL have you been' I could only reply — 'Sorry Sir, I was under Monty's orders!'

General Alexander

General Alexander, or 'Alex' as he was affectionately known throughout the army, was said to be the most gifted and the best loved commander of the British Forces.

I drew his portrait in Cassibile, Sicily, on the day that American and British armies entered Messina, after clearing the whole of Sicily of the German and Italian forces. The Army Commander is wearing an 'army issue' bush shirt on which is pinned the American Legion of Merit ribbon, awarded by the Americans in honour of the day.

Alex himself greeted me as I approached his tent, in front of which his batman had unrolled a stretch of artificial grass resembling an English lawn. He suggested immediately that I might like to have a swim with him in a nearby bay before beginning the portrait. The Sicilian temperatures had been in the nineties for several days.

Unfurling a small Union Jack on the bonnet of his jeep, he took the wheel and, unaccompanied by anyone else, he drove me to a small bay where we both donned borrowed bathing trunks and had a refreshing swim. A vivid memory of this swim was the re-appearance of the army commander's head after his preliminary 'ducking'. His wet hair streamed downward over a noble and most impressive forehead.

Alex had brought an army 'ablution bowl' with him in the jeep, and while using this bowl to wash the sand off his feet before putting on his socks, he pointed out to me the remains of several army gliders that had been released too soon during the recent amphibious invasion and now lay half-submerged and derelict two or three hundred yards from the beach.

We drove back to the H.Q., again unaccompanied by an escort, and I began the portrait immediately.

Conversation during the one-and-a-half hour sitting was largely about painting. No one would have thought that such an important event as the Allied conquest of Sicily had just been completed.

Although Alex himself did not refer to the fighting in Sicily at any time while I was at his H.Q., his Chief of Staff General Richardson gave me some first hand accounts of it. I was able to do one of my best portraits of this distinguished and popular soldier before I returned to my unit. He was to die of cancer soon after the end of the war.

It was at General Alexander's Mess that I heard two amusing stories about him, related to me by Colonel Douglas Scott, Military Secretary to the Army Commander and brother of the Duchess of Gloucester.

'Alex confided in me', said Colonel Douglas Scott, 'I have Montgomery on my right flank, and Patton on my left flank, both racing for Messina. Providence has placed a high range of mountains between them!'

DRAWN FROM LIFE, IN SICILY, ON THE
DAY ALLIED FORCES ENTERED MESSINA

DRAWN IN SICILY ON THE DAY
ALLIED FORCES ENTERED MESSINA (from life)

The second story shows the special relationship that General Alexander was privileged to share with the King.

On one of his periodic visits to the battle fronts, King George noticed that General Alexander looked unusually pre-occupied.

'Everything going all right, Alex?'

'Yes Sir. Everything is under control.'

'Come, come, Alex . . . what's worrying you? You know you can be frank with me.'

'Well Sir . . . It is this fellow Monty, Sir.'

'Monty?' said the King, 'What's the matter with Monty?'

'Well Sir . . . I think he is after my job.'

'Thank God for that', said the King, 'I thought he was after mine!'

History has confirmed that one of General Alexander's outstanding qualities was his ability to direct and control the able and sometimes fiery commanders who served under him, not grudging them the credit for winning campaigns for which he himself had had over-all responsibility.

His modesty, tact and consideration for others were very apparent to me while I was with him, and no artist could have had a more understanding sitter. In acknowledgement of the reproduction of his portrait which the R.A.F. had made for me on captured Luftwaffe paper, the Army Commander wrote me two pages in his own handwriting.

This letter was written during the anxious days of the Anzio landings and made my Colonel exclaim on reading it — 'What a man!'

R. D. Raikes

Battle of Salerno

(From a letter home to his father)

In one of your recent letters you expressed a desire to know something about the Battle of Salerno as I saw it. (What I saw of it—which wasn't an awful lot).

We didn't land with the first wave, in fact my troop and another of my battery were the last troops of the Regiment to land, with what is known as the 'first follow-up', on the evening of D+5. We had made the crossing from a port in N. Africa in landing-craft of a certain type, without incident, except that we were attacked once from the air—of course I would have to be Troops Watch Officer on the bridge at the time, but nothing came of it. We made a practically dryshod landing, which was very satisfactory, and went up off the beaches, knowing, of course, nothing at all of the situation. We eventually found our way to an orchard, 3 miles or so inland, in the small hours, where we lay up for the rest of the night, while the Bty. Cmdr. went for orders. He returned about dawn, and was able to tell us the situation. It was not until then that we realised that things had not gone quite according to plan, and we were able to set up our maps, and find out where we were, and where everybody else was. We discovered that we were some way S. of Salerno, about 3 miles inland at a spot where the beachhead was about 5 miles deep. The B.C. told us that he had been told for certain that we were not going into action, and in all probability would not move from our present location, for 3 days. You will readily understand that that appeared to us a certain indication of a move into the line in a matter of hours; and so, indeed, it turned out.

We got the order to move about 1100 hrs to a fresh harbour area, moving back onto the main road, turning right (i.e. north) through the towns of Pontaraquamo (of which you may have heard), on for a short way, and turning right again (i.e. East) up a valley. It was understood that we were to take up positions somewhere in this valley, and after a short time I received a 'flap order' to recce and get the guns into position within half an hour. This would be rather a tall order in most circumstances, but here siting was very easy, and I was well within my time limit. To get a *very* rough picture of this valley, imagine the road going up towards Bulch from Frickhowell. Put Half-Way House about ¾ mile from the Road junction at the bottom of Bulch Hill (I've forgotten how far it is in actual fact). The hill on your left is higher and more rugged, and at the forward end there is a little knob with a castle on. The country is covered, except for the higher slopes of the hill on your right in vineyards and orange groves. The hill on the right is partly open and partly wooded. My guns were roughly in the area of Half-Way House, which might well have been a little Welsh farmhouse, whitewashed, with a few outhouses and a litlle farmyard—all, of course deserted. It was in one of these outhouses that I made my troop H.Q.

Well, as I say, I got the troop settled in, about 1300 hrs, and then went off to see what I could find out. The main discoveries I made were not particularly reassuring. Apparently this morning a recce patrol of light A.F.V.s[1] had gone on to the road junction, and turned left, (i.e. towards Llangynidr) and had stirred up a fair sized hornet's nest, with the result that, in the end, our chaps were pushed out of the castle, a very vital spot, and also off most of the hill on the left.

---

[1]Armoured Fighting Vehicles.

The Forward Localities of our chaps now was approx 300 yards ahead, but this was little more than a pleasant thought, as the Infantry Company concerned was down to 37 men all told. We had a few tanks 100 yds forward of Half-Way House—in fact it was from the Officer in one of these that I got my information. He also told me that somewhere around the Bosche had 40 tanks, and anything up to 1,000 infantry, ready for an attack. I had been aware of this already—in fact it was in preparation for this that I had come up. Had they put in that attack in full strength, I don't know what would have happened, and one doesn't like to think. This Tank Officer pointed out to me a cloud of dust on top of Bulch Hill, in which I could just distinguish about half a dozen Bosche tanks having a sort of private rodeo, and after some time they began to go down the hill. They were out of range, but it did look as if we were going to get our chance. However, they went down to Llangynidr, and I later gathered that they were suitably dealt with. It was a disappointment, but we certainly weren't getting bored. There was a good deal of stuff flying about in both directions, and I returned to the troop to see how they were getting on in the way of digging slit-trenches and other vital activities. All were doing well, full of the 'one that landed over there', and in excellent form. There were the usual rumours of enemy patrols and 'infiltration', and the chaps in front of us in the vineyards were firing Brens intermittently, but nothing particular materialised that day. About evening, I began to be slightly worried—the infantry in front of us were little more than a token, and did not seem to be getting reinforced which suggested that, if anything, as they say, 'developed' during the night, it might be a bit awkward.

I was hardly reassured when the handful of infantry that were still in front of me moved about 400 yards to the right. The fact that their new positions were tactically sounder was cold comfort. However, at dusk, I was delighted to see a few Armoured Cars of the Recce Regiment, roll up and park in the grove a short way behind us, and their occupants dismount, and still more to see that their officer was an old friend of mine, Monckton, whom I had known well. His boys had come to act as infantry in our area, which was a great relief.

It was a night of continued alarms and excursions, of periods of intense quiet, when there mightn't have been a soul for miles, and then someone would send up a Verey light, or let off a Tommy-gun for no particular reason, and every firearm in the valley would open up, the tracer would fly across from one side to the other. Monckton's boys and mine would loose off with no particular object in view, with the rather vague intention of giving the impression that there were more of us than was the case. I don't for a minute believe it would have mattered anyway, but at the time it seemed rather a good idea. A house a bit to the right of us was set on fire but otherwise no damage was done. As far as I can make out, there were in fact no patrol or any other activity of any kind on foot the whole night and all this random and extremely nerve-racking firing was chiefly the result of nervous tension on both sides. Monckton and I spent most of the night in my troop H.Q., where, since it was completely under cover, my batman was able to brew tea practically continuously, or else we would wander up and down his little sector, and occasionally go into my 'O.P.'[2]. A word about my 'O.P.'. This consisted of an outside staircase of brick on the forward wall of Half-Way House, with a good solid brick balustrade, about 2 feet high. One could get up the staircase, either sit on the 'landing' and look over the top of the balustrade, or sit on the stairs and look round it. In any case, the view was excellent, and the brick was proof against most things.

The night, surprisingly enough, did not last for ever, the light of the waning moon gave place to a glimmer from the East, and we were treated to the most wonderful sunrise I have ever seen. The next few hours were very peaceful and in fact nothing happened at all till mid-day, and most of us were able to get a bit of sleep. Monckton and his boys, after a bit of sleep, got back into their recce cars, preparatory to resuming their normal role, so I was deprived of his support, but some of the infantry began to spread out a bit round us, and my friend with the Shermans was once more a few yards up the road, so things weren't too bad. About noon some rounds of mortar fell in the neighbourhood of the house, and it occurred to me at the time that he might be registering, but for various reasons, which I still consider adequate, I did not move T.H.Q.

About 1400 hrs, the fun started once more. It lasted about 3 or 4 hours, and during the whole I don't think anybody had the faintest idea what was happening.

All we could make out from various sources were that a fair number of small parties of Bosche were trying to infiltrate down the valley. Bear in mind that because of the vineyards and oranges, our maximum vision at ground level was about 100 yds. You could look through the stalks of the vines, and the stakes which supported them, and it was like looking through a wood of saplings or young birches in England. You know how it is, you see a bit of movement between the trees, but you have no means of telling how far away it was, or even in which direction it was going. Well it was rather like that here. So that whenever anybody saw anything they would open up and the chap next door would say 'What the hell are you firing at?' and the answer would be 'I thought I saw something over there'.

Before leaving Africa I had issued myself with a Tommy-gun (the distribution of arms to members of the troop, within the allotted scale, is at the discretion of the Troop Commander) and I had a lot of fun with it, but I shall never know if I did any good. I spent most of the time in the 'O.P.' where the view of the immediate neighbourhood, being from above looking down

---

[2]Observation Post.

through the vines, was no better than from the ground, but we had a good view of the general scene, and the road. The Bosche was supporting his little attack with heavy but very inaccurate M.G. fire, and there was a continual 'pewt-pewt-pewt' over our heads, and an occasional 'ping-ping-ping' on the wall behind me. He was also sending over plenty of mortar bombs, etc., though none very near the house.

People were, of course, firing all over the place, all the time, but we were occasionally able to make out that the main activity was a few hundred yards to our right front.

Then it moved to our right flank, then to our right rear, and then it all seemed to be right behind us. This was rather disconcerting, but each time we began to feel certain we must be cut off and surrounded, some D.R. jeep[3], or armoured car would arrive up the road on his lawful business and indicate that the road was still open. One of my chaps got a bit of mortar in the boo-hoo. Everyone thought this was the funniest thing in the world, including the chap himself—because it so happened that he was the sort of fellow to whom a bit of shrapnel in the boo-hoo *would* be the funniest thing in the world. We bundled him, amid hosts of merriment, upside down into a jeep that happened to be about the place, and packed him off. I must say, en passant, that I was very grateful all the time I was there for the fact that my guns were all within an exceptionally small area, so it was not hard to keep an eye on them.

On several occasions during that afternoon our Colonel came up the road on a motor bike to see how we were getting on. He was very cheeful and of course his presence went down very well with the men, because it was not everybody who would have taken a ride up that road on a bike that afternoon when they didn't have to. He spent quite a lot of time in the O.P., having the time of his life (as, indeed we all were).

All this went on, as I say, for several hours, with an unceasing concerto of Bren, Tommy-gun, Spandau, but it began to grow less about 1630 or so, and finally died away completely about 1800. This, I gathered, was largely due to the counter-attack which had been put in from the other side of the hill on our left, and drove the Bosche once more out of the castle.

We had, it is true, heard a good deal of noise from up there during the afternoon, complete with a fairly heavy artillery concentration, but hadn't paid much attention to it.
P.S. Incidentally, on speaking afterwards to others who were on the hill on the right that p.m., I gather that they had quite given us up for good.

The Infantry established themselves a little way ahead of us, so we weren't in

---

[3]Dispatch Rider Jeep.

quite so exposed a position as we had been the previous night. The night itself was very similar to the previous one, only slightly more so. I took the opportunity to shift one of my guns which, to judge by the unwelcome attention it had come in for just before sunset, I imagined must have been spotted. As it turned out, it was just as well I did. I was up all the night, so was nearly everybody, but, as I say, it was like the previous one—plenty of noise, but nothing more. Came, at last, the dawn. After it was fully light, I got down to a short sleep, till breakfast was ready, but was disturbed by my Battery Commander, whom I hadn't seen for 24 hours, he having been extremely busy since then elsewhere. He stayed for a cup of tea and a chat, and pushed off. We had breakfast about 0700 hours, after which, I began to notice signs of something brewing up on the hill on the right. I knew one of our other troops was up there, so I was naturally interested in what was going on, so I went into the farmyard, from which I could get a good view (the O.P. not being any good except for looking to the front). There was certainly a lot going on on the right hand hillside.

I saw quite a number of Bosche advancing along the slope, and coming under very heavy fire. They tried to put down smoke, but the wind was wrong, and they were sending over a lot of mortar and Arty shells. They didn't seem to be making much headway, and had mostly gone to ground,—remember I said that the hillside was partly open and partly wooded? Well, they seemed to be lying low near one of the edges of the woods, and were drawing a lot of M.G. fire. I was absolutely fascinated by all this, and was watching intently through my field glasses, kneeling on one knee by the farmyard fence, when all of a sudden somebody lifted me up and threw me about 3 yards backwards, at the same time giving me a colossal clout on the right hand with a two-foot ruler, and being extremely noisy about the whole business. More indignant than hurt, I looked round, a trifle dazed to see who had perpetrated this outrage, and could only see a large hole in the ground a few yards away. I then realised that there were others dropping in the neighbourhood, so I got into the hole. It was then that I realised there was a certain amount of good Raike's blood about the place, and also that my right hand was not behaving as it should. When things quietened down, I got out of my hole, and walked gingerly back to my T.H.Q., where I found my batman extremely distressed, he seemed to think (a) that I had about 5 minutes to live, and (b) that it was all his fault and started fussing around with field dressings etc., for all he was worth. He soon fixed me up, and using my field glasses as a sling, I took a quick look round, gave a few instructions to my Troop Sgt., summoned my driver, and set off back to the R.A.P. (Regimental Aid Post) where the M.O. bandaged me up proper, gave me some hitherto unsuspected 3-star French brandy, and took me down to the nearest Main Dressing Station.

Here I sat in a tent till I went in and had the hand tidied up, and redressed.

They were not particularly busy there, and there was an extremely nice M.O. who was a pipe smoker. At my request he fished my pipe and baccy out of my right-hand trouser pocket, and filled the pipe. This was the last time I had anything in that pocket for 3 months. It was the only time I have ever had someone else fill my pipe for me—I managed left-handed after that. I stayed there till there was an ambulance going to the Casualty Clearing Station, which was merely another M.D.S. being used as a C.C.S., there being no C.C.S.'s functioning at that time. When I got to the C.C.S., the first person I saw there was Monckton, who had been hit in the leg that morning.

I saw the reception officer who immediately said 'Evacuate', and wrote 'EVAC' on my card, and I was taken off to a part of the orchard roped off for those awaiting evacuation; Monckton was there, and about a dozen other officers including 2 Germans, and a lot of other ranks. They gave us stretchers to lie on, and blankets and pillows, but it was very hot, and there wasn't much shade. A C.C.S. on a beach-head is not a very pleasant place, and we were all disappointed when we were told that there wouldn't be a hospital ship in that day, and we would have to wait 24 hours. I didn't enjoy those 24 hours, and I was one of the more fortunate ones. The serious cases were kept away in a tent; in our compound were those who would not need immediate attention. They gave me a spot of morphia, but I didn't feel like sleeping, nor eating, for that matter—it was just as well I had had my breakfast, as I had nothing else till I got onto the hospital ship.

Michael Melford came and saw me in the afternoon, and brought my washing things and writing case in a haversack. Otherwise, I had only what I was wearing—i.e. 1 shirt tropical, 1 pr trousers long tropical, 1 cap S.D.[4], 1 pr boots and gaiters. I had a restless night, and about 1000 hrs the following morning (18.9.43) we went off in ambulances to the beach where we got onto a landing craft and were taken out to the Hospital ship. So ended my 60-hour Italian tour.

Well, it's been an awful long tale in the telling and I don't know if it interests you at all. It has been quite fun writing it, anyway. Your impressions of it will probably be
(i)   That at most times I had not the foggiest idea what it was all about
(ii) That if I had, there was nothing much to do about it
(iii) That I was lucky to get away as I did.
All three are quite true.
P.S.   Please bear in mind that where I was it was only a very minor section of the beach-head. The main fighting was going on elsewhere—at Vietri, at Salerno itself, at Battipaglia, etc. Our little valley was only a sideshow.

---

[4]Service Dress.

Henry Reed

The Place and the Person

The place not worth describing, but like every empty place.
So much like other empty places, you yourself
Must paint its picture, who have your own such places,
Which lie, their whitening eyes turned upwards to the sky,
On the remoter side of a continent,
Under a burning sun. Their streets and hovels
Have lost all memory, and their harbours rot.
Paint it, and vary it as you like, but only
Always paint this: the solitary figure,
Who lies or squats or sits, facing the sun,
Now in bewilderment or a vacant calm,
In filthy rags, the ancient garb of exiles,
The casual mixture of others' memories,
Legacy or theft; and the mind perplexed and eroded.
In such a one, at the edge of his world, desire
Is buried or burned in lust, and love is banished
Beyond the creeping jungle; in the noontime heat,
Since even these can be lost, they are far away.
You will know all this, and can paint it as suits you best,
But paint alone the central figure faithfully;
His surroundings do not matter: they are yours or mine,
The walls perhaps with greying notices
Of the bygone sales of heifers, or the concourse
Of a troupe of vanished singers, singing there,
The carrion birds shuffling upon the roof,
The empty expanse of ocean confronting him,
The harbour steps, the empty sands below,
And the movement of water on the harbour bar.
And from the emptiness, still mute but moving,
Emerge the dancers who will not be still.
Nearest at hand two scuffling figures, who
Saunter a little and scuffle again and dance,
Or lie on the paving-stones and yawn at each other,
A daily ritual; if not with them, with others.
This is a dance, with ritual and celebration.
Others join in its windings as the day
Passes through noon and afternoon and evening
And wave on wave of heat and sunlight fall,

Illuminating and transfixing, and at last
The dreadful pattern of their lives disclosing.
From out of rocks and paths they come, the dancers:
One who walks solitary and shuns the gaze
Of the scuffling pair, now languid in the heat,
Until, withdrawn, he looks about and secretly
Seizing a dead shark's jawbone out of air,
Makes it a trap with stones and vegetation
For yet another who walks on the level beaches.
They congregate, beseeching or resentful,
Till the empty place is crowded with silent ghosts.
They are intangible, but he is one with them,
As with their proud, vindictive admonitions,
And sensual taunts, and gestures of possession,
They separate, part, return, link arms again,
Familiarly, yet not with reconcilement.
And, one with them, he cannot turn away,
Or forget in the motions of song and prayer and dance
The great dried fountains of their sombre eyes.

Fed on such visions, how shall a man recover
Between the dancing dream and the dream of departure?
For the dancers go, and their silent song and prayer
Go with them; and the ship goes from the harbour,
Vanishes in sea, or drowns in air, but goes.
The waves of noon can barely reach the shore,
And the jungle approaches always a little nearer.
This is the captive. And paint him as you will.
These are my images. The place not worth describing.

J. H. Rehill

An Account of the Landing at Salerno

When I landed on the beach at Salerno on the morning of September 9th 1943, quite apart from the danger and the hectic atmosphere, I was still asking myself how I ever got myself into this situation. Only a few days earlier I had been quietly and quite happily rotting away in an ammunition depot in Benghazi. A month earlier shortly after returning from a week's leave in Alexandria I had been told that my application to join the Parachute Regt. was being considered and I was called for Medical Examination and Interview. I had been accepted and then awaited posting.

Four days later the Major confronted me. I was burnt black from days in an open lorry up and down from Benghazi to Tobruk. 'I had you brought back,' and repeated! 'I had you brought back—it has been a mistake—*you cannot* transfer from the R.A.O.C.[1], you are an army tradesman! I'm afraid that you must regard it as one of those things and forget about it!'

However, only days after this interview with my O.C. when he appeared to have squashed any last attempts to get into a front-line Unit, I was called into his office and asked 'Do you still long to get in among the shot and shell?' When I agreed he told me to pack my kit and report to R.A.F. Benghazi on the following morning to join a Beach Group. Two privates were to join me. Why these two were chosen I do not know—they were subsequently court-martialled in Anzio after being A.W.O.L. for some hours—but they agreed to go. We flew in an overcrowded Dakota and landed at Tripoli (Bennina Airport). We proceeded to the A.A.D (Advanced Ammo Depot) where we collected two more R.A.O.C. privates and a W.O.II, a regular soldier. I had a vague idea that we would join the Beach Group and undergo some training but that night we went to a staging area near the water-front and joined a motley throng of people in a field. They were checking equipment—drivers were checking the water-proofing on their vehicles. I was shattered. I asked what we were all doing there. A cheerful Sapper replied—'We're all going on a landing—embarking tomorrow—dunno where—maybe—Yugoslavia—somewhere?'

Early next afternoon we joined a massive queue on the jetty—out in the bay landing craft of all sizes and shapes swayed on the gentle swell.

On board the Landing Ship Tank the upper deck was packed with various troops and lorries and some Bofors Guns and half of the unit I was joining. The Ordnance Bench detachment consisted of Stores and Ammo. Half of the unit was on this craft the other half on another L.S.T. Everyone was in high spirits there were R.A.O.C., R.A.S.C.[2], R.E.[3]s, Royal Artillery Light Ack Ack and a number of American C.B.[4]s with their DUKW[5]s. The DUKWs were stowed in the large hold and would be launched from the bows of the LST when we were some two miles from the beach. I met my new comrades. They were a Beach

---

[1]Royal Army Ordinance Corps.
[2]Royal Army Service Corps.
[3]Royal Engineers.
[4]American assault engineers.
[5]Amphibious craft.

detachment all had served considerable time in Corsham Base Ammo Depot and had then transferred to the Beach Group. They had spent much time on exercises in Scotland (Beith) climbing cliffs, marching, battle exercises etc. They had come out from England at the same time as the Canadians 1st Div for the Sicily landing. They had landed near Pachino, Gulf of Noto—the landing had been easy the Infantry advancing far ahead in a few hours. They had little trouble and were very, very confident. They regarded me with some mixture of pity and a little contempt. After Sicily they had gone over to Sfax and from thence to Tripoli. All this excitement and travel had done wonders for their collective ego. They had various items of equipment issued to Combined Ops troops like water-proof gas-masks etc. They asked me how long I had been abroad and when I replied two and a half years one said, 'We've only been out 7 weeks but we've seen more in that time than a lot of people who have been out a long time!' The old, old army game of 'getting one's knees brown'.

While we lay at anchor waiting for the convoy to assemble we lazed about or swam from the side of the LST climbing a net to return. But within a day we set off. Only a hour or so out and still with land in sight the O.C. Stores section, Capt. Woodbine, assembled us in a hot sweaty cabin—there was scarcely room for us all. There on a board was a map of Southern Italy. He got down to business right away after the usual 'Can you all hear me?' We were off to Italy to a place 'here—h'm called Salerno—it is near Naples—we will be part of a force with the American 5th Army—the General is Mark Clark—we will be in support of the 56th British Division and I understand they insist on being called '56th LONDON Division—their badge is a black cat.' He fumbled in a large envelope marked 'Most Secret' and produced a string of photos—like large postcards. These showed a beach taken at low height—about thirty feet—a low flying aeroplane? There was a sort of Martello Tower and the mouth of a small river—there were also low sand dunes and the beach was quite narrow. Some of the ribald characters quickly noticed that a couple had somehow been photographed at the same time and speculated enthusiastically on the fellow's chances. There were also aerial pictures of the landing area over-marked with lines and notes. 'H' hour would be 3.30 on morning of Sept 9th, some Commandos would go in early towards Salerno also U.S. Rangers—with the first Infantry would be 'some unfortunate pioneers' whose job it would be to lay Somerfeld tracking (a sort of wire mesh to bind soft sand into some sort of track). Our immediate objective was this town here at the cross-roads 'Battipaglia'—so we land in between the tower and the river and set up the dump in the fields of the beach! The Captain glibly used some terms familiar to those specialising in sea-borne landings while the men listened with complete understanding. But all this left me feeling more bewildered than ever.

We filed out on deck and I sat eavesdropping on a typical American College Boy Officer complete with square rimless glasses who was giving a brief talk on first-aid and resuscitation to his men who sprawled casually on the deck. Then he got on to the problem of the tyres on the DUKWs—apparently on the Sicily landing the over-inflated tyres caused the craft to bounce and ride high on the water—'If we sink we're no good to the British or to ourselves—let's go down now and let those tyres down!' One of his men remarked 'If you do that you'll just cut them "toobs"'. 'You'll do WHAT!' snapped the Officer. Another man suggested going down at 'H' hour minus two and letting the tyres down using a pencil torch in the blackness.

What they finally did I will never know. I saw them on the morning of the landing launching off the open bows of our L.S.T. setting out bravely for the beach.

On the evening of the 8th Sept we passed a fiery volcano flaring in the dusk possibly Stromboli—the darkness fell and suddenly cheers rang out around the convoy—the news spread 'Italy had surrendered'. There was a surge of euphoria. Men talked wildly of what they would do in Naples.

Now I am a pessimist. I had a sense of foreboding—it surely couldn't be so easy, there must be a catch somewhere—all these rejoicings could be as ashes tomorrow.

Many of the troops on the L.S.T. had had a fairly easy time in Sicily—certainly the Beach group had. For many it had been their first time in action and now they had a concept of a landing where the Infantry swept inland and everything went smoothly—they had great confidence—'This landing will be easy—each landing would be easier than the last one!' Now this surrender news must have pushed them further into this frame of mind.

An hour later there was an air raid on the far side of the convoy. Booms and flashes—the steady dum-dum-dum of Bofors and Pom-poms and the strange laziness of the stream of tracer curling into the night sky.

This should have sobered them—but it did not. Early next morning we woke from a fitful doze. It was still almost dark. I could just make out some very high mountains—they looked blue-black and very near. There were bangs and dull flashes and crackling of small arms a long way off. I was still dozy and half awake and felt I must be dreaming. We stood to in full marching order—as it grew lighter we could see the long sweep of the shore. There was smoke everywhere; some was from smoke pots but I could see craft burning also. A young sailor was going around the deck with an old English newspaper, he had folded it to an article on health with the headline 'How are your nerves?' Nobody was very amused. Shells started to pass on both sides of the L.S.T.—the sea was filled with scurrying craft. A cruiser fired all her guns on our left and a rocket-firing LCT loosed off a woosh of rockets. All the craft proceeded steadily to the beach. Our DUKWs took off with hearty cheers from all aboard—over on the American beach things looked very confused. Landing craft appeared to be milling around—there was much smoke and quite a lot of burning·craft—already it was quite obvious that the landing was very much opposed. I did not feel very happy—the troops taking part on this landing were not the hardened veterans of the Eighth Army—some like 46th Div had fought in the Tunisian campaign, some troops had been in Sicily only. The 56th Division as far as I knew had been in Iraq and in a holding position in the Mareth Line—only a small number of 7th Armoured would land early, the rest almost a week later. A single plane flew over the fleet. Everybody opened up and the sky darkened with bursting ack-ack shells. The Bofors on our deck appeared to hit the plane one could see the path of the tracers going straight on target and their Officer cried out 'Hey!' in his excitment. But the 'plane turned to show R.A.F. roundels—how we failed to bring one of our own planes down I do not know—there were hundreds of bursts all over the sky.

We neared the beach. There were L.S.T.s and L.T.C.s along the entire length. Men stumbled on the soft sand. There was a great number sitting on the edge of the dunes. I tried to make out what they were doing there. Early wounded awaiting evacuation; people who had lost their units; some German prisoners. Some German wounded. There was one badly wounded German being tended to by two R.A.M.C. men. One man I remember seeing was a Dental Corps Officer sitting looking completely lost.

From the deck of the L.S.T. one could see quite a long way. There was the narrow beach and the sand dunes beyond these some sandy fields and orchards. Lanes and a narrow metalled road. Beyond the beach a mile away could be seen the dotted figures of the Infantry. Almost on the beach—just beyond the sand dunes there was a 25 pdr battery in action I could hear the Battery commander calling out the ranges—overhead there was the angry distant zoom and rattle of aerial dog-fights—we were using P40 Lightnings—they had two fuselages and carried extra fuel tanks. German ack-ack—4 Cm dotted the sky with their closely grouped four bursts. There were long loose white tapes marking the swept area of the beach but sappers were still sweeping—a Bofors gun was sticking in the sand. We lined up to go down the steel steps to the ramp now out. I remarked to the Captain that the ack-ack was German—'Don't be a bloody fool' he snapped, then when I told him that I had seen it before he said after thought 'I believe you're right'. We got onto the beach. There was a dead sailor lying there with his rifle stuck in the sand by the bayonet. There were some other inert forms. One of our number stared in horror while another taking a more realistic view remarked that it wasn't a picnic. We had a small handcart with stores which we pulled up the beach with great difficulty. Around us vehicles revved and slithered. There was a huge, burly Beachmaster (Naval). He was fierce and bearded. He was holding a dog on a leash with one hand and a stick or cane in the other. He roared all about almost blasting stuck vehicles with his voice. One got the instant impression that he owned the beach and was chasing everybody else from it.

As we were leaving the beach I heard a noise behind. There was a huge Basuto Pioneer with two comrades on either side of him. He had lost his nerve which wasn't surprising—there was much noise of explosions and small arms and the air battle overhead. The Basuto was trying to stay on the ramp of the L.S.T. and shouting 'No! No!' digging his heels in. A rather elderly British Major apparently their O.C. went back to urge him off. We crossed the sand dunes and passed by the 25 pdrs. To my amazement one of the Officers with us remarked casually 'H'm! Practice camp!' I thought that he was surely joking—but he was not. There was no doubt they had a fixed idea that somehow it would be like Sicily again; that the real artillery was further inland and the infantry miles away. We made our way through an orchard filled with trees laden with red apples—there was, incredibly, a very old woman standing there nodding pleasantly—this was something we were to meet many times in Italy—the Italians somehow reasoned that they were no longer in the war so if they lived in a battle zone they wouldn't get killed because it was between the British and Americans and the Germans—this became even more evident in Anzio later. We turned up a metalled road and trooped into a field which had high edges and dry ditches all around. This field was on the left of the road which ran up to Battipaglia we spread out in some sort of defensive order. I had a bren gun in the top right hand corner where I could see up the road. The battle cracked and banged ahead from time to time, stray shots passed overhead. The other half of the Beach Detachment arrived to join us. They had been in the part of the convoy attacked by German planes the previous evening—one man on their craft had died of wounds. A sandy haired W.O. II walked about with a young lieutenant—he surveyed the field and I was amazed to hear him say 'This will do, I think—we'll have the Sergeants mess over there'. One would have thought that we were in an area miles behind the lines instead of a very shaky position indeed. Nothing much happened for an hour and we began to feel fairly confident. The 56th Division appeared to be making ground up the road. Soon the first ammo started to come up from the beach. It was mainly .303 rifle and some 75 mm H.E.[6] We started to make our dump on both sides of the road. For the first time in my career I met British Pioneers. Their purpose to supply labour. My stay in the U.K. after joining the army had been very brief—three months from joining up to overseas draft. In Africa I had seen only Swahili or Basuto or Mauritian Pioneers.

By early afternoon confidence was growing, a lively R.A.S.C. driver passed down the road with a captured German horse and cart (with balloon tyres) on seeing me he called 'Cab sir?' then added the punch line of a doubtful Music Hall joke about a persistent Edwardian Cabbie—'Horse an' all sir?'

---

[6]High Explosive.

I went up the road with the W.O. II who had joined us from Tripoli. He appeared to be surplus to establishment although a senior W.O. and they seemed to be at a loss to know what to do with him. We checked the supply of .303 ammo. There was renewed firing ahead and I could see infantry in action. Again stray shots passed over and what seemed like a mortar shell burst very near. I wondered how see-saw the battle was—the line had seemed further forward earlier in the day. Vehicles going up and down the road did so at full speed. All day the 25 pdrs almost on the beach kept up a ceaseless barrage—it was a very hot day and I remember at this point filling my water bottle with water from a ditch and putting in the tablets provided to sterilise it—somehow at that moment the fear of getting typhoid seemed not as bad as getting suddenly obliterated by one of the shells exploding in various places.

By early evening we went back to the bivouac area in the field. Our cook had made a makeshift meal and we ate sheltering in a shallow ditch with the continuous noise of battle all around. The O.C. of the beach detachment came up to give us the latest picture from H.Q. Beach Group. Things were going well: the 56th had captured the small town of Battipaglia; we hoped also to take Montecorvino airfield on our left; R.A.F. and R.E.s would be making a landing strip for fighters to land and refuel. We were consolidating the bridgehead. Also the Eighth Army were making good progress from the south and were hurrying to link up with us—much more ammo would be coming up from the beach we must work without respite.

The W.O. then divided us up into three groups to stand to in shifts, two groups resting while one was on duty—the former to be ready for instant call if needed.

I was now beginning to see what the work of an Ordnance Beach Detachment entailed. The ammo was placed around the edges of fields in small stacks of about 2½ tons. It should be noted that British ammo like 25 pdr and Medium Artillery was very stable and a shell landing on a small stack might scatter it without actually exploding it. Cordite was an entirely different matter. It would burn with a terrible swiftness, the heat sufficient to incinerate anyone even 30 yards away—yet even there I have seen a single box ignite blowing the lid off without setting fire to the rest of the stack. P.I.A.T.[7] ammo could go up with total devastation. (I was later, in Anzio, to see an entire stack go from a single shell.) It will be realised that without any plan ammo could be dumped anywhere and total confusion result. Even with a careful plan of the area things could go wrong if somebody panicked and dumped a mixed load anywhere. Some ammo came ashore in American DUKWs. These often loaded out to sea and then 'swam' ashore. For those of us who had revelled in the wide

---

[7] Anti-tank.

open spaces of the Desert, the narrow lanes of Europe suddenly presented us with problems not encountered before. A DUKW is quite a clumsy vehicle especially in narrow lanes. They had high sides. To unload one was quite a physical feat. A box containing two complete rounds of 3.7 A.A.[8] weighed 118 lbs; a box of 25 pdr shell (×4) 120 lbs; loose shells for 5.5 Medium Guns weighed 100 lbs each—they were difficult to hold especially when wet; they were also difficult to stack—and loose in a lorry they would roll all over the place. The copper driving band on these was protected by a rope 'grummet'—so often these were missing and the soft copper designed to give spin to the shell when fired was often damaged.

That first night we dozed fitfully despite the crescendo of guns. Next day some R.A.F. 'Commandos' arrived—it said 'Commando' on the side of their lorry. A farm building was blown up and with R.E.s they made a landing strip about a mile from the beach.

As is well know people in action have very little idea of the general situation; they see only their immediate area and in the absence of true information rumours abound. Most of our 'news' came from 56th Div, 201 Guards, R.E.s etc, who came to draw ammo on that second day. There was a distinct pessimism the battle was not going well. One man said the Germans were using flame-throwers. Another from 56th Div said that they were placing captured British soldiers on the front of their tanks—the truth of this I will never know. The British Forces at Salerno were 46th Div and 56th Div with 201 Guards Brigade and Corps troops. Of these 201 Guards were the élite unit. None of them had the longer experience of the Eighth Army veterans. I found that very quickly people were beginning to ask how far away the Eighth Army were and they would look to the mountains on their left as if they expected to see them suddenly appear.

About mid-day on Sept 13th things seemed to get much worse; shelling was very heavy and there were many sudden low flying air-raids. Units came in, in great haste for ammo—gloom and doom in the air—talk among the more dispirited was that 'we had had it here!' As that afternoon wore on things got much worse with much hurrying to and fro of lorries and staff cars. I was checking 75 mm H.E. with an Irish Pioneer. About 5.0 p.m. a bren gun carrier went by swaying dangerously with men clinging all over it: down the road it went out of control and lurched into a ditch—then came a group of men running wildly. The Pioneer asked 'Where are all these fellers goin'?' Stupidly and fearing the worst I said perhaps they had been relieved—he replied 'Why are they in such a bloody hurry?'

We stepped out onto the road. A lorry sped by loaded with men— one of

---

[8] Anti-aircraft.

them fired a pistol in the general direction of the beach where there was a wavering curtain of flashes from the never-ending 25 pdr barrage. More running men followed and we were brushed aside as we tried to stop them. Although they were now well into the rear area they ran crouching and dodging. Bits of twig and stones blown by the artillery fell about them. I tried to tell them this was British Artillery but one called, wildly 'Don't listen to him, Charlie!' Finally we stopped one of them. He was haggard, dishevelled and sweat-soaked. He grabbed my water bottle and gulped it all greedily. 'Where are youse fellers going' asked the Pioneer. 'We're in full retreat!' he gasped. 'It's bloody murder up there—we've bloody had it!' He ran on after the others toward the beach.

We decided to follow instructions issued earlier to report to 'assembly area'. This was in our field by the orchard. A shell had just exploded and the air was hazy with smoke in the gathering gloom—a young Officer stood with arms akimbo staring ahead. I asked if this was the assembly area: without moving he said in a flat voice 'This *is* the assembly area'.

Growing panic and confusion on all sides; I saw a fire-eating Staff-sergeant—I remember him from the boat—'you play ball with me and I'll play ball with you!'—he was huffing and puffing as he inflated his lifebelt. He must have kept this since we had landed 4 days earlier! He was gasping something about 'the beach!' and 'being used as bloody Infantry!'

I moved over to find the W.O. II. I found him issuing S.T. Grenades to an R.S.M. Coldstreams from 201 Guards. The R.S.M. was not a young man; he looked well over 40 but there was nothing wrong with his military bearing.

I gasped out my story of the Infantry in full flight, the R.S.M. snorted 'Full!—full retreat—rubbish!'—'The boys are fighting—very hard—very hard!—retreat—rubbish!' Fearing that I would be charged with spreading alarm and despondency I repeated my story carefully. The R.S.M. looked fiercely disbelieving and left to rejoin his men. When the battle at Salerno was finally won I believe the 201 Guards Bde played the key part. One of the Coldstream's C.S.M.s was awarded a D.C.M. which at the request of King George VI was raised to the Victoria Cross—his Majesty had been so impressed when reading the citation.

We assembled and were told that the line had broken, we would be taking up a position as infantry. A few moments before that I had felt as low as could be—it seemed for a brief period that everything was lost. But, although scared, it was a great relief to be doing something positive. We went up the road. Over on the right in the gloom I could make out the lines of a tank and I could hear the squealing noise that these vehicles make—it paused to fire and then swayed forward. It must have been a German tank because of the handful of Scots Greys Tanks ashore I had seen none in our area. We went up the road and a cheerful M.P. called 'Good luck' then he added with a hint of sarcasm 'Don't worry, the

Yanks are bringing a combat team up here—' he added more saracsticaslly 'A combat team!!' We entered a field which ended in a tobacco plantation and lay down with our rifles. From this position we could not be seen—we could not see anything either! One man remarked 'Well if Gerry comes he'll bloody well fall over us!' We lay there in a long line like something from the Alma or Waterloo. We were not strategically deployed. It seemed suddenly to go quiet. I wondered what the hell we would really do if some of the hard-bitten Germans showed up. Captain Thompson O.C. ammo section came up to boost morale. I told him that my rifle was sticking—the spring in the magazine was faulty. He remarked that it was a bit late in the day to report it and brought me a bren gun. He moved me forward to some sort of thatched shed and placed me by a corner of it. As I crouched there waiting I heard men marching in the field across the road. Then came the voice of an Officer—I say an Officer because as well as being a Military voice there was public school and Sandhurst all wrapped up in it. He was drilling these unseen men. 'Attention!—about—turn!' 'Forward—march!!' This went on for quite some time. I was afterwards told that he was a Senior Officer of the Scots Greys (I have no proof of this) drilling the rounded-up runaways I had seen earlier—before they went back into the line.

I lay there in the darkness waiting for something to happen. It was so quiet I began to fear that I had fallen asleep and was now quite alone, my comrades having withdrawn. Indeed, it seems impossible to believe that one could fall asleep standing up but when totally exhausted it is very possible.

I heard a footfall nearby and challenged. It was a British soldier probing from another position—it transpired that I WAS alone! When I explained to him that I was with these men—'here'—he assured me that I was the only one there. They had withdrawn quietly and had missed me.

I returned to the orchard to find them sleeping like dead men still holding their rifles.

Next day we were moved to another location over to the right and quite near to the disputed Montecorvino Airfield. We were placed in a field with banked ditches on three sides. There was another road which seemed to run roughly parallel to the road to Battipaglia it went over a humped bridge over a deep ravine with a shallow stream at the bottom. Up the road were three new graves on the verges—all men of the Queen's Own—one I noted was L/Cpl Tuck killed 9/9/43. They had been in a bren carrier hit by an 88 as they rounded the corner. I stood with an Indian soldier, one of the number sent to help as labour—the steel helmet of one of the fallen on his shallow grave badly ripped by the shell. The man's pay-book was underneath. The Indian soldier shook his head and regarded the general scene—'This war—no good, Sahib!' I believe he meant that the battle was going all wrong. We started to put ammo along this road which wound around at right angles and—somewhere it must have joined the road to Battipaglia. We camouflaged the stacks with tobacco leaves.

Back at the bivouac we received small two-man bivouac tents. These we pitched and borrowing a spade from a friendly farmer (his name was Giuseppe - Forte) we hollowed the insides and banked earth around them.

Across the road was a battery of 3.7 A.A. guns manned by coloured soldiers and since there were many air-raids one could hear them calling out ranges etc in the typical accents. There was always plenty of that stuff called 'window', I believe, strips of tin foil designed to jam RADAR. It must have been dropped by Germans in high level raids on the shipping.

Our new position was rather further forward than the previous one and Montecorvino airfield was clearly in view. On the morning of the 15th some fighter bombers—they looked like Lightning P40—three in number swooped over the airfield and dropped small calibre bombs—it seemed quite mad—I was convinced that we held it but I could see no personnel—the planes dropped their bombs by a small hangar and made off. I was sure that it had been bombed in error and it was typical of the bewildering confusion in such a confused battle. About this time the massed B25 USAAF bombers started to attack Battipaglia—it was rather like pre Alamein when our army was reeling but the Desert Force was intact and deadly. Also the heavy guns of the Warspite and others plastered the small town.

On the night of the 15th there was a steady stream of 'planes going over and flares started to fall over the mountains. This was the men of the U.S. 82 Airborne over Avellino.

On the 17th the bulk of the Armour of 7th Armoured started to come ashore. The shelling that day was intense. Shells seemed to slither and whine everywhere. And now, away from the noise of the 25 pdrs we could hear the moaning noise of our own heavy 16 inch naval shells—'like a freight car' as one American C.B. put it. It was a mad, mad day. One of our number was killed in the bivouac by an airburst. I remember fragments of earth showering over me as a real shell burst nearby. I paused by the Italian farmhouse where a shell had burst smothering the farmyard with smoke. At the same time a crowd of shabby baggy-trousered Italian soldiers appeared scrambling wildly over the banks. There were crowds of them—I well remember how some of them were quite old—with premature bald heads—they were badly frightened—somehow they had got through the German lines on the road from Naples through Pontecagnano—some of them actually dragged suitcases—they drank water from the farmers' bucket and from what they said they had come from Naples and were heading home to Reggio di Calabria in the deep South. One very young man had written on his cap in marking ink 'Ritornero, Mamma!' 'Come é vero'[9]. I remarked—I was rather puzzled by the mass of fleeing Italians—they

---

[9]'Will come back, Mother' 'How true!'

had no wish to fight—the Germans had disarmed them and then ignored them and they flooded home like a crowd from a football match. Yet a few days later, when we had returned to our old location some were brought in by M.P.s as prisoners and were made to work as labour moving the ammo. When I asked why, the M.P.s said that they had been still carrying arms when taken. Since many of them were local they were constantly escaping into the woods and scurrying home. Later that day I saw some of the 7th Armoured coming shore under very heavy shelling.

I was no admirer of Military Police but that day I saw one on duty just up from the beach moving traffic to clear a way for the tanks. In a very exposed spot he stood smart as paint in his Red-cap a model of discipline and quite ruthless efficiency—shouting, directing, threatening all sorts of dire punishment on those too slow to respond. With the tanks came some of the supporting troops.

How different they seemed from the battle-weary survivors of the past week, some of them came into our billet area—fresh and cheerful their casual dress bringing a nostalgic breath of the old Western Desert. They had all the confidence of the experienced craftsman soldier. Like any other job—the longer you do it the better you become—it was somehow like when you have been trying to fix the plumbing at home and a real plumber turns up.

People still looked for the 8th Army but things began to improve that day. The planes continued to plaster the Germans and one day I could see on a road on the rising ground above Montecorvino long lines of German transport, they were nose to tail and that distance—about 3 miles I could hardly make them out clearly but there they were moving very slowly. The mass of B25 Bombers pounded them without mercy—huge clouds of smoke engulfed the massive convoy but it went on looking from that distance like a very long crocodile which somehow kept going despite the bombing—although some vehicles burned and appeared to be pushed off the road the bulk of them went on and at that moment I could see that although we were going to survive and move out from the beach-head we had not stopped the enemy and trapped him in Southern Italy. I watched for a long time with a terrible fascination as this convoy moved on what must have been the thinnest of corridors taking a terrible pounding but somehow getting away.

The next day we moved back to the first location on the Battipaglia Road. The Germans pulled out of Battipaglia and shortly afterwards the lines of prisoners came down the road.

They were a terrible sight. There were not many of them and they reeled about drunkenly some laughed madly, some cried—it was very frightening to see men reduced to such a state. They had fought some 12 days in a terrible battle and had been shelled and bombed without mercy. Now they appeared totally broken men.

It was hard to believe that danger had passed. The whole force was moving

North. The next day a young Minister of the Church of Scotland held an impromptu service in our orchard. He spoke movingly of the dead. 'These young men who are now as if they had never been'—somehow this seemed just right—it had been a terrible battle—human life was very cheap. Later that day we went up the road to see the town that had cost so many lives—it was 90% destroyed, the bomb craters were so close together they overlapped each other and the ground looked like the leftover pastry after the baker had cut out the pastry with a ring. All about in fields and on the grass verges were shallow graves. I noticed also the extraordinary amount of paper lying about—letters and photographs—little religious cards in Italian—I picked one up it was a sort of Sunday school picture card of 'Gesu Bambino' with a little prayer on the reverse—there were scattered letters and photographs—very mixed —German, Italian—British—it was all very, very sad to see, the fond hopes of wives and sweethearts lying strewn like so much debris. Nearly a year later I went back to the new cemetery at Pontecagnano, sadly, to bury one of our number who had survived Salerno only to be killed accidentally. After the burial I walked around the masses of graves. Some of the names read like Debrett—the Duke of Wellington and many other titled names side by side with the working lads from London and the Home Counties.

They had come with high hopes of an easy battle; they had not all had long battle experience but they had given all that man could give. Not for them the sight of Naples and Capri so fondly imagined less than a day or so before they met their end. As time went by they would be slowly forgotten except by those whom they left behind and I would live to see the day when I would hear a young man say—'The War? It was all a long time ago!'

FOOTNOTE: Reading these notes over I reflect, with some regret, that basically I remained a 'base wallah' for the rest of my service even though I landed at Anzio on 'D' day and later at Megara while the Germans were still in Athens and went through the Greek Civil War. I remained firmly shackled to the R.A.O.C. At Salerno our brief spell as 'infantry' lasted about 5 hours. Summing up our contribution to the operation we probably did a reasonable job—no more. Yet, some 10 days after most of the troops had left the beach area our O.C. told us that the O.B.D. had been mentioned in despatches and that 13 individual mentions had been awarded. These were given out in order of seniority—Officers, Warrant Officers, some senior N.C.O.s, the odd one out went to the O.C.s driver. I couldn't help wondering how many of the brave lads lying in their scattered graves had had any mention or, indeed, if anyone knew they were there at all.

I should have mentioned in the account being amazed to see Ladies of the Q.A. Nurses on the beach in battledress towards the end of the battle—some sort of field hospital having been set up.

The O.B.D. after Salerno did sundry base 'filling in' jobs at Torre Annunziata Docks; some at the B.O.D. Naples; Ammo Section at new B.A.D Nola (near Naples). C. Major Walker a Tobruk veteran: A small number with W.O. II including myself at the Railhead Cancello (line was unusable after Cancello) finally returning to Castellamare di Stabia before going on the Anzio landing.

I don't know whether I would have been a good infantryman. Most of the time on Salerno I was scared stiff.

R. M. Roberts

Italian Road

Down the road they came,
The women of Italy.
The children, and the old,
Old men of memories.
Stumbling with their torn feet
On this broken road;
And we watched in silence
From the high turrets
Of our brutal armour.
Slowly they passed
Weary with children,
And the faltering footsteps of age.
Burdened with shock
And their pitiful bundles.
Treasured salvaged hopes
Of the home-makers.
These women of Italy
Powdered with dust,
Heavy with fear and fatigue
Trail past.
Only their eyes raised briefly
To the sun—and us,
From out the sweat, mud and pain
Speak mutely, of the beauty,
The gentleness that must have been.
In them is no hate
Yet must we avert our gaze
Lest our pride be dry in our mouths
And the sweetness of our dreams
Be bloodied by their wounded feet.
And as they pass in the bitter dust
Of trucks and noise of distant guns
Our column moves
As the advance grinds on.
We leave them
These weary women of Italy
Lost in the harsh world of men
And our hearts grow a little tired
A little old.

Geoffrey L. Robinson

Sorrento for Health

Come, she said, sit in the warm of evening
And see me dance, you know he'll be there,
His wound's healed now, tomorrow he's leaving;
Sit by the trees with your wine and share
Joy before danger, love before parting.
All right; get on with your dancing, dancing,
Inhabit the lamplight, laughing, laughing,
Put night advancing back in its shell.
Through luminous leaves and hard to tell,
Came a wall, black-grilled, crouching to stare
Nearer and nearer, a convent there
Secret and dark beside all this larking;
It shouldered among us, hearken, hearken,
The toll of its midnight bell.

N. Robinson

P.O.W. Camp, Italy

We stare across the wire
at the close of empty days
to where the wheatlands glisten
and the haughty cattle gaze;

To where the ploughman turns
his horse at the broken wall—
but the visions that meet our eyes
mean nothing to us at all.

For we live in a shadowland
like the audience at a show
while the play upon the stage
is the world we used to know.

Kenneth Rowe

Barrack Room Nocturne

On leaden hands and knees the thoughts
Go crawling round the raw red brain
In weary penance through the night
Locked in their circling cells of pain
    —I shall not sleep again!

The lightning stabs the sky with knives
And rips a memory from its tomb:
The sleeping faces in the flash
Spring out and seem to fill the room
    —They linger in the gloom.

The whipping lightning flays the flesh
Lays bare the shining bones beneath;
The unconscious faces spring to life
With vacant eyes and grinning teeth
    —O, not for me the wreath!

Stalking the dark oppressive clouds
The thunder shouts its stupid threat:
The bleaching bones upon the beds
Shake like a rattling marionette
    —Why must man know regret?

Then through the weeping whispering rain
Your quiet lonely face appears:
My darling, surely you will end
The fever of these chafing fears?
    —But dreams are spun from tears.

The searing lightning stabs again
And melts the vision of your face;
The lifeless bones, the sneering skull
Leap out to mock me in its place
    —The ultimate disgrace.

And still the leaden weary thoughts
Go wailing round the raw red brain
In endless penance through the night
Locked in their circling cells of pain
    —I shall not sleep again.

Sue Ryder

Letter Home

No. 1 Special Force,
C.M.F., 1943.

In case my earlier letters have not got through I am writing again.

Glorious skies made up for a great deal, and at last we even had a tap and even at another place some gas came on but no light. How luxurious this all seems now! P. and I flew on about midday, bit bumpy, though we are getting quite used to this mode of travelling. The volcanoes looked like I thought they would, also the mountains. Landed some hours later to discover that none of the two or three FANYS[1] was here, in fact no-one to meet us. Incidentally, an accident happened about their transport, so they are apparently coming on by a slower method. Therefore, this meant that we were waiting around until evening in a dirty town and arrived at this place ultimately in darkness. To our immense joy I actually found some post! Wish you could have seen us reading the first letter from England at the place we have now reached, sitting on somebody else's kitbag (for mine has been lost or stolen) in a very bare outside place holding a spluttering candle. I can't thank you or Simmy enough for writing and sending so many warm wishes from people.

Along these unending roads, scattered villages and little houses at intervals, difficulties are innumerable. We have an oil lamp, however, and the stone floor can be cleaned *when* we find the cold water. Surrounded by everyone other than English and somewhat confused by their divers tongues. Attended Mass out of doors. A most memorable Mass. I wonder later on whether you will be rehearsing for carols and, if you are, then no doubt you will be out every night singing.

Today continues to be bitterly cold and the wind is really indescribable and so, too, the snow blizzards which blew tents down. We have been well informed that this is the worst winter for very many years in these parts. Some of the locals say well over 40 years.

Our previous C.O. ceased to be in command last week and we miss him a lot. The population becomes rather hysterical at times—partly through ignorance. Poor things, they are incredibly poor and dirty. We have to go for long, long drives right up into the hills and mountains and then, of course, one realises the many problems there are for other people as well as ourselves, but the former are having a wretched time.

In case you do not hear from me again, and it may well be impossible to write

---

[1] A women's volunteer service.

for several weeks, I hope you enjoy Christmas. You will be especially in my prayers and thoughts and I will be imagining you all and what you are doing, also all my loving wishes and prayers for 1944, when perhaps we will be reunited—who knows, only God. Meanwhile, may God bless you always.

Ever your loving Sue.

This letter was written whilst serving with S.O.E. (Special Operations Executive) in Italy from where the operation in Poland was organised, including the sending of a DC3 (Dakota) to pick up a German rocket prototype which the Polish underground had acquired from the German research station. The plane was so heavy with rocket and passengers that it took forty minutes to take off from a field in occupied Poland. In the end logs had to be embedded into the soil to make a take-off strip. This heroism of the Poles and S.O.E. alerted London and saved many lives in the rocket attacks that followed.

Harry Secombe

The Expendables

The unit had established a temporary H.Q. in a reasonably roofed farmhouse north of Termoli and the battery commander was trying to catch up with some office work between barrages. He waved a piece of paper at the R.S.M. who sat on an empty ammunition box opposite him.

'Div. H.Q. want us to send an N.C.O. back to Tunis to join a party to pick up the kitbags we left behind there. We haven't got one to spare have we?'

'Lance Bombardier Secombe,' said the R.S.M. promptly. 'He's getting to be a bit of a bloody nuisance.'

He was right, too, as I agreed with the battery clerk who relayed the above conversation to me as he handed me my orders. I was getting a bit jumpy and had taken to throwing myself into slit trenches at the slightest sound of a plane—ours or theirs. One of these trenches had contained the R.S.M. I had also wrecked his motor bike by running it into a three-ton truck while looking over my shoulder for signs of German infantry. We were in convoy on a road thirty miles south of the front line at the time.

The battery commander also had good reason to remember me. I had overturned a Bren Carrier in Scotland on manoeuvres and he had happened to be my only passenger. He distrusted my ability as a soldier from then on. 'You're a damned idiot,' he had said on the occasion as we lay upside down tangled in camouflage netting, our heads inches above the swift-flowing burn over which the Carrier had formed a temporary bridge. 'Yessir' I had replied, feeling that under the circumstances he was justified in saying so.

The rendezvous was at Divisional Headquarters, which was comfortably situated well away from trouble and which carried an atmosphere of unhurried calm compared with the frenzied clatter and banging of a twenty-five pounder artillery battery in action. I jumped from the truck, stood upright for the first time in weeks and took stock of my surroundings. The farm buildings were virtually untouched and because it had been static for a reasonably long time, the headquarter's staff had made itself very much at home. Painted signs were everywhere and pointed to such Aladdin's caves as 'NAAFI', 'Corporals' Mess' and 'Cookhouse'. 'I'm going to like it here,' I thought, stretching luxuriously before picking up my kit.

'You there!' shouted an irate voice, and suddenly I was not so sure. A red-faced corporal advanced on me at a brisk walk, and within minutes I was presenting myself and my papers to a languid lieutenant who looked us both over briefly and waved me off to a tent near a pig sty. There I met three of my fellow companions for the journey south to Tunis. They were a curious looking bunch, and I wondered why we had all been chosen for the job.

One of them was a short, stocky corporal from the Buffs who had a flattened nose and an air of bewildered belligerence. He shook hands briefly, introduced himself as Corporal Frampton and ordered the other two occupants of the tent to get up off their ground sheets and meet me.

'Fusilier Black,' said the taller of the two reluctantly. He had bushy black hair, a long narrow face with a pendulous lower lip and a nervous tic in his right eyelid. This gave him the appearance of winking wisely and was a potential source of misunderstanding.

The other soldier was about my height with a small moustache and projecting teeth and looked like a rabbit. He held out is hand and smiled tentatively. 'Gu-gu-gu Gunner Wuh-wuh...'.

Outside a motor bike backfired and with one accord the three of us threw ourselves on the floor. We stayed down for a few seconds then slowly raised our heads and looked into each others' eyes and knew why we were expendable.

'Wuh—Williams,' finished the rabbit-toothed one, 'Anti-Tank.'

'Secombe,' I said adjusting my steel spectacles, 'Anti-War.'

The following day we met the final member of the party. He was the Royal Signals Lieutenant who was to be in charge of us, but when we saw him, we knew from the smell of alcohol on his breath at 0900 hours, the stains on his battledress blouse and the marks on his epaulettes where his third pips had been, that we were going to have to look after each other.

Our orders were to get to Tunis by any available transport. A truck was going to be provided as far as Taranto, and from then on we had to take whatever ship was going. Headquarters was anxious to get rid of us and we had no time to savour its delights. Within twenty-four hours we were loaded aboard an open three-ton lorry with the lieutenant in the cab next to the driver. Corporal Frampton had tried to get in there first, but the officer summoned up enough sobriety to order him out again. We suffered from this for a time as the Corporal roared and shouted orders as we loaded our kit. He mistook Fusilier Black's twitch for insolence until I pointed out to him that the man couldn't help it. After a while he seemed to forget, and he slumped against the tailboard and went to sleep. We other three were too busy searching the sky for non-existent enemy fighters to follow his example.

'Lucky bleeders,' said the lorry driver as he unloaded us at the docks at Taranto. We gave him the age-old two-finger salute and picked up our rifles and webbing equipment.

'Take these documents and try and find the traffic Officer,' said the Lieutenant to Frampton. 'I'll go to the bar over there and see if I can use the phone.' He addressed this remark to Fusilier Black who winked. 'Don't be so damned cheeky,' said the officer with a show of indignation and crossed the street, squaring his shoulders as he did so.

The corporal aimed a savage kick at a dog which was rummaging around his kit. 'That's the last we'll see of that bastard officer today.' He handed the papers to me. 'Don't see why I shouldn't get pissed as well,' he said. 'You take charge of this lot and report to me when you've sorted something out. I'll be over there to keep an eye on him.'

'Just a minute,' I said, overwhelmed with responsibility, 'What about all the kit?'

Frampton turned to the twitching fusilier. 'Come on, you bring the gear over. And Williams, you go with Secombe.'

It was hours later that the Gunner and I finally returned, having talked myself hoarse trying to find space on a boat to Tunis. Eventually I had to settle for a disabled infantry landing craft which was going as far as Catania in Sicily.

The news was received in total silence by the other three, who were seated at a table in the seedy bar. Frampton and Black had their heads down in the pools of cheap vino they had spilled, and only the Lieutenant was sitting upright. I gave him the news and handed him our sailing orders. He nodded sagely, without taking them from me, tapped his nose with his finger and fell off the chair to the cigarette-end-littered floor where he immediately fell asleep.

'If you can't lick 'em, join 'em, I said to Gunner Williams, and seating ourselves at an adjoining table we ordered a bottle of Chianti.

The sea trip to Catania should have been uncomfortable because we had to sleep on the deck, but it was a smooth passage, the weather was fine and the fresh sea air cleared away a lot of the wine mist from our heads. Frampton became almost human, and even Black smiled between tics. Williams and I had become firm friends during our exhausting day at the docks, and he allowed me now to finish his sentences for him.

The Lieutenant, of course, was found a berth in the ship's officers quarters, and we saw nothing of him until we berthed at Catania. There we had the same trouble getting transport for the next stage of the journey, and all Williams and I could muster was a lift as far as Malta in a listing Greek tramp steamer which was going to Valetta for repairs.

We turfed the others out of a waterfront café only just in time to save Black from getting knifed by a Sicilian fisherman who thought he was winking at his girl friend. Corporal Frampton, who had been doing worse things under the table to her and meeting no resistance, was reluctant to leave.

'I was doin' well there, Taff,' he complained over my shoulder as I carried him out.

The Lieutenant was delivered to the boat with some distaste by a smartly uniformed Military Police Officer. We'd had difficulty tracking him down until, as a last resort, we tried the transit officers' Mess where they found him asleep in the Gents.

From Catania to Malta was a nightmare voyage. We were confined to one of the holds where the angle of the deck was at a permanent forty-five degrees. Fortunately we had been given a box of 'compo' rations before we left, and we did not have to rely on the ship's galley for our meals. These ration boxes contained tins of bully beef and vegetable stew, soya bean sausages and bacon along with a tin of cigarettes, chocolate, hard tack biscuits, and, if you were lucky, a tin of golden syrupy sponge. There was also a tin which contained tea, sugar and powdered milk already mixed.

We had to use the galley's facilities to boil our cans after we had been severely chastised by the first mate for trying to light a fire in the hold. The food we had was, as I said, far better than that which the crew had to eat, and as a result the rats on the ship came down to join us. They even tried to dine on us. A nightmare journey indeed, further darkened by Corporal Frampton's increasingly erratic behaviour. He kept leading charges up Long Stop Hill in his sleep, sometimes cutting off the careful line of retreat I had been making in mine. Fusilier Black refused to take off his Mae West throughout the trip, and God knows what private hell the Lieutenant was going through in his cabin above us.

We were all relieved and delighted to get to Valetta. The boming had stopped and life was returning to some kind of normality on the island. From the deck we looked expectantly at the odd cafés still open amidst the rubble. The Lieutenant joined us as we docked, bleary-eyed and scruffy.

'When do we go ashore, sir?' asked Frampton anxiously.

The officer focused slowly on his face as if seeing him for the first time. 'Yes,' he replied at length, choosing the word carefully.

'Gawd blimey.' The Corporal spat over the side in disgust.

Across the harbour H.M.S. *Rodney* lay in all her glory, and lean grey warships and frigates floated arrogantly around us.

We were not permitted to go ashore by the Naval Officer who boarded the ship. He examined our papers and told us that accommodation on the island was extremely limited and that we would be told as soon as room had been found for us on a boat to Tunis. We greeted this news with groans and were only slightly mollified by his sending us some bottles of beer and a bottle of whisky for the Lieutenant. Back in the hold, the rats scurried towards us like old friends.

The next morning Williams and I were on deck carrying on a nearly one-sided conversation, when he stopped in mid-stutter and stared across the harbour at HMS *Rodney*. He pointed to an Aldis Lamp which had just started sending a message in morse.

'Th-th. they are sig-sig-signalling t-to us.'

I knew he was a signaller, and was far more eloquent in dots and dashes than he could ever be in speech. I had no idea of what was being sent, but he started to get excited and motioned that I should get the Lieutenant.

I ran down to his cabin and half dragged him on deck. He peered uncertainly at the battleship which was now repeating the message and spelled it out.

'TO S.S. PYRAMUS AM PREPARED TO TAKE ABOARD ARMY PARTY FOR TUNIS.'

He turned away and his eyes seemed to be clear. 'Do you realise Bombardier, that we are to be invited aboard one of His Majesty's battleships. We're going to finish our little trip in style.'

It was the longest statement he had ever made and it surprised Williams and myself by its careful clarity.

I thought he'd finally gone round the twist, but Williams nodded vigorously in confirmation.

'We'll have to smarten up,' he said. 'Get the men on deck as soon as you can, and looking ship-shape.' He gave a little laugh. 'Ship-shape,' he repeated.

Williams and I clambered down into the hold and aroused the other two who were as excited as they could be after six bottles of beer apiece. I took my other suit of battledress from my big pack and put a fresh shine on my scuffed boots. The others did the same—suddenly soldiers again, a spark of pride beginning to smoulder in our demilitarised breasts.

We stood in a happy group near the gangway waiting for further news. Behind us a voice said 'All right chaps, fall in.'

The Lieutenant was a changed man. He had put on his service dress, shaved off the stubble he had acquired on the trip from Catania and wore an air of authority we had never suspected he possessed.

'You heard the officer. Fall in there.' Corporal Frampton, smart and shining, was anxious to prove his own transformation.

'Now listen, lads,' said the Lieutenant, 'we've all had a pretty rough time on this little outing, and it's fairly obvious to all of us why we have been chosen for this kitbag operation . . .'

We looked away from each other and nodded.

'But today we have been offered a most signal honour.' He emphasised the word 'signal' and we all laughed. 'We are going to be the guests of the Royal Navy and it's up to us to show them that we khaki jobs are as good as they are. It's very rare for this kind of thing to happen and we as representatives of the Army must be on our best behaviour. Thank you.' He saluted.

It was not a very good speech, but I was so carried away that I asked for three cheers. Williams was still on the last Hooray when the ship's radio operator came out of his cabin with a message in his hand. He gave it to the Lieutenant who read it, stony-faced. When he had done so he handed it without a word to Frampton, turned away and went below.

We crowded round the Corporal and read the message over his shoulder. It was headed 'MESSAGE RELAYED BY H.M.S. RODNEY FROM S.S. EXCELSIOR.' That was enough for me. Obviously what Williams and the Lietenant had read was not from the battleship itself. As it turned out later, the wireless on the S.S. *Excelsior* was out of commission and also out of Aldis range of our ship. There was to be no glory road to Tunis, no white bread from the ship's bakery, no fresh vegetables and no free issue Navy grog.

The S.S. *Excelsior* turned out to be another tramp steamer and though the trip to Tunis was a little more comfortable than our epic voyage on the *Pyramus*, it was no picnic. We never saw the Lieutenant again and were told that he was put ashore in Bizerta with a bad case of D.T.s.

When we got to Tunis we found that the warehouse where all the kitbags had been stored had been broken into and the contents scattered. We became aware of this before we actually arrived at the door of the building when Corporal Frampton spotted one Arab going past wearing an officer's Sam Browne, and I saw a veiled lady with a jug of water balanced on her head and a pair of stout Army boots on her feet.

All I found of my own belongings was my Palgrave's *Golden Treasury*, which was some consolation at least.

It took us only two days to get the stuff loaded on a lorry and we were back in Italy for Christmas.

It was great to see the old faces again, and the disappointment about not having any kit left soon faded from the minds of the lads.

'Marvellous to be back with you fellers,' I said that night as we sat around the fire we had cautiously lit. Then a shell landed nearby and I wasn't so sure.

Shelldrake

Wake No More

From 46 Div. magazine *The Oak*. Shelldrake (David Morgan) was the staff poet

Sleep on, soldier! Sleep on!
Another day is here: sirens
of dawn beckon you. Ignore the
alluring sun, firing
the early chill with a new warmth,
the brown hillsides flushed with gold,
the grey stream changed to silver-
        blue.
Dismiss the fable, dispel the old
mockery each morning brings anew—
'Awake to my joy, the sink
of darkness is empty, dawn is aglow
with the freshness of beauty. Drink,
drink of the sparkle of youth!' No!
Shatter the glass, break the illusion,
seductively tempting—see! gone
is the spell. Only confusion
follows the image, chaos
awaits you. Cheat it, for
it has cheated you, this living death
called life. Sleep on! Before
you lies an unknown world—
heaven or nothing—the chance is
        yours
to seize. Choose, the choice is
        hurled
at you. Wake to a world of eternal
        wars
or take a risk and let your sleep
        grow deep.
Sleep on. Sleep on. Sleep . . .

Richard Shuckburgh

Sonnet from a Slit Trench

How quickly comes the dawn! One moment gone
and now grey fingers creep across the gloom,
like strange ethereal heralds of the morn,
that come to presage what? What dreadful doom,
do they lead on today? What terror born,
when night to day's realities gives room,
and casts its cloak aside that hides forlorn
man's hopeless quest, shows up the battered plume
of tired respectability, outworn,
outclassed, defeated! Ah! to whom
shall life seem stable in the light of morn,
having but just emerged from the tomb
of this pitch blackness! Yet comes with the light
the strongest, coldest, soberest delight!

P. T. Sinker

The Invasion of Sicily 1943
With a S.P.[1] Artillery Regiment

Benghazi: Friday 26th June 1943

At the conference I copied out lists of personnel going on landing craft, tanks (L.C.T.s). I was to be officer commanding (O.C.O.) troops on L.C.T.2.

It was a sense of relief when we got everything loaded up. It was all done very efficiently. Had conference with friendly skipper (R.N.V.R.) on water, sanitation, ack-ack, accommodation etc. I was to sleep in the wheelhouse (a pastime I did not look forward to remembering the occasion with my brother-in-law as undergraduates in a fishing drifter in the Outer Minch by the Hebrides). However as one officer was always on the bridge, it was later decided I should sleep in the vacant bunk.

Sunday 28th June was a lovely calm day. Next day the sea started to get up. Wrote letters home and wolfed 'The Old Century' (Siegfried Sassoon). Felt a bit queasy but supper held it down. Drank innumerable cups of tea. Difficulty in keeping clean; everywhere one goes the hands get filthy. Next day was

---

[1] Self-propelled 105 mm gun-howitzer in a Grant tank chassis.

uneventful except for a mine that appeared. All ships had a poop at it, but all missed. The temperature was in the mid-80's, but the menus were as for the Dogger Bank: beef and suet pudding followed by duff, relieved by cups of tea.

Tripoli sighted at 8 o'clock: a lovely sight with the morning sun shining on minarets and houses. Passed several cruisers on the way in and masses of L.C.T.s. There was a bit of a shemozzle getting into the harbour, skipper blinding and swearing at everyone.

July 1st and 2nd and there was the first and second day of bathing and feeding. Weather terribly hot: very fine sand everywhere. One just lives for cups of tea. Reading a good book 'Cactus' by Ethel Mannin. Flap in the night. Everyone hauled out of bed: Jerry parachutes and submarine landing expected. Camp left empty.

At last got money to pay the guards left on the boats in the harbour. Saw my first American troops: they looked like men from Mars. Ate tinned sausages before turning in, and left some in case I woke hungry, but ants polished off the remainder. Went to evening service: Parson exhorted people 'don't be over-confident, like Peter', which I thought a silly text just before an invasion, when you want a little extra confidence: typical C of E!

Next morning we were briefed for the invasion; all very dramatic. IT'S TO BE SICILY and the mainland of Italy. Monty in command. He was terrific in a special address to all troops. 'The time has now come to carry the war into Italy and into the Continent of Europe. The Italian Overseas Empire has been exterminated. We will set about the Italians in no uncertain way . . . With faith in God and with enthusiasm for our cause and for the day of battle, let us all enter into this contest with stout hearts and with determination to conquer. To each of you GOOD LUCK AND GOOD HUNTING IN THE HOME COUNTRY OF ITALY'.

That night there was a 'blind' on the boat and the skipper got terribly tight. We sailed for Sicily next day. Pulled out of harbour at 15.30 hours and cruised up and down outside till 19.30 (as one gunner remarked—'just to let fifth-columnists know we'd started'). Went alongside L.C.T.1 where the rest of our troop was; they gave us a terrific cheer. I briefed our blokes that evening and read them Monty's address which really did go down well with them. (He knew how to handle the men: but officers not always. We found him difficult to swallow; whereas we worshipped General Alexander (Alex) who was General Officer Commanding (G.O.C.)).

The weather got a bit rough and I had to struggle against being sick: did not get much sleep. The convoys collected at Malta before going on to Sicily; an impressive array of L.C.T.s, which were joined later in the evening by L.S.I.s and L.S.T.s[2], and liners from Alexandria.

Saturday, 'D' Day. I hardly slept a wink and very nearly seasick: terribly hot in cabin. The tea tasted disgusting with rum in it and the water hadn't boiled. Later it became clear we were going to be pretty late in. At midnight a force of 'planes towing gliders passed overhead (this particular operation was disastrous with un-tried American pilots). There were flashes in the sky but no noise.

Then it started to get light and we were off Sicily: at first we thought (and hoped) off Avola but we were nowhere near: saw white towns and villages; a big fire in one of them. A lovely morning as we cruised completely unmolested along the coast: a green and pleasant land in contrast with the barren, ochre aridity of North Africa.

Behind us on the horizon were anchored the big ships, and naval guns were firing over our heads. No aeroplanes: apart from those with the gliders; only saw two the whole time we were at sea. The peace and calm of everything was uncanny. The attack seemed to have started late—by three hours—and I was apprehensive especially, as the skipper didn't know where he was. He couldn't read a land map and went by sounding whereas I, though not a brilliant artillery officer, could tell from the map more or less where we were. However between the two of us we decided on a spot and beached at 0700 hours. Whereupon all the carriers and the portes got stuck in the sea (so much for the water-proofing), and of the two Priests,[3] one broke a track immediately on landing: Sergeant Stringer remained with it to repair it but it was out of action till late that evening.

I was hot and rather desperate. The party on the beach had seemed casual and informal, like a point-to-point crowd at home, except for a horrible, mangled corpse like so much meat being carried away to an Advanced Dressing Station (A.D.S.): obviously a hopeless case. A L.S.T. had beached and been hit by artillery—5 out of 7 shots—bridge blown away. (Later I learned that our Survey Officer and Assistant Adjutant had been killed in it.)

A very narrow track led up through a lemon orchard (later I collected pocketsful). We had to get the guns and vehicles through. Came out into a field and to my great relief ran into three officers from my regiment, so fitted in with their guns. My guns must have been about the first artillery landed in the invasion of Europe. First call for gun-fire came at 3 o'clock: 5 rounds 'gun-fire'. (Later heard that we had fired at some Yankee troops. However they said they just lay 'doggo'. We were also fired on by Yanks: so all square.) That was the nearest I got to firing a gun in the whole war—one gun in anger.

A bombardier was badly hurt and we couldn't get an ambulance for him though eventually found a battery ammo. truck. The 'Compo rations' were

---

[2] Landing Ships, Infantry, Landing Ships, Tanks.
[3] Guns were known as 'Priests' because of their comfortable outline.

pretty good—biscuits, boiled sweets, four bars of chocolate; also bully-beef, dripping, cheese, tea and milk powder.

Drove through the almost deserted streets of Avola with martial clatter, feeling very gallant British! Any inhabitants about waved cheerily and one or two clapped. New gun position in a vineyard. Turned in early to get some sleep before my turn on at 11. An amazing day so much less fierce than expected. It will come soon no doubt. Thank God for bringing me safe to the end of this day.

The Itis up to now seem to have fled. It was broadcast: British, American and Canadian troops had attacked Sicily and that everything was going to plan, in fact there had been pretty good chaos and my guns were the only guns of my regiment landed on the correct beach.

Went out this morning with the Commanding Officer (C.O.) (I had been called in to take the place of the Asst. Adjutant killed in the landing) to see the results of concentrated fire by one of the batteries. They had done terrific damage. The C.O. went right into the front line (forward defence lines—f.d.ls)—in fact beyond them. I followed in Jeep. I had got up quite unprepared for this expedition and was in gym shoes. Two company commanders wounded and I raced back for the Medical Officer (M.O.). There was an Iti body burning, making a nasty smell, and a blazing ammo truck going off with periodic bangs. The advancing infantry were no doubt surprised and relieved to see a British Jeep in front of them. There was a dead Iti officer in his bottle-green uniform lying on the edge of the ditch by the roadside—a mere boy of about 18—gouts of blood; poor child.

Now-abouts appeared a figure in a D.U.K.W. (an amphibious armoured car) with a Tank Corps. beret and 2 badges—he waved. It was Monty having a look-see. He appeared relaxed and completely in charge and seemed to give me a piercing look. I must admit my morale was greatly raised.

Later that afternoon I missed my chance of winning an M.C.: a small Italian tank came roaring down the main street of Florida looking for all the world like a small, black, angry rhinoceros. Everyone dived for cover, they were so astonished. It was stopped further down the street. Then I'm afraid I fraternised with the civilians, accepted wine (v. good) and a jug of water (forbidden).

After Lentini had been given a good shelling, the C.O. with the Commander Royal Artillery (C.R.A.), a few Bren gun carriers and self in the C.O.'s tank, made up advance guard into the town. Greeted with cheers and clapping—really quite embarrassing. Some scenes of havoc en route. One of our guns had knocked out a Jerry 88mm gun, a weapon much dreaded by the Allies. When one got out of the tank Itis came running to embrace him but really to beg for 'cigaretti'. Proceeded towards Catania and got bombed on the way. Next position on ridge above Catania with marvellous view away over to Mount Etna with its volcanic plume of smoke. I didn't realise till next day that we were the most forward troops. Next day up at first light—I, in tank, and C.O. in Jeep to have a 'recce'. Quite a lot of shit flying around. Watched shelling, then tank had petrol trouble and got stuck en plein vu and appeared to be being ranged on (by enemy artillery). However the C.O.2 arrived with sustenance for my 'baby' and we got away.

I saw one man over-come with hysteria. Lots of wounded in a culvert and a terrible blackened corpse lying on its back on the road with its bowels sticking out like a bunch of bananas. It's been there two days now and I can't help looking at it every time I pass.

Mail arrived to-day. Terrific thrill. Put aside till I had time to savour it properly and as it turned out very nearly never read it. I was detailed to take the Honey (C.O.'s tank) to advanced R.H.Q., a few hundred yards from Primasole bridge which was still in enemy hands. The position was behind a large out-crop of rock somewhat like the Calf rock of the Cow and Calf at Ilkley.

Well the driver overshot the entrance, and as a well-trained OCTU officer, I got out to direct his turning and all Hell was let loose; Spandau bullets and Mauser bullets whined past and spat on the rock and richocheted off—if ever my guardian angel was by, it was then. I scrambled back into the Honey and we made it.

I was now sent off by the C.O. to gather equipment for the officers' mess. The truck with the mess stuff had 'brewed up' in the invasion—an official looting party! Found a marvellous Hun cook-house—a pig and lots of bottles of wine . . . but empty—and the kit of a captured English soldier. Later I was tipped off about a wine cellar and found vats over 12 feet high; so filled a gigantic cask full and took it back. Also I found yesterday, quite near our farmhouse, the terribly smashed up corpse of a German parachutist. His parachute must have failed to open properly—one of his legs wrapped round his neck—a great, big, fine man—from a crack German para. regiment. There was a Mauser automatic on his belt which I removed. Got shelled twice—an 88mm gun doing harassing fire, bits of shrapnel fell quite near: not pleasant.

Two quick moves; just got settled in the second one and the C.O. and Adjutant had gone with the C.R.A. to a cocktail party when the order 'prepare to move' came. I dashed over on a motor cycle to warn them. They were having 'rosso vino' on the balcony of a lovely house—in Hollywood style.

The next location was in an orchard sloping down to the plain, with Mt. Etna as back-drop—f.d.ls. in between. Feeding very well—break-fast—sausage, tomatoes and roast chicken, melon, washed down with strong tea. Told to-day we may mention Sicily in our letters home.

Douglas Street

Cassino Revisited

This place did catch a vast pox from off the Moon;
Crater and wrinkle all are here,
And we are travellers from another Time;
This place still keeps its own infected counsel;
The most thin atmospheres of loneliness and fear
Still make a heavy labour for the heart;
Yet tribes, I know, lived here, those loved and clumsy tribes
That men call regiments; one tribe would start
The day with telling of its beads; the men of one
Would talk of killings with the knives, and rum;
Yet others talked of the clean unchronicled Antipodes,
Of pasture and a blue haze of trees;
Some had left their private silken skies behind,
Folded neatly with the storemen, out of mind;
And all read letters smelling of the mules,
And talked of two myth-planets, Rome and Home;
For battle cries they used shy word—'Perhaps' or 'Fairly soon'.

After Anaesthetic in Rome

Those wise people you spoke to, when you swallowed sleep,
Did they tell you the ultimate politics are
The mourners' fidget round a grave's clay scar,
Spandaus tittering into fits of laughter,
The sneer and distant malice of a shell?

Did they phrase, as I had never phrased before,
The wooden whisper of the beaded curtain at the door,
The suddenly true ribbon for your hair,
True even by lamplight? Did they phrase
The time we sheltered in the debonair
Bandstand from a shy indefinite rain,

The locket and the keepsakes lost
Behind the echo in the hangars of the brain?
Did they explain those two ceramic seagulls
Against a fading Wedgwood sky and sea,
Two, for metaphoring you and me?

Those wise people you spoke to when you swallowed sleep,
Spoke to with the runes of the soul,
Did they mock the world's suburban Spring of two dwarf hyacinths
   in a bowl?
Or did they speak just nothing,
And speak it with sad hands?

John Strick

Vineyard Reverie

A lemon-coloured house, lying
   Cross-wise upon the rising slopes;
Vine-green, wine-red, always
   A column of sweet smoke
Rising, rising, and the broad
   Blue water of the Southern sea.

Who came here, and why, and when?
   Whose voice calling in the vineyard?
Where are those who lived here?
   What memory have they carried
Into the dim land whence
   They are departed?

The Germans were here, grey-faced,
   Grim-helmeted, their guns
Remain behind the balustrade, round
   The corner of the road.
A thick, black-barrelled tube
   Lurks in the alley-way.

The beach is attractive, opalescent water,
    And the cold, clear virility
Of the mountain stream,
    Piles of 'S' mines, plates
And tapes—the strange silence
    Of deserted fortifications—unused.

Blood has sunk into soil,
    This year the new wine
Stamped under boot, is richer.
    Children gaze with saucer eyes,
'Sicilia bara'—jump and run
    Playing dive-bombers in the glittering sun.

Yes now, look now!
    There is a house standing.
Yes, this was Messina,
    Stone on stone—
They say it was
A large and prosperous city.

Sicily, 1943

Extract from Diaries

103 General Hospital—Nocera. Jan 14–22 1944.

Jan 22nd: The day has been immensely long and rather monotonous—indeed a sort of monotony hangs over everything. Only two people in the ward are really ill, a Norwegian Sea Captain, wounded during the Bari raid, and a Commando lad. The rest are more or less convalescent, apart from myself—who feels listless and sick in mind. Every now and again the deadly river, with its steep sapling covered banks rises before me—the river which defeated our efforts and which swallowed Sgt. Budd—our first loss. I live through the hideous scenes outside Castelforte again and marvel that I could have acted with so little wisdom. At first I was inclined to discount the 'bomb-happy' explanation myself, but in view of my four breakdowns, I begin to wonder and must try and see a psychologist. I wonder if Sgt. Murphy has been found, how terrible if he had died from loss of blood—but I think that the Germans or the Italians must have taken him in. But to go back over the history of the last two weeks. Gradually information began to seep through—parties arrived at Bn. H.Q. (Battalion Headquarters) in Caregliano requiring guides—most of whom were provided by us. Our operational tasks were more or less at an end with the abortive attempt at crossing on which Sgt. Budd was drowned. It all happened so quickly. Sgt. Woolf and I had made six attempts—each time the same result. We would go upstream and turn out into the current and be swept down into the bushes on our own bank. It was a somehow ludicrous journey some two miles from our own outposts. Luckily, no moon—the night being inky black—I sitting perched at one end of the useless rubber boat—my behind in two inches of water, searching the opposite bank with anxious eye and poised TSMG[1]—dead meat if anyone had fired at us. At last, exhausted and disappointed, I came ashore and Sgt. Budd took a turn in my place. On a previous occasion the rope had broken, so Abehurst (who was to be killed two days later on a mine) and I made it fast. All went well to begin with until the boat got caught in the current, then it seems that Sgt. Budd must have lost his head and stood up in the boat. I heard Woolf saying 'Take it easy', then a moment later, 'O.K. bale out'—we at once began to haul in the rope, thinking they would cling to the boat and two men, Wilson and Jack Armstrong dived in—everything was rather chaotic because of the darkness.

Eventually they got Sgt. Woolf to the bank, but Budd had disappeared. (J told me later that he had risen once, his canteen still in his hand—and then disappeared for ever.) All those who had been in the water were totally exhausted, shivering, distraught and had to be sent back. A certain gloom fell on us and I felt that any further attempts would be a waste of time. I remembered the General that morning—very musical comedy— with his anecdote which I had thought remarkably erudite until I discovered that it came straight from the Illustrated London News—he would be angry at this failure. In spite of the ear splitting noise we had made, nothing stirred—the river flowed on just the same. We withdrew, carrying the boats to the base and held a council of war with the covering party. Thence I travelled an immense distance with a guide and talked to the C.O. who agreed to our having a crack at the German post we had discovered. The raid was a failure—all life had been driven out of us—everyone was cold, sitting about the base and disheartened. When we got there we found the ground had absolutely no cover from mortar or SAA[2]. We should have been most grimly placed and as it happened, nothing

---

[1] Thompson Sub Machine-gun.
[2] Small Arms Ammunition.

presented itself as a target. Away on our left there was a great deal of noise occasioned by the Scottish attacking the small German Salient this side of the river—Sotto, Sopre and the rest. That same night C.S.M. Budd (newly commissioned) was killed (as for us, 13 known) a melancholy coincidence. I withdrew the force to a safer locality and we fired Bren at various places where we expected enemy—there was no response—but I am told the next day they mortared the points from which we had fired. This showed that observation was maintained on the area. I had begun to wander since my numerous journeys in civilian clothes along the bank. This failure was our last expedition. After I took Major ... and various Queens parties to the banks and a successful reconnaissance was made. More and more people kept pouring into our straggling village of Caregliano. To our horror a party of 95 Sappers went to work on the ruined Power House and filled in holes in the road. Previously only small patrols had visited the area, but there was no mishap. A bad cold brought back by Terry from leave, still had me in its clutches and J was very unwell, which he tried to conceal from me. Eventually we had a few hours of uneasy slumber. Next day began in a leisurely fashion as the General, his red hat on the back of his head, after giving us the broad outlines of the battle, had spoken of two days time. Alas a sudden change sent us scurrying in all directions. I went with the C.O. to 167 H.Q. which, after a great deal of difficulty, we found right forward, overlooking the plain. A most exposed position. I was not surprised to hear that it was later dive-bombed.

A party of German prisoners were just being questioned and photographed and orders were unsatisfactorily vague. I walked back to the canal bank and re-read the route which had to be taken that night and arrived very tired and footsore about 3 p.m. While Cpl. Young and I were making some Oxo, some planes dived right over us and I thought our time had come, as they could have riddled us with bullets but they didn't fire—fortunately. Among so many doings, an incident of that type seemed nothing, though further back it would no doubt have provided conversation for days. In such a way, things are unjust and R.A.S.C. and similar people receive medals for doing what the Infantry have to do every day.

Amazing to relate we got supper before setting out. It was an immense distance and we found a whole queue of people waiting to cross the river. A very long time elapsed before the Bn. appeared, during which I became extrememly cold and resorted to all kinds of expedients to keep warm. There had been a great controversy as to whether overcoats should be taken—climbing in the sun would have been terrible, but I think they could have been dumped. At last the main column arrived and we stood like policemen, dividing them into batches. At last I could stand them no more and went across—the journey was remarkably simple, compared with our rubber boat excursions, and then we trundled along a tape for about a mile before reaching the village of St. Luca. On the way we passed various huddled shapes which I suspected were bodies. It was just as well we did not realise we were traversing a mine field. The areas was incredibly crowded. However, we found a stable and fitted in well enough. I was so tired that despite the cold and stone floor I fell asleep at once. Alas it was not to be, and after an hour I was summoned to the Presence. Our assignment was to investigate Castelforte and to see whether it was occupied.

The distance was rather formidable and as it was already 1 o'clock and the moon well up—we set off at once. It will be long before I forget that moonlit journey which was to end so disastrously. First we passed C+B boys[3] who had taken positions that evening in villages well sheltered on the slopes of the rough slope. First a pause at the crossroads, where one went right down to Tibaldi—the other to Castelforte—that white sprawling town that we had gazed at for so long. My plan had been to proceed with scouts to the hairpin bend—thence across country. All along the road were houses and at any moment we expected to be fired on—it was impossible to investigate them all. At the first bend we halted suddenly, an ominous ditch to the left of the road. After a while, leaving the Bren Group, I investigated the houses and we came upon one area where voices could be heard. Eventually I decided that the only course was a bold one and we forced an entry to find about twenty Italians sleeping. An old man greeted us with embraces, which I relished, on hearing we were English. He gave us some information. The Germans had moved out pretty quickly the day before, but might still be in Castelforte. Many mines had been sown although the main road was clear. This was a clear warning and yet looking back I do not know what else we could have done. To go straight up the main road would have been suicide, so we struck across country behind a row of dwellings fronting on the road. Another scare was caused by a sinister click being heard. This noise required investigation and must have some natural source. The events of the next half-hour are still painful to describe, though I have already done so in several letters. First we were amazed to hear on our right the sound of a long column moving up a road, where we knew of no road. Sgt. Murphy and I stalked some distance towards it to listen, but beyond the fact that at least a company was passing and an occasional word of command which sounded like English, we were none the wiser. As far as I know, this mystery has yet to be solved, though in view of subsequent events they were almost certainly German. When we came to the edge of the olive groves we were about 200 yards from the town. An open field with lines of tiny, leafless saplings stretched ahead. I divided the patrol into two—Sgt. M to take the other half; and for some unaccountable reason put Pile, the bren gunner, directly behind

---

[3] American assault engineers.

me instead of J. Sgt. M, I remember, queried this. It was indeed fortunate for J that I did so. We were not looking for mines any more and indeed would have been unlikely to see them. I had covered a few paces when there was an appalling explosion behind me and I shot about 8ft through the air into the field, thinking as I went—I suppose this is a mine. How long, whether seconds or minutes I don't know, I lay is uncertain. But then staggered up to see what had happened. Pile lay moaning on the ground and I strode over him to contact the others. I had been blown backwards but apart from cuts and a piece in the eye, was O.K. Cpl. P came up and we found that Pile had lost one foot and both legs were broken. He was very brave and cool and cannot have felt much pain. I started back to collect the others and we got Pile onto a rough stretcher when there was some firing (TSMG or Schmeisser) and another explosion and we realised Sgt. M was missing. My nerves were in pieces and I felt completely panic-stricken and could not go back into the vineyard. Cpl. P however rose to the occasion and took a search party which however failed to find any trace. Just before this I thought I heard voices and a German shouting 'Allo'—it may be that they took Sgt. M in—I hope so. I waited until they were all out and then hobbled back beside the stretcher—every piece of grass looked deadly now. When we eventually reached C Coy—a stretcher had come out and I had my arm bound up—the wounds were numerous but not deep. I kept breaking into tears, which was alarming and J and I eventually got back to Bn. H.Q. where the same scene recurred. The C.O. was very kind and fatherly—thanking me for what we had tried to do—I remember Allan looking at me in horror as well he might. The doctor did not think much of my injuries but prescribed bed or hospital—so I chose the former. The hysterical fits came on for about two hours, after which I was O.K.

We had a rough post-mortem, but I cannot escape a feeling of guilt over Sgt. M—It is terrible what blast can do to one. An attack was being planned, so after a rest and and food we started the long journey back but we were delayed by a long evening air raid of about an hour. They kept sending planes over and had previously damaged the bridge and such as in Exercise Bombay. The return was not pleasant. All along the route were bodies of the original attacking force and to stray off the tape meant to go into a minefield. We went considerably astray in our boat and passed the General coming up. The boat party was rather nervous having been repeatedly 'straffed'. On the way we passed a band of reporters and did not get a lift till the last turn, thence to the rear Bde., where we were both given lunch and entertained and I borrowed the Staff Captain's Jeep to return to A Ech. Which proved to be right the other side of Cascano.

Here again we were the centre of attention and old Cleave looked after us magnificently. In the evening to B Ech., where the miserable R.Q.M.S. was supposed to have prepared a room. A gaunt upper chamber without furniture or windows disgusted me, but Perkins came down to help. C probably rightly insisted on my wounds being dressed, so we drove to the M.O.'s at . . . where I saw Major Macewan who insisted I go to hospital. A deluge of medicines—M & B, Hyoscine, anti-typhus etc., and then back to B Ech. I was absolutely drunk when I got there and could hardly walk—so strong was the drug. Next morning we had a big leaisurely breakfast and then by truck to the C.C.S. J was very depressed at my departure. I commanded him to stay at A Ech., but very much fear that in present circumstances he will have been called to the front again. However it is better not to consider what one cannot prevent. The C.C.S. proved to be at Francois and tented—I thought of the Div. School which I expect has now been dissolved owing to the number of casualties. J had his eye seen by a specialist who pronounced that there was no serious damage—a relief. I sat for some time in the reception talking to two young and not unpleasant Germans. 'If this war were over, things would be very different', one said. They belonged to the 94th Div. who had been our main opponents up to date. I bade farewell to J and Cleave and was 'admitted'. The day passed quickly with X-Rays and rest. It transpired that my bone was O.K. and nothing serious had penetrated. What a blessing X-Rays are. A doctor being treated there frightened me by saying it looked like a fracture. Opposite me was a D.L.I.[4] officer of swarthy complexion and few words, whom I could not make out. As he was beside me in hospital I discovered he was a Jewish Italian called Gutten and a pleasant type. He had had a hard life of persecution and believed his people were 'concentrated' near Rome. It had been laid down that I was a stretcher case, so was carried everywhere—a peculiar and rather tiresome business.

We were driven to the station and remained for hours in the van, being almost the last on board. It was my first experience of a hospital train and not too bad. Except that we became very cramped in a stretcher. I was on the top rung—there were three each side and could hardly move. Food, however was good and I had something to read. Moreover there were two Germans below who kept up a conversation of moderate interest. It seems they had been short of food and were surprised at their good treatment and not annoyed that the war was over for them. Far from going to Caserta, we passed Naples and after an eight hour journey stopped at Nocera, a dismal place which we had passed through on the original journey from Salerno in carriers. Thank Heaven my day with these vehicles is ended. I had a further talk with a German in the ambulance. Very young and it seemed had not been in the Hitler Youth, which is curious. Then we were classified quickly and I was carried to one of the men's wards by mistake—thence to the officers' ward where an excellent reception was to be found of food, attention and warmth and have been here ever since.

'To succeed in the world you must appear to have succeeded already.'

---

[4] Durham Light Infantry.

Rifleman Jack Armstrong's Letter to his Mother

20/2/44.

My dear Mother,

As I sit here and writing you these few lines, I am more brokenhearted. You will, and probably all at home will be the same, when you hear the same ghastly news as I heard yesterday on returning from hospital. *Capt. Strick was killed.* It was the first time I had ever left him whilst we were in battle—a few days before he was killed, he sent me back to hospital, because I had a fever and a very high temperature, 102 degrees. When I left him, he shook hands with me and said: 'Good luck. Look after yourself.' I told him it was he who needed all the luck. I didn't know how right I was.

Mother, I don't know what I shall do now. There just isn't any future for me. On the three occasions when he was wounded before, I was with him each time. We always said to each other, we were each other's luck. There was something in that, mother, because we never left each other's side, no matter how bad the circumstances were.

Everyone in the Bn. liked him for his daring and skill and cool courage. If ever anyone deserved a medal, it was him. To think that during the past few months the dangerous corners which the platoon had been in—he always got us out of them, and yet when he goes back into a company, and was not in what one would call a dangerous corner, he was killed. I might not have mentioned it before, but we were in 'C' Company at the time. He had just been out of hospital a week or so, after having his last wounds attended to.

Yes, Mother, I have lost my best friend—the best in the world. Everywhere he went I was with him. Don't ever lose that photograph of him—get it enlarged as big as you can, so that when the day comes and I will be back home again, I shall be able to walk into the house and salute the most gallant soldier and friend I have ever known.

I shall write to his mother as soon as I can. I hope she does not take it too hard.

Randall Swingler
Infantry Coming out of the Line

So must the ancient dead
Have climbed from Acheron
Or Aeneas' ditch of blood,
Their ineffectual substance
Still spangled with fine dust
Like phosphor that reflects
And holds the wistful light
A little longer, a little
Longer—Brittle the tension now
Between the real and the dream
Dewed with the bloom of death
Still, these drained faces,
(Embrasures of the eyes
Frame the long bore of guns)
And every feature bleak,
The nerves withdrawn and hiding,
Blind walls of a beleaguered city
That has not realised
The siege is raised, the invaders
Gone with the sly night.
They do not look. They walk
Like blind men, boots shuffling.
Maybe one shouts a greeting
But the sound is detached, wild,
Has another meaning than ours
Like a gull's cry.
          Inside
The skull their riot begins,
The mob of memory straining
Against the cordon of pride.
Rest will be no rest
But a fear of falling, till
Sleep softly supervenes
And slips the knot of will,
Horror with laughter mingling,
And the frontier melt
Between despair and longing
And felt things be but things
Divested of emotion

And reason slowly wake
To find the world is still
The only world, and what
Was done and what encountered
Was the unavoidable run
Of life as it is given
To make of it what we can.
Dream-locked, grotesque survivors,
They will know least of all
How animal behaviour
Is made by circumstance
A superhuman feat,
And by historic chance
A month of hell becomes
In memory's colour-filter
Framed in heroic gilt:
Or what dim calculus
Works out the indifferent sum
That they should be the one
In every ten who now
Painfully to resume
The fallible of life.
Limps back from Acheron.

Anzio, March 1944

Richard Trudgett

A Note in my Diary – Shipwreck

Some spoke of the oil that lay like a lagoon
On the threaded sea
Some of the thought of sharks
Mr. J. thought he saw one
And commented on its arrow teeth.
I upbraided him with skeletons
Pointing to the woman floating by
Her body white and happy in death.

So we both laughed
When the Captain's hat
Floated by with a note to his wife
Tucked neatly inside.

Alan White

Lily Marlene

I am hearing it again,
Lily Marlene,
      Lily Marlene,
song that I heard
the German soldiers sing,
to the compound marching,
pounding up the dust
of a Tunisian road.

I am hearing it again,
Lily Marlene,
      Lily Marlene,
song that I heard
an Italian violinist play,
remembering wryly the requests
of his late overlords,
wringing the melody
from polished wood and catgut
in a club where Allied officers
were maudlin with wine.

Lily Marlene,
song of the German soldier's
faithless girl,
a wanton of the barracks,
who can feel another's body,
while her former lovers
feel the bite of Russian snow
in day and night retreat.

226

I am hearing it again,
Lily Marlene,
            Lily Marlene,
as I hitchhike my way
from hospital to war.
The driver of the truck
is humming it,
as we ascend the mountains,
and the windscreen blurs with rain.
Lily Marlene . . . . . . Lily Marlene.

Portrait of a Conscript

Poem for an Italian Child Blown up by a Mine

The undetected, uncleared mine
was your disaster.
Unknowingly you led the docile goats
along a fatal track.
And now no tears of stricken mother,
nor of village mourning,
can ever bring you back.
Blame this war,
beginning in a beachhead,
dabbling the holiday sand with blood,
lingering with its treacherous devices
in green grass, in tarmac and in mud.
Tread of a child at play,
tread of a man at work,
tread of a lumbering cart,
all suffice to free the pointed plunger,
tearing flesh or framework,
creation or construction,
viciously apart.
War can lurk in the unlikely places,
straggling behind a fluctuating front.
Sown by the enemy in retreat
are mines, alive and waiting
for the impress of haphazard feet.
The general on his reconnaissance,
the shepherd guiding sheep along a lane,
the soldier on his usual scrounge,
are sure to tread sometime . . .
and to children, unaware,
it is bound to happen again.

Monastery Hill

Away from the temptation of the town,
in disapproval of the valley's vice,
the monastery crowns the hill,
austere and celibate,
its isolation only pierced
by a deterrent, winding road.
Now its tranquil vespers are supplanted
by the wailing agony of nebelwerfers[1],
and its inmates are the paratrooper
and the panzergrenadier,
who finger bandoliers of ball and tracer,
the rosaries of their fanaticism.

Even in mountain mist, night gloom
or fog of smoke-shells
still the monastery persists,
an outline lit occasionally by flares.
Below there sprawls Cassino,
hiding its rubble carcase
underneath a winding sheet of smoke,
and in among the ruined maze
the infantry play hide-and-seek.

Hidden in the olive-grove
and on the forward slope of our own sector,
we observe . . .
and are observed ourselves.
In our student minds we strive to find
a means to break this deadlock
in a difficult campaign,
to burst the lock-gates
that will lead to Rome.
We wonder too if monks will ever
resurrect the spirit of the monastery,
or if it will be forbidden them,
forever branded as an evil monument,
a bastion, fêted by historians,
and once a valuable accomplice
in the art of war.

[1]Smoke-shell Mortar

Anonymous

The D-Day Dodgers

We are the D-Day Dodgers out in Italy,
Always drinking Vino, always on the spree.
8th Army skyvers and the Yanks,
6th Armoured Div and all their tanks.
For we are the D-Day Dodgers, the lads that D-Day dodged.

We landed at Salerno, a holiday with pay,
Jerry brought the band down to cheer us on our way.
We all sung the songs and the beer was free.
We kissed all the girls in Napoli.
For we are the D-Day Dodgers.

The Volturno and Cassino were taken in our stride
We didn't have to fight there. We just went for the ride.
Anzio and Sangro were all forlorn.
We did not do a thing from dusk to dawn.
For we are the D-Day Dodgers.

On our way to Florence we had a lovely time.
We run a bus to Rimini through the Gothic line.
All the winter sports amid the snow.
Then we went bathing in the Po.
For we are the D-Day Dodgers.

Once we had a blue light that we were going home
Back to dear old Blighty never more to roam.
Then somebody said in France you'll fight.
We said never mind we'll just sit tight,
The windy D-Day Dodgers in sunny Italy.

Now Lady Astor get a load of this.
Don't stand on a platform and talk a load of piss.
You're the nation's sweetheart, the nation's pride
But your lovely mouth is far too wide
For we are the D-Day Dodgers in sunny Italy.

If you look around the mountains, through the mud and rain
You'll find battered crosses, some which bear no name.
Heart break, toil and suffering gone
The boys beneath just slumber on
For they were the D–Day Dodgers.

So listen all you people, over land and foam
Even though we've parted, our hearts are close to home.
When we return we hope you'll say
'You did your little bit, though far away
All of the D–Day Dodgers out in Italy.'

The last verses to be sung with vino on your lips and tears in your eyes.

"When they call us D-Day Dodgers—which D-Day do they mean, old man?"

Poems from Campo 53

A RESTLESS NIGHT HAS JUST BEEN PAST.
WE'RE AWAKENED BY THE WHISTLE'S BLAST,
THE SERJEANT'S VOICE COMES CLEAR AND SHAKY.
THE USUAL CRY OF "WAKEY, WAKEY"
THE MORNING AIR'S COLD TO OUR FEET,
FOR ONCE THE MORNING COFFEE'S SWEET.
WE CLIMB ONCE MORE BACK INTO BED.
AND LISTEN FOR THE CRY OF "BREAD".

ONCE MORE WE HEAR THE WHISTLES BLOW.
WITH A BLANKET TO DRAW BREAD THEY GO.
THE CALL IS HEARD "ONE FROM EACH SIX",
WE DRAW A CARD AND TAKE OUR PICK,
FOR SOME ARE BIG AND SOME ARE SMALL,
BUT MOST OF THEM NO SHAPE AT ALL.
WE PULL THE BLANKETS ROUND OUR KNEES
AND PATIENTLY WAIT FOR OUR CHEESE.

AND SOON THE CHEESE IS ISSUED OUT.
THE GROUP COMMANDER'S GIVE A SHOUT,
THE PIECE WE GET FOR SIX IS SMALL.
IT'S A WONDER WE GET ANY AT ALL.
FOR EACH PIECE IS A DIFFERENT SIZE,
IT'S BARE FACED ROBBERY IN OUR EYES,
BUT THE CHEESE ITSELF IS HARD TO BEAT
THEY STOP IT TWICE AND ISSUE MEAT.

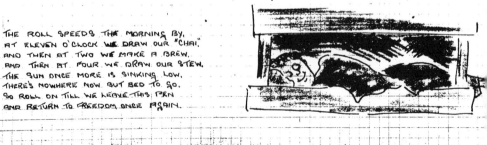

THE ROLL SPEEDS THE MORNING BY,
AT ELEVEN O'CLOCK WE DRAW OUR "CHAI,"
AND THEN AT TWO WE MAKE A BREW.
AND THEN AT FOUR WE DRAW OUR STEW.
THE SUN ONCE MORE IS SINKING LOW,
THERE'S NOWHERE NOW BUT BED TO GO.
SO ROLL ON TILL WE LEAVE THIS PEN
AND RETURN TO FREEDOM ONCE AGAIN.

For me, the brave do not have to scale the heights or take on a company with a solitary gun. On the contrary, it is often the unarmed and unprotected, quietly taking risk beyond any call of duty— so quietly for they must not be known for what they do—who quality for inclusion among the heroic.

One such man was Giovanni Leoni, of peasant family in Olibra, Ascoli, in Central Italy, who with his companions found three escaped British P.O.W.s, hiding asleep in a field in October 1943, took them to his home and, aided by his family and others in the tiny village of Olibra, hid the men until the British line moved up to Ascoli ten months later.

The people of Olibra enjoyed no Geneva Convention, no uniform, no rights. They were among the many Italian families who sheltered the Allied P.O.W.s who had walked out of the camps in September 1943, when Italian guards sloped off, deciding their war was over and the Germans had yet to replace them. The families took horrendous risks. When the war ended investigators were sent out from Britain to collect evidence on war crimes. I accompanied one, a former London detective. After a while one could write the script. For the German Army, even when it was virtually all over and they were pulling out in retreat, took vengeance on the local civilian population, rounding up anyone they suspected of aiding the Allied cause or helping P.O.W.s. Soldiers tortured and hanged victims from trees. The evidence was too consistent to be doubted. And significantly just before the executioners left, they would leave a message with a survivor: 'Tell anyone who asks, "nur unsere pflucht tun" (we are only doing our duty)'. And Austrians sometimes proved to be more ruthless than the Germans. Still, the Fuehrer was an Austrian.

The civilian heroes earned no medals. They acted for no reward[1]. True, compensation was paid to a few who looked after P.O.W.s but this was not organised until it was all over and even then not many knew of it.

In Olibra the three British P.O.W.s moved from shelter to shelter. But one of the trio, Ernest Court, an RASC driver, taken prisoner in Tobruk, had more to hide than himself. He had taken with him from Campo 53 a book of poems and sketches he had compiled which he hid in the safest place in the village—under a manure heap in a barn. The poems and sketches in this book are reproductions of the originals on the squared Italian exercise book paper from Campo 53, which lay hidden for nearly a year and today resides in a suburban semi near London, waiting to be presented to the Imperial War Museum.

The man who collected the poems had no literary pretensions. There was a large notice board in Campo 53. P.O.W.s wrote poems and pinned them to the board. They were sentimental, nostalgic, ironic, hardly likely to qualify for any classic collection.

But Ernest Court was so taken with them that he copied them into his exercise book and then bribed a colleague to illustrate each poem. The illustrator's fee was a day's bread ration (a loaf) per poem. What the Italian guards called a loaf amounted to a small bread roll but it was like gold. They were always hungry. Ernest Court had a privileged position. He drew rations and firewood for thirty men of his group. He made a special pocket in his coat and at the stores he would involve a guard in argument or trade coffee and chocolate from the Red Cross parcels. He also stuffed onions and fruit into that bread pocket.

The two poems reproduced above, tell their own story. Others from the exercise book show such items as the Italian Medical Officer puncturing a tin of bully, so that men could not hoard it for escape—and then using the same needle to inject the men. The last picture is of a P.O.W.'s dream of home... his feet up on the mantel-piece and tins and tins of luxury—condensed milk!

When Ernest Court finally left the Army, a grateful country gave him a gratuity of sixty months at ten shillings a month, making a magnificent £33, to which they added a long deferred post-war credit of £37.16.6. Sixteen years after the war ended, he took his wife Olive and two sons back to Olibra to thank those who had sheltered him, his mates and his poems. It cost £600. He raised the money from weeks at the dogs, following the tips from a London evening paper. He began with a £24 float, from his money as a London cab driver. Each night he banked the winnings, to take the £24 float back next night to the track and begin again. The day the £24 went, he stopped. He had won and banked enough to thank Giovanni Leoni and the people of Olibra.

V.S.

---

[1] To my list of the brave in this context let me add the priests in Rome who sheltered P.O.W.s, their work made even more perilous by certain agents blowing their cover before the Allies entered Rome in June 1944. One priest, Brother Robert Pace, from Malta, was actually lined up before a German firing squad before Partisans rescued him. Years later I met Brother Robert again on an island in the traffic in Berkeley Square, London. He had just collected his B.E.M. from the Palace. With his hat on he only came up to my shoulder. He must have hidden twenty or more of our P.O.W.s.

The Circle

War begets Poverty,
Poverty Peace;
Peace begets Plenty
then riches increase.
Riches bring Pride
and Pride is War's ground,
War begets Poverty—
so goes the Round!

A Fitter's Lament

My toolbox is minus a padlock,
My padlock is minus a key,
My tools are all over the car-park,
Oh, bring back my padlock to me.

My Whitworth is gone and my shifter,
My screwdriver, where can it be?
I've looked all around for my feelers,
Oh, bring back my Whitworth to me.

My six millimeter has vanished,
My pliers have gone on the spree,
My wire cutters also have left me,
Oh, bring back my pliers to me.

When I get released back to England
How happy at home I will be.
I will buy me a steel-plated tool box
With a steel-plated padlock and key.

A. H. from *The Oak*

Two Songs from the Partisans

Pieta l'e morta

Lassú sulle montagne
Bandiera nera
È morto un partigiano
Nel far la guerra

È morto un partigiano
Nel far la guerra
Un altro italiano
Va sotto terra

Laggiú sotto terra
Trova un alpino
Caduto nella Russia
Con il 'Cervino'[1]

È morto nella steppa
Assiderato
Ferito o da amputare
Congelato

Ma prima di morire
Ha ancor pregato
Che Dio maledica
Quell'alleato

Che Dio maledica
Chi ci ha tradito
Lasciandoci sul Don
E poi è fuggito

Pity is Dead

Up there on the mountains
A black flag
A partisan died
Making war

A partisan died
Making war
Another Italian
Goes under the ground

There under the ground
there lies another Alpine
Who fell in Russia
With the 'Cervino'[1]

He dies on the steppe
Made cinders
Wounded and for amputation
Frozen

But before he died
He again asked God
To curse
That ally

That God should curse
Whoever had betrayed him
Leaving him on the Don
And running away

---

[1] Il battaglione alpini 'Cervino' faceva parte, in un primo tempo, del CSIR, poi dell'ARMIR. Subí perdite gravissime e i superstiti, dopo la ritirata del gennaio 1943, furono pochissimi.

[1] The Alpine battalion 'Cervino', formed part, originally of the CSIR, then of the ARMIR. It suffered severe losses and had few survivors, after the retreat of January 1943.

Tedeschi traditori	Treacherous Germans
L'alpino è morto	The Alpine is dead
Ma un altro combattente	But another fighter
Oggi è risorto	Takes his place today
Combatte la sua guerra	He fights his war
Da vecchio alpino	Of an Alpine veteran
Fatiche, freddo e fame	Fatigues cold and hunger
Gli son compagne	Are his companions
Combatte il partigiano	The partisan fights
La sua battaglia	His battle
Tedeschi e fascisti	Germans and fascists
Fuori d'Italia	Out of Italy
Tedeschi e fascisti	Germans and fascists
Fuori d'Italia	Out of Italy
Gridiamo a tutta forza	We shout with all our might
'Pietà l'e morta!'	'Pity is dead!'

Alla vigilia deì rastrellamento del 20 aprile 1944, il comando del II settore Giustizia e Liberta, bandisce un concorso per una canzone partigiana. Il I° premio è assegnato alla 4ᵃ banda del Vallone dell' Arma (Valle Stura) e la canzone diventa poi il canto della I divisione alpina Giustizia e Libertà. Le parole sono di Nuto Revelli e va cantata sull' aria Sul ponte di Bassano bandiera nera (gli alpini della divisione 'Julia' in Grecia nel 1940 riprendono lo stesso motivo, per dar vita a sul ponte di Perati bandiera nera).

Publicata sul n. 1, del 6 aprile 1944, di Quelli della montagna, Gruppo bande 'Italia Libera'. (Cumunicazione e testimonianza di Revelli.)

On the eve of the Search of April 20th 1944, the Command of the 2nd Section Justice and Liberty arranged a competition for partisan songs. The first prize went to the 4th band from the Vallone d'Arma (Valle Stura) and the song then became the song of the 1st Alpine Division Justice and Liberty. The words are by Nuto Revelli and is sung to the tune of Sul ponte di Bassano bandiera nera (in 1940 the Alpines of the Julia Division in Greece took up the same theme).

Published as no. 1 of April 6th 1944 of Quelli della Montagna, group of Italia Libera bands.

Sul Pónte Fiume Sangro

Sull' arid de 'Sul Ponte di Pereti'

Sul ponte fiume Sangro
bandiera nera
è il lutto della Maiella
che va alla guerra.

La Meglio gioventú
che va sotto terra.

Quelli che son partiti
non son tornati
sui monti dell'Abruzzo
sono restati.

Sui monti della Romagna
sono caduti.

Questo fu in un certo senso l'inno ufficiale
della formazione 'Maiella', cantato in varie
occasioni, soprattutto nei momenti di
ricordo, e nella cerimonia dello scioglimento
del gruppo, avvenuta il 15 luglio 1945 a
Brisighella (Ravenna). Il motivo è ricavato
dalla notissima cazone della Julia piú volte
citata e la rielaborazione delle parole è opera
collettiva. (Testimonianza e notizie di
Troilo.)

On the Bridge over the Sangro

To the tune of Sul Ponte di Pereti

On the bridge over the Sangro
a black flag
and the struggle of the Maiella
going to war.

The finest youth
which is going underground.

Those who are gone
have not come back
they have remained in the hills
of the Abruzzi.

They fell on the hills
of the Romagna.

This may be considered the signature tune of
the Maiella group and was sung on various
occasions, especially at memorial meetings
and at the ceremony when the group was
disbanded. on July 15th 1945 at Brisighella,
Ravenna. The motif is taken from the well-
known song 'Julia' to which frequent
reference has been made and the working out
of the words is a collective operation.

IV
Yugoslavia and Greece

Robin Benn

Dalmatian Islanders

These were peaceful people, and the hills, their world,
hedged in by changing seas, to rocky breasts
took prints of intimacy with gentle feet.
These rocks, white-piled a million gleaming cairns,
or walled around with meagre fields they hid,
saw silent fortitude reach dogged mastery,
and grimly watched, amazed, a people grow.
These waters, savaging the stranger craft,
conspiring with the rocks to spoil their keels,
took fathers to their death, and saw the sons
tight-lipped at dawn confront their rage anew.
Through centuries the thirsty sun beat down on them,
parching their vineyards; from their hard-hewn wells
spirited off the precious hoarded drops
of water. Yet they'll say they loved the sun.
For these were peaceful people. In their hearts
no bitterness that Nature was so harsh,
no whined complaint to Heaven in need they raised.
Man had not harmed them; therefore friends of Man,
and all men friends, their life was hard but glad.
And Man has struck them, vilely, from behind,
thinking to bend them, beaten, to his will.
These are quiet people, but their eyes are hard,
and sounds we know can number none to tear
and chill the heart as when their women mourn.

R. Killian Brady

Ghajn Tuffieha

Draw in to the tent and make a little room,
There's Lonchar at the door—he lost his eyes,
And his arm, too (only the left one, but)
And his job as well, I suspect,
Somewhere in Bosnia.

Come in, Lonchar, on Vladimir's mano
And take the Boy Scout's shoulder.
He'll speak this lingua franca of Italiano
Sweet-voiced as a girl, but bolder
And more blest and strong to support
A man without his eyes, a real good sort,
Like you, my Loncharico.
Step right in, amico!

I, Lonchar, had—avevo—when I had my sight,
Ragazza, capite? do you understand?
A girl lassù in Bosnia, tall and grand,
She could read and write.
She called herself Velazia.
But I was a cobbler in Dalmazia—
I no speak English well, nor 'taliano:

'Dalmatinska—' com' è lontano!
'Domovina—' oh, how bright
Were the days there of estate—
Sing up, cantate,
Camerata, to-night
Sing out
The songs the Partigiani made,
While Lonchar who is blind
(He traded his sight with a hand-grenade,
Be kind)
Sits smiling, with his arm enfatico
Resting on the scarf's red flame
Of Anthony, the Maltese Scout.
Ah, Toni, thou art molto simpatico!

Lonchar occhi non ha più,
Sing the Partigiani song!
Non ha più, his eyes have long
Been pulp in Bosnia, so no more
He'll cobble on Dalmatic shore
In the back room of his mother's store.

Lonchar is nineteen now (a noble age)
And he had a way with the girls
Up there, lassù!
He was all the rage:
But Lonchar occhi non ha più.

Ah, Toni, thou art . . . ! Alas . . . !
'Domovina zove nas,'
The throng
Sing the Partigiani song!
All, tutti, raise its sound—

Hark, in the Women Partisans' compound
The strains of mixed voices are rising, proud,
In the Battle Hymn! the Battle Hymn!
Sing, all the crowd,
Sing loud, sing higher
The marching song of those who fight,
And lose their eyes in Bosnia. Oh, sing!

. . . Whilst the Tiger Patrol, beside the fire,
Are cooking macaroni this lovely night of Spring,
And broth, and bully, and other things are there,
For the Yugo-Slavs to share.

Donald Everett

Jimmy Gardner

Even in mid-October at Dhekelia
in half-shade of a Carob Grove
under the double canvas
of the Company Office tent
it was hot. I sat and baked
painfully typing Company Orders
on an ancient machine, the oldest
typewriter in the world, scavenged
from a dustbin at Mena Camp.
The Company Officer watched
as the keyboard rose and fell
noise thunderous, progress minimal
mesmerised equally
by heat and the antediluvian Oliver.
Out of this drowsy atmosphere
unheard and unannounced, came Jim.
He shuffled to a gangling halt.
We all looked up, he stiffened
saluted with surprising smartness
through split lips croaked the prescribed formula:
'727214 Private Gardner, Sir!'

We all three stopped and stared
upon the figure, still at attention
which swayed precariously before us.
He was ugly, dirty, and stank
of stale brandy and sweat
(sweat our common denominator, but his
stronger and older than ours).
With face puffed and scratched
his forehead wore
a wide and hideous scar, blood still oozing
between the many stitches, making
a weak red rivulet which dripped
slowly from his chin.
We were aware that Jimmy grinned,
there was a movement
as in an earthquake-ruined city,

243

the damaged features of his face
shifted and settled as he said:
'Bit of an accident, Sir . . .'
'At ease!' shouted the R.S.M.
for the little Cockney bastard
was first to regain his normal self
after the shock of Jimmy,
'So you're Gardner,' sarcastically
eyeing the extent of Jim
which was considerable
'the Trained Nurse of wide experience,
outstanding ability, but who is'
he looked at the officer
'a little inclined to go astray
outside the Company Lines?'
'Yessir, but I've given that up,
learned my lesson' said Jim.
'I hope so,' remarked the Captain
an American, and rather amused
at the British conception
of a man of exceptional ability.
'But what's that ribbon, soldier?'
pointing to a greasy flash of crimson
clinging to the khaki drill.
'Oh that,' a shamefaced Jimmy said
'they give it me at Liverpool—
I dunno what it's for.' He lied
and I knew too when I had later looked
in his Military Conduct Sheet
and found the citation:
'For conspicuous bravery
in saving the lives of his comrades
at the sinking of the Troopship Collonade.'
But the Officers showed
no further interest, and Jim was sent
to report for duty in the Wards.

His scars soon healed, his crooked grin
came easier. Trouble he contrived to keep
at arm's length, and when his thirst prevailed
and a little madness came to him

we, his new friends, took certain care
no Red Cap ever saw
what devildom came out.
Taffy's head shook sadly over Jim
in mock reproof and resignation
but helped me, taking one arm
to drag one night his drunk insensibility
out of a Larnaca ditch
into the anonymity of our truck
which noble act
earned us his undying gratitude.

One day I saw the ward
of which he was now the master
and marvelled at the neatness it possessed:
how clean the grassy floor
the intricacies of barriers
against the enemy—dust
around the spotless instruments.
Laughing contented patients, confident
in Jim to care for them
and cure them of their Dysentery
or the malignant type of Malaria
of which so many died
but not in Jimmy's Ward.

When virulent Diphtheria struck
we were in disarray, set up
large tents upon the hill
and there the patients went
and there was Big Jim too
his twisted grin never so wide
as when he painted a throat
swabbed out the mucous
so that, among many, a certain Havildar
doomed by his unit, measured for his grave
cracked unintelligible jokes with Jim
after three days, and in a week
blessed him in Urdu, bowing low
as he strode away.

Cyprus, 1943.

Kyrenia

Saw far below
glitter of white churches
among grey of Castle
grey of Mosque
and two piers enclosing
the blue deep harbour
with Pharos, the little guardian
sturdily standing.

We descended into the little city
bathed in cool of sea
beneath the Pharos
rested upon surface to see above
green of gardens
red of Bougainvillea
eyes reaching to inland crags
dominating the sky
to castles floating among the ranges.

Completeness of beauty
we had never known
an absolute of perfection
for us this once.

Brian D. Garland

X.18

Sometimes beyond the long Dalmatian isles
I saw the moonshine on Dinaric snow
Gleaming like milk-glaze where the crowding piles
Of lightning-reddened cloud-tops were aglow.

These were the haunts of mysteries in the night,
—The tautened lightning like a vibrant spring,
Or cold-fired flame of blue St. Elmo's light
Like a stuck dart on tip of gun or wing.

Here was the secret anvil of the sky
Where storms and rains and sea-mist all were made;
This was the realm of spell and lore, which I,
Unwanted, but unheeded, would invade.

Over the moon-green hills and sandy bars,
Where only the Partisan knew how to go,
I ranged remotely with the clouds and stars
Looking on things which Men ought not to know.

Alec Grant

Randolph's Gethsemane

A Churchill stands beneath the trees
Silent, while Adriatic breeze
Sends scudding clouds across the moon,
Decision now, and 'take-off' soon.

'My Father sends me, his Only Son,
Save Comrade Tito from the Hun.
The Red Flag to be my Calvary?
This moment, my Gethsemane?'

624 Squadron (Halifaxes) S.D. (Special Duty) C.M.F.

When Winston Churchill sent his son, Major Randolph Churchill, on a mission to Tito, the writer, one of the ground crew of his aircraft, watched him standing in the moonlight outside the Operations Room, in a strong wind, while he made the 'go—not go' decision.

Colin McIntyre

Motor Transport Officer

Pyatt had something to do with horses.
No, that's not what I mean,
   wipe that smirk off your face.
I mean that in Civvy Street he had
   something to do with horses.
Not as a Trainer, you know, but in
   the buying and selling line.
A horse-chandler, or something.

We didn't have any horses in The Regiment,
   though we had some mules with us in Greece.
So we made him our Motor Transport Officer,
   as he was a Captain, and none of the other
   companies wanted him, not being a Gent.

He made a damn good transport officer, actually.
'Not afraid to get his head under the bonnet,'
   the Colonel always said.
And he could nurse a three-tonner back on the road,
   like a horse with an injured fetlock.

He didn't like the fighting much, and when shells
   fell, managed to be back with 'B' Echelon;
   and he drank too much.

But I wouldn't have wished his end, on man or beast.
Slewed a 15-hundredweight across the road, into a wall
   when he came upon a sudden roadblock.
Trapped in the cab, when the bastard truck caught fire.

Well, they shoot horses, don't they?

Infantryman

When you have walked through a town, as an infantryman,
You'll never go through streets the same way again.

There is shoulder-ache from rifle-sling, and sore
butt-bruise, of bolt, on hip and thigh.

The walk comes somewhere between lope and slow hike,
a wary step, splay-footed, as drawers cellular,
catch in the crotch, twist centrifugally around.

Our lot moved at slow deliberate plod, eyes down, look out.
Ted walked on the left, looks right; I took the right,
looked left. Well spaced out, bloody tired all the time.

Ted and I had a reputation, in Four Section, for hitting
the deck, together, quick as a flash, at the first shell.
Ted had a nose for crossroads ranged by guns.

Infantrymen grow fat in later years, from never walking.
Ted would have become quite gross. But Ted's dead.
Stepped on an AP mine in champagne country.
Cheers, Ted, you old sod, you.

Hey, Joe!

Hey, Joe!
Wanta my sister,
        wanta jog-a-jig-jig?
Hey, Joe!
        you cumma with me.
My sister, fine clean girl,
        only forty thousand...
                        drachma/lire/marks/days.

249

P. Savage

The Island

There grow the gnarled archaic olive-trees,
With Cretan grannies croaking in their shade,
Wimpled in rusty black, impassively
Watching, while old worlds pass and new are made,
Watching from wizened cheeks with jet-keen eyes,
While far away the fleeting fashions fade,
The weary panicked people deifies
New godless gods, and yesterdays are laid
In nameless graves. But they unceasingly,
Aged with their ageing ageless earth, have played
Their thankless part, since Minos ruled the seas
Or Zeus was born—and they are not afraid

Crete

John Waller

Spring in Athens

Cities that death inhabits contain memories
Like vanquished garments on a pauper's knees,
So Athens waking from her death gave out
Sad flavours of the lost who lived without
The lore of loving, reckless, halted doom,
Leaving a legend for an empty room,
A friendly hand to wander over books,
Friend's eyes to catch the careful whim of looks
In shining windows, calling from the blue
Sky of whole pity that they died for you
Whom they thought perfect; so to lose a friend
Is in each loss to find the fabled end.

But Athens for me was Katsimbalis, Seferis, Antoniou,
New friends for merry places, though reflecting you
Who lived not here nor there. Moments were glad
That moments held for you were no more sad.

The dead are always present like the stars
Dancing on the Acropolis or outside bars
Of small tavernas. In the Grecian night
It seemed small journey from the dare or fright
Of your disasters. So with Antoniou
A small white girl and Mozart were still you
Pirouetting in a cellar; you were the Russian
Who played the music on the hills, so certain
That loneliness would go, when deaths would leave
The still, parched cities to their silent grief.

This was the last relief, a kind of curtain
Repeal of sadness where new lives make certain
New places and new friends.

       See in Antoniou
All of the silly loss I felt for you
Who were not there, or in Katsimbalis
Calling to cocks from the Acropolis,
Roaring through nightfall, a Gryphonic phantom
Who knew the world not he was the more wanton,
Like you too in his way of making friends
Knowing that lives not loves are certain ends
To all adventures

       Wars with their applause
May break both human and more god-like laws
Of life and beauty. The drunkard's web we use
Will keep the past not present from abuse—
It is a kind of weary voyaging
From one place to another, though we sing
Songs of an evening, imitation brave
Who are not lost, whom only we can save.

Now Athens also fades, Seferis, an image
Shines distantly before me, a still visage
Of brightness in dull life. Goodbye to friends—
Like deaths—departures to uncertain ends.

         April, 1945.

A.M.

Death Passed Me By

Death passed me by, but I
Caught his swift glance and knew
He saw me too.

When shall we meet again—
In the soft April rain?
When the first swallows wing?
In time of harvesting?
It may be then:
When the last lacquered leaf
Falls to the mud beneath?
When, in a time of woe,
All the land lies in snow?
Then, perhaps then.

This do I know, we shall
Meet, but I know not now
What time— or how.

Memo from Maj. Gen. T. B. Churchill

When a Commando Brigade was put onto Vis Island in the Adriatic in 1943 to strengthen its
Yugoslav Partisan garrison, the British troops set up a local news-sheet which was called the Vis-
à-Vis. At some date in 1944—probably around April or May—a poem was submitted by one of
the British garrison called *Death passed me by.* Some years ago I tried to find out who the poet
'A.M.' was, but nobody who was there at the time, and still alive, could offer any help.

THE QUARTERMASTER

Historical Background

Part One

If we are to appreciate fully the writings in this book we must know their setting, the history of their time, the back-cloth against which the events occur.

The campaigns in North Africa and in Italy represented Churchill's answer to those—American, Russian and British, including Lord Beaverbrook—who called for a Second Front across the Channel in 1942. After the invasion of Russia in June 1941, the German Army had inflicted horrendous casualties[1] on the Red Army, which retreated, trading space for time. Moscow and Leningrad were threatened. If the Germans could take Stalingrad and sweep through the Caucasas and so to the Persian Gulf they could cut off our Middle East Forces—and supplies, especially oil—and eventually link with the Japanese in South East Asia.

On December 8th 1941, the date of Pearl Harbour, the USA entered the War. Britain had been going it alone from the fall of France in May 1940 until Germany invaded Russia. The main British and Commonwealth action in that time took place in the Western Desert in a seesaw campaign of advance and retreat, with troops siphoned off in the Spring of 1941 to disasters in Crete and Greece.

Churchill went to Washington in January 1942. The first two weeks of that January shaped not only World War Two but the world ever since. There would be a combined Chiefs of Staff Committee in Washington. Later, when in answer to the American General Marshall's demand for an invasion of France to relieve pressure on the Russian front, Churchill persuaded the Americans to undertake an allied invasion of North Africa (code named *Torch*) instead, the Commander of the operation had to be an American, General Eisenhower, who had risen rapidly on the staff of the United States Army.

Operation Torch was scheduled for 8th November 1942, two weeks after the start of El Alamein, over two thousand miles to the east, from where the 8th Army, led by General Montgomery advanced all the way to Tunis.

The territory to be invaded was held by the French, who had made their peace with Germany. The United States had stayed on terms with this regime and so it was held that a United States led operation would prove more acceptable.

---

[1] The Russians were to lose over 20 million men and 15 million civilians.

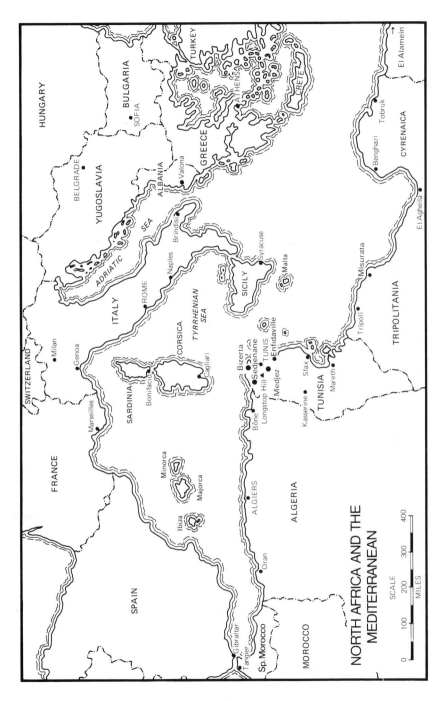

NORTH AFRICA AND THE
MEDITERRANEAN

The operation, which was to link up with the British and Commonwealth 8th Army advancing from the Western Desert and drive the Axis out of Africa, lasted until May the following year. It meant a comparatively short campaign, six months, for the British 1st Army. If Admiral Cunningham had had his way, it would have been a shorter campaign. He proposed landing troops at Bizerta, a short run by fast road to Tunis. But the Americans feared bottling up ships in the Mediterranean. Their Chiefs of Staff also overruled a plan of General Eisenhower to land forces at Bône, 260 miles further on from Algiers. The British 1st Army and American 34th Red Bull infantry Division finally landed near Algiers. Two other landings were made by the Americans even further away from the main objective of Tunis—at Oran and Casablanca, landings that cost the Americans dearly.

General Kenneth Anderson, commanding the British 1st Army, was ordered to move his forces 560 miles to Tunis, by road. Promised paratroop support, to be landed further along the coast, did not happen. No planes were available. In the end the parachutists came by sea from Gibraltar, where they had waited. As later in Italy—part of the 'soft underbelly of Europe' in Churchill's phrase—the stretch from Algiers to the break in the mountains just before Tunis, proved ideal terrain for any intelligent, tenacious defender. And there were no better defenders than the Germans. It would be a costly campaign, for the British and the Americans, with names like Longstop and Kasserine, key points taken, lost and taken again. These names are in the poems and prose of this book.

The operation was bedevilled by politics, intrigues with the Vichy French in North Africa, that infuriated public opinion in Britain. The deal that rankled most was concluded on 13th March 1943, between the then Major Gen Mark Clark (USA) and Admiral Darlan. Darlan was appointed Civil Head of all French North Africa. Later he was to be assassinated by a young Frenchman. (The man who directed his hand was a senior member of British Intelligence. That does not mean Whitehall knew or approved.)

The campaign in North Africa firstly ended any independence, if it could be called that, of the Vichy regime in France. The Germans occupied the whole country. The Germans and Italians also poured troops into Africa. By the end it would cost them 300,000 casualties in killed, wounded and missing, four times the Allied total. And there were the prisoners.

The final scenario was to be played out in a joint operation with the 8th Army. General Alexander directed the operation of the two British armies, 1st and 8th. General Montgomery, after the 1,850 miles from El Alamein, found the fortified line of Mareth a tough nut to crack and then by-passed it in his famed 'left hook'. Units of the 8th Army were transferred to the 1st, including the 7th Armoured Division.

The winding up of the 1st Army now began. By the time the troops reached

Italy, divisions of the 1st Army, beginning with the 78th (Battleaxe) Division, became part of the 8th Army, followed by the 56th London (Black Cat) Division and the 46th. It was the fate of these units to be thrown into action after action.

Part Two

Before the landings in Italy, Sicily was captured in July. The North African campaign had drawn Axis forces away from the mainland of Europe and this eased the invasion. Even so the island cost 23,000 casualties, killed, wounded and missing. Malaria also struck. In the process Mafia power was restored in a deal with the American underworld through Lucky Luciano, enabling the American troops to move more swiftly on their front.

On September 3rd 1943, four years to the day from the day that Britain had declared war, Allied forces landed on the toe of Italy. Six days later, landings began at Salerno, to be fiercely resisted.

Earlier on 25th July 1943, King Victor Emmanuele III had ordered the arrest of Mussolini and directed Marshal Badoglio to form a Government. On October 13th 1943 Marshal Badoglio, by agreement with General Eisenhower, declared war on Germany. By then the Italian army had long decided it was not their war and those guarding POW camps sloped off, enabling some POWs to walk out in the short time before the Germans took over. (See notes on poems and sketches from POW Campo 53 near Macerata, pp 232-234.)

Later, Italian Partisans aided the Allied Advance. A British Intelligence Officer who worked with them, Hamish Henderson, is one of our poets.

The weather remains a dominant memory of the Italian campaign. In Italy it rained. In sunny Italy it rained. For two winters the British 8th Army, alongside the American 5th, fought in the cold, wet and mud in a country tailor-made for defence. One of Germany's ablest commanders, Marshal Kesselring, unaware of Italy being regarded as the soft underbelly of Europe, took every advantage of the terrain—Italy with its mountain spine from North to South, with lateral spurs and mountain outcrops, its rapid rivers and its wide rivers flowing across the front of the Allied Armies proceeding North, with high banks on the far side, easily fortified.

Rivers were to etch their names into regimental history, the Sangro, Garigliano and Anzio and mountain strong points like Cassino, nature presented to opponents who blew up everything in sight on their retreat.

So, it became, too, an engineer's war. The German engineers constructed the Gustav line from north of the Garigliano, through Cassino and east to the Adriatic—and later in the north a Gothic line, from a point between Pisa and La Spezia to south of Rimini of the silver sands. To counter that, Allied engineers flung Bailey bridges across the ravines and rivers. Trucks bounced the guts out

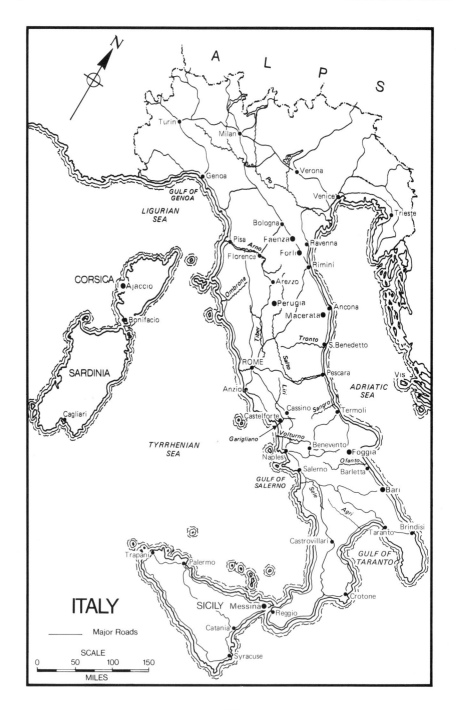

of their occupants as they were forced onto lengthy diversions. Some bright man had hit on the idea of a submersible bridge, a hidden concrete strip across the river bed, that allowed a foot of river to flow over it and ensure anxious moments to anyone traversing it, especially in fog—and for real fog, little can beat Northern Italy—and gave a surprise shock to many a driver stabbing at his wet brakes at the far end only to find nothing happened. His truck sped on.

The British 8th Army had left a sparse dry desert and then Tunisia for a populous country, with towns and villages, fine roads, narrow roads and rough tracks clinging to hill-sides, churches and ancient buildings and rough wine and people who sang, and protected women (respectable) and other women. But the 8th Army, that had fought from Egypt to Tunis would not long remain that same Army. Within months of landing in Italy, the Army Commander, General Montgomery would be recalled to England to prepare for Normandy. And with him went the 50th and 51st (Highland)—and the 7th Armoured Division, which after all the years in the Desert would now take the long route from Normandy to Germany.

In such a restricted terrain, flexibility proved difficult. The campaign became a slogging match. The main diversion was at Anzio, a landing there on 22nd January 1944, to by-pass Cassino on the road to Rome. Politely we can only say it was mismanaged. If the first momentum of landings had been pursued, months could have been clipped off the campaign. As it was the Germans had time to react and Allied soldiers clung by their finger-nails to a strip of beach. Cassino eventually fell on 18th May 1944, the Polish Corps of the 8th Army, fighting their way up the mountain side, achieved at great cost what other action and American bombing, which also hit our own troops, failed to do.

The Allies entered Rome on 5th June 1944, the day before the Normandy landings and the Germans retreated fast first to Arezzo and then to the opaque green of the River Arno at Florence. There they destroyed the most graceful bridge of the 14th Century, the Ponte Santa Trinita, before retreating to the Gothic line. The bridge had no strategic value.

The war ended in Italy on 2nd May 1945. At the Brenner Pass, the 8th Army ceased. It was now the British Troops in Austria.

Mussolini, one half of the axis, had been deposed in July 1943, to be held under arrest in the mountains only for a German Commando-type operation to airlift him to the north to set up another government. As the war ended he tried to flee the country. Partisans caught up with him and his mistress Clara Petacci, who in her day had shocked the gentility of Rome. The pair were shot and hanged upside down in Milan. Still, his heritage remained: the civil law he created stayed more or less unscathed, and mostly remains thirty one governments and forty years later. The Allies seemed bent on restoring the status quo. A quasi-military organisation named AMGOT , (a plum job for those involved like that of Town Major) followed the Allied armies to set up a civilian administration.

The troops were still needed, although Victory in Europe had been won. New Zealanders went full speed to Trieste on the Adriatic to head off the Yugo-Slavs—Marshal Tito's Partisans, who had tied down twenty three German Divisions in a brutal war—from their taking a slice of Italian (now friendly) land at the port of Trieste. Trieste is today the oil terminal for a quarter of Europe.

52,895 soldiers of the 8th Army were killed, wounded or missing in Italy, as were 25,742 soldiers of the 1st Army in North Africa. At El Alamein the 8th Army suffered 13,560 casualties and 12,348 in Tunisia.

Harry Secombe's Airgraph letter home to his sister Carol, on her 20th birthday.

Biographies

The editors regret that they have been unable to include biographies of all poets due to lack of information.

T. I. F. ARMSTRONG, better known as poet John Gawsworth. G. S. Fraser called him 'the last of the Jacobites'. Merchant Taylors' School and briefly with publishers Ernest Benn. Died from alcoholism. (See *Return to Oasis*)

J. H. BAILEY, drove Sherman tank for General Sir John Hackett in Western Desert. Post-war with Unilever.

J. BEVAN, born 1920. Left English studies at Cambridge for 6½ years war service in Royal Artillery. Gunnery Officer in Italy. Post-war, teacher, published poet and translator of Salvatore Quasimodo. Lives at Tettenhall, Wolverhampton.

Dennis BIRCH (Robert Dennis), born 1913, educated Clifton. South Staffs Regt. and Royal Artillery in North Africa, Italy and Greece. Solicitor, chairman Incorporated Church Building Society, member Grants Ctee Historic Churches. Editor of anthologies *Poets in Battledress* and *Home is the Soldier*.

H. I. BRANSOM, Brigadier, C.B.E., D.S.O., T.D., D.L., author of *Inferior Verse* and *Still Inferior Verse*. President 124 (Northumberland) Field Regt. R.A. (T.A.) Old Comrades Association. *Inferior Verse* raised money in war to send parcels to P.O.W.s.

J. E. BROOKES, born 1920, London. Worked passage to Australia, landing with 2/6d. Walked from Broken Hill to Melbourne to join up. Served with 2/5th Bn as private in Middle East. Taken P.O.W. in Crete. Post-war, Colonial Police, Kenya, Ghana and Sierra Leone, retiring as Superintendant. Joined De La Rue on formation of Security Express.

B. W. BROWN, enlisted Redhill, Surrey, 928 AA Brig. Coy RASC, (T.A.), 6th Division as fitter. Dunkirk. Sent to Suez, MEF, as 13th Corps, Troop Supply Col., then on loan to Sudan Defence Force. Contributor to monthly magazine *Mobile Home*. Writing joint biography with German wife.

K. BURROWS, 16/5 Lancers in 6th Armoured Division, Middle East. Writes: 'I used to amuse myself writing poems on scraps of paper, but most were lost or thrown away'. Lives at Alvaston, Derby.

W. H. BURT, Lieut. in 51st Highland Recce Regt., when he wrote Stane Jock. Killed in Germany shortly before end of the War.

Michael CARVER, Field Marshal Lord. In Middle East, GSO 1, 7th Armoured Division at El Alamein. First Royal Tank Regt. Officer to become Chief of Defence Staff. Writer and literary critic. Books include: *El Alamein, Tobruk, War Lords, Policy for Peace*.

Louis CHALLONER, born 1911 in Blackpool. Educated Preston and University College, Southampton. Pre-war teaching in London, post-war headmaster in Newham. Served with 2 R.H.A. (25 pounders) in North African campaigns.

J. K. CLARK, born Scunthorpe, 1922. St. Edmund Hall, Oxford, modern languages. Commissioned, 6th Bn Lincolnshire Regt., Platoon Commander, Rifle Company. Captured at Sedjenane, Tunisia during 'Ochsenkopf'. Post-war builder's labourer under ganger who had gone on patrol with him as L/Cpl. Later, teacher.

B. COLE, private, 4th Battalion, Royal Sussex, wounded at El Alamein. Sent as reinforcement to Salerno. Retired now after twenty five years in Fleet Street.

Henry COMPTON, born Coventry 1909. Journalist. Intelligence Corps., North Africa, Sicily, France and Germany. Edited Bournville Works Magazine. Lecturer in Communication, College of Advanced Technology, now University of Aston. Books of poems include: *Kindred Points* (1951) and *Overtones* (1982).

E. COURT, London Taxi Driver (retired), left Liverpool on the *Oronsay* October 5 1940, ship bombed. Left on *Samaria* arrived Egypt March 5 1941. Taken P.O.W. at Tobruk, June 21 1942, moved to Campo 53 in Italy, near Macerata. On 15 September 1943 walked out of camp, sheltering in Olibra until British line moved up, ten months later.

R. COX, educated Fettes College. As 2 i/c 31st (Perth) Lt. A.A. Regt. R.A., sailed from the Clyde with Canadian Division to meet 8th Army off Gozo, for landings in Sicily, having lost three ships off Cap Bon. With Land Forces Adriatic to clear Dalmatian Islands, in combined operation with Tito's Partisans.

Dan DAVIN, M.B.E., born New Zealand. Rhodes Scholar. Fellow Balliol College, Oxford. Platoon Commander 23rd N.Z. Battalion in Greece, wounded in Crete 1941, transferred to Intelligence. Official N.Z. historian Crete campaign. Served at Cassino. Intelligence representative in the Joint Control Commission until end of war. Oxford Academic Publisher. Short story writer and novelist.

Erik de MAUNY, born 1920 in London, French and English parents. Educated New Zealand, Victoria University College, Wellington: School of Slavonic and East European Studies, University of London. Pre-war journalist in New Zealand, 1940-5, served with N.Z. Expeditonary Force in Pacific, Middle East and Italy. B.B.C. Foreign correspondent for thirty years. Novelist. Living in Normandy.

C. P. S. DENHOLM-YOUNG, Colonel, O.B.E., F.C.I.S. Commanded the Signal Regt. of the 51st Highland Division. Post-war returned to accountancy, now genealogist.

B. ETHERINGTON, born 1906, Torquay, Mill Hill School, Wadham College, Oxford. Half Blue Athletics, Hockey. Taught classics. Infantry Officer at Tobruk. Died Edinburgh 1971.

D. EVERETT, born 1911, Bodmin, Cornwall. Joined Midland Bank in 1928, and returned after War to become Manager until retirement in 1970. Joined R.A.M.C. in 1940, with 57th and 82nd General Hospitals, Egypt, Palestine, Cyprus. Western Desert. *A World Stretching Out*, collection of poems, 1974.

Ian FLETCHER, born London, 1920. Professor of English, Arizona University, U.S.A., formerly, Reading University. Served in Middle East, including Sudan. Poetry includes: *Orisons, Picaresque & Metaphysical* and *Motets: Twenty One Poems*.

F. K. (Freddie) FORRESTER, M.B.E., born 1915, Danbury, Essex. Chigwell School and Queens College, Cambridge, Asst. Cataloguer, British Museum, 1938-40. Pioneer Corps. 1940-6, Adjutant 15 Airfield Construction Group. Asst. Director of Labour G.H.Q. C.M.F. Principal, later Assistant Secretary in Government Social Security Depts., 1946-75. Member of Society of Civil Service Authors.

A. FREEDMAN, London Editor *Manchester Evening News* and chairman of the Newspaper Conference. Served in R.A.F. Intelligence, M.E.F., later posted to Air Attache's Office, British Embassy, Ankara.

Brian GALLIE, Captain, Royal Navy, D.S.C., served in Mediterranean now living in Portugal.

R. GARIOCH, captured near Tobruk, while serving as a private with 201 Guards Motor Brigade and spent rest of war in P.O.W. camps in Italy and Germany. Books include: *Chuckies on a Cairn*, 1949, *The Masque of Edinburgh*, 1954, *Scots Verse Translations of Buchanan's Jepthah and the Baptist*, 1959; *Selected Poems*, 1966.

William GODFREY, Mons Star, bicycle despatch rider in World War One, K.R.R.C. in M.E.F. in the Second.

John HACKETT, General Sir. In Middle East, G.S.O. 1, Raiding Forces M.E.F. Commander-in-Chief British Army of the Rhine 1966-68. Visiting Professor in Classics, Kings College London. Books include: *The Third World War, I was a Stranger, The Untold Story*.

Norman HAMPSON, born 1922, educated Manchester Grammer School, University College, Oxford, Ord. seaman in H.M.S. *Carnation*, sub-lieut. H.M.S. *Easton* in Eastern Med., escorting convoys. Liason with Free French and landing in South of France. Professor of History, York. Various books on the Enlightenment and the French Revolution.

Hamish HENDERSON, born 1919, Blairgowrie, Perthshire, educated Blairgowrie High School, Dulwich College and Downing College, Cambridge. Intelligence Officer with 1st South African Division at Alamein and with 51st Highland Division in Libya, Tunisia and Sicily. Mentioned in despatches. On Anzio beachhead with 1st British Infantry Division. Operated with Italian Partisans, arranging Graziani's surrender. School of Scottish Studies, Edinburgh.

Quintin HOGG, Viscount Hailsham of St. Marylebone, C.H., F.R.S., Lord Chancellor. President Oxford Union. Rifle Brigade, Middle East. Poems published under title *The Devil's Own Story*.

Richard HOGGART, born 1918, Warden, Goldsmith's College, London University. Royal Artillery 1940-6, Staff Captain, organised publications and Arts Centre for the Forces in Naples. Professor of English Birmingham University 1961-73, Vice Chairman, Arts Council 1976-81. Books include: *The Uses of Literacy, How and Why we do Learn, W. H. Auden*, (jointly) *The Future of Broadcasting*.

W. G. HOLLOWAY, Royal Artillery Regiment hammered at Alamein. Returned to base, Almaza, Cairo, to write his war-time verse.

Michael HOWARD, Regius Professor of Modern History & Fellow of Oriel College, Oxford. Professor of War Studies 1963-68.

Coldstream Guards. Books include: *The Theory and Practice of War, The Mediterranean Strategy in World War Two, War and the Liberal Conscience*.

John JARMAIN, Officer with 51st Highland Division anti-tank unit. Served in Desert, only to return to England and then be killed in Normandy, 26 June 1944. The night before he worked through the records of his unit, assessing each man and recommending promotions. He did so as if like Keith Douglas he foresaw his own end. Against advice but to make sure he went on a recce into Ste Honorine la Chardonnerette to be killed by a German mortar bomb. One of the truly great but neglected poets of the war.

B. G. J. JOHNSTON, born 1913, Bethnal Green, London, fifth of eight children. Prewar, electrical fitter, Wimbledon Corporation. 57th Anti Tank Regt. R.A. Sergeant. Attached U.S. Special Services, Italy, 1944. Control Commission, Germany, Transport Supervisor. Manager Group Office Services, General Motors.

L. K. LAWLER, former B.B.C. executive, living at Henley-on-Thames, Oxon.

Ronald LEWIN, C.B.E., F.R. Hist. S., F.R.S.L., military historian. Royal Artillery 1939-45, North Africa and North-West Europe. Wounded and mentioned in despatches. B.B.C. 1946-64, Head of Home Service 1957-64. Books include: *Slim the Standard Bearer*, official biography of Field Marshal Lord Slim. W. H. Smith Literary Award 1977. Gold Medallist, Royal United Service Institute, 1982.

Lawrie LITTLE, born 1921, London. Alleyn's School. Served North Africa, Italy, Austria. Wrote novel, *Dear Boys*. Caxton Trust, an educational charity, based in Pimlico.

A. M. Bell MACDONALD, born Montreal 1914, Charterhouse and Clare College, Cambridge. Law degree. Qualified as solicitor. 32nd Field Regt. R.A. in France 1939. 159th Field Regt. R.A. with 6th Indian Division. Posted to Italy on attachment. Postwar, two years with Judge Advocate General preparing cases for Nuremberg.

Dennis McHARRIE, O.B.E., Wing Commander R.A.F. posted to 38 Bomber Squadron, Middle East, 1942, as a Flight-Lieutenant, moving to Barce near Benghazi. Now lives at Blackpool, Lancs.

Colin McINTYRE, Black Watch, Company Commander, Lovat Scouts. Journalist.

George MEDDEMMEN, cousin of *Oasis* poet, J. G. Meddemmen. Born South London, 1920. Elementary education, scholarship to Haberdashers Askes. Left at fifteen to become dogsbody in commercial art studio. Six years with 66th Medium Regt. R.A., the assault regt. in the invasions of Sicily and Italy, drew and painted in Command Posts and O.P.'s, lost work before 1944. One man exhibitor in Rome, 1945. Post-war studied at Hornsey School of Art, painting diploma. Royal Academy exhibitor. Vic Feather purchased painting for T.U.C. Eight war paintings in Imperial War Museum collection. Became director of large London studio. Principal lecturer, Graphic Design, East Ham College of Technology.

J. G. MEDDEMMEN (pen-name of J. G. Barker), *Oasis* poet, cousin of George Meddemmen, artist. Conscripted into army 'and marriage' in 1940. Post-war, British Rail shipping.

Spike MILLIGAN, born India, film actor, radio and T.V. comedian and script writer, including the Goon Show. Bombadier, Royal Artillery, North Africa and Italy. Wrote: *Monty, His Part in My Victory, Mussolini, His Part in My Downfall, Rommel? Gunner Who?*

Norman T. MORRIS, born 1912, Cheshire. Lancaster Royal Grammer School. Teacher. Enlisted September 1940, 50th Royal Tank Regt., Western Desert, Sicily, Italy & Greece. Post-war, Headmaster for thirty years, including school at Elephant and Castle, London. College lecturer and examiner.

William E. MORRIS, N.C.O., N.Z.E.F. in Western Desert and Italy. When the 2nd N.Z. Division needed railway lines to run military stock in the Western Desert volunteered from Public Works Dept. in

New Zealand to join Construction Unit in June 1940 (12th Railway Survey Company). Member of International Poetry organisations including Tagore Institute and New Zealand Poetry Society. Poems translated into Hindi and Russian.

Sam MORSE-BROWN, in Italy Adjutant of Royal Engineers, Major, Staff of Rome Area Allied Command, War Artist. Now in Bermuda.

Jack NEILSON, North Irish Horse (Tank Regt.), North Africa and Italy.

Jack PARTRIDGE, trained as artist, Queens West Surrey Regt., Alamein. Post-war estate agent, Rottingdean.

Ivor F. PORTER, O.B.E., S.O.E., trained Middle East, jumped into Romania (Operation Autonomous), caught but released when King Michael overthrew the Antonescu regime in August 1944. Finished war as major. Joined the Foreign Service.

ENOCH POWELL, Rt. Hon., M.P., P.C., M.B.E. Fellow of Trinity College, Cambridge, Professor of Greek, University of Sydney, Australia, 1937-9. In World War Two, Brigadier, General Staff. Poems published under title, *Dancer's End*.

M. RAWLINSON, with Royal Tank Regt., Western Desert, 8th Army.

James H. REHILL, born 1915, Liverpool. History teacher, now retired after thirty three years service. R.A.O.C., Egypt, Italy and Greece. 8 Ord. Beach Dept., Salerno, Anzio.

Newman ROBINSON, served with South African Medical Corps., (L/Cpl), taken P.O.W., Western Desert. Wrote reminiscences *In the Bag* (Macmillan SA 1975) from which poem 'P.O.W. Camp, Italy' is taken.

John ROPES, Brigadier at G.H.Q., Cairo, put on entertainments for the troops.

Sue RYDER, Baroness of Warsaw, C.M.G., O.B.E., born 1923. Second World War with F.A.N.Y. and Special Ops. Executive.

Founder and social worker, Sue Ryder Foundation, world wide. Golden Order of Merit, Polish People's Republic, married Group Capt. Cheshire. Autobiography: *And the Morrow is Their's*.

Harry SECOMBE, Sir, C.B.E., born South Wales, L/Bdr., Royal Artillery, North Africa and Italy; stage career began at Windmill Theatre 1946; In Goon Show with Milligan, Sellers and Bentine. An ex-choirboy, sang the lead in stage musical *Pickwick*. Radio, T.V., films, books.

Victor SELWYN, journalist and researcher, written on subjects from map reading to investment and business in Western Europe. Founder, joint-editor, *Oasis*, with Denis Saunders (Almendro) and David Burk, Cairo 1942/3. Manages The Salamander Oasis Trust, lives in Brighton.

SHELLDRAKE (David Morgan), staff poet and assitant editor of *The Oak*, 46th Division magazine. Died two weeks after handing over files of magazine to The Salamander Oasis Trust.

P. T. SINKER, Subaltern in Surrey and Sussex Yeomanry (Queen Mary's Regt.), Royal Artillery. Writes, 'The guns were 105mm howitzers, firing a 37lb shell, mounted on a Grant chassis'. Sicily to Cassino. Merton College, Cambridge.

Douglas Arthur Manatanus STREET, born 1915, mother, Belgian artist, father, member Air Council. Scholar Hertford College, Oxford. French Foreign Legion, extricated by Foreign Office, 1938. Commissioned 1/7 Mdx. (M.M.G.) T.A.,

B.E.F., 3rd Division Dunkirk. Chief Instructor Intelligence Staff Course. Liason with General Leclerc, Free French. G.S.O. 1 Intelligence 8th Army. S.O.E. Yugoslavia and Greece, liason in Trieste. Commanded Allied Information Services under the then General Sir John Harding. Foreign Office.

John Richard STRICK, educated Rottingdean, Sussex, Wellington and London University. London Irish Rifles, i/c Battle Patrol twice wounded. Killed by shell at Anzio.

R. N. WALKER, born 1917 in Stoke-on-Trent, Headmaster. R.A.M.C. Middle East, retrained as cypher operator, Persia, India, Burma, H.Q., B.A.O.R., at Nuremberg for the trial.

John WALLER, seventh baronet, descendant of Edmund Waller, 17th century poet. Born 1917, educated Weymouth College and Worcester College, Oxford, where he edited *Kingdom Come* 1939-41. Served in R.A.S.C., Middle East. Features Editor in Ministry of Information, Middle East 1943-5.

Founder Member of the Salamander Society, Cairo. Greenwood Prize for Poetry 1947, Keats Prize 1947. Information Officer, Overseas Press Division, C.O.I. 1954-9. Principal volumes of verse, *The Confessions of Peter Pan*, 1941, *Fortunate Hamlet*, 1941, *The Merry Ghosts*, 1946.

Alan WHITE, born 1920. Poems collected in *Garlands and Ash*. Second collection *Gentle Baptism* cut short by death. Killed at age of 24 at Cassino, May 12 1944. He was at that time a Lieutenant in the Royal Artillery.

FOREVER....

from *The Oak*, 1946

Major General Francis de Guingand, Monty's Chief-of-Staff, Eighth Army